The Third Force

GLOBAL POLICY BOOKS FROM
THE CARNEGIE ENDOWMENT FOR INTERNATIONAL PEACE

Africa's New Leaders: Democracy or State Reconstruction?
  Marina Ottaway

Aiding Democracy Abroad: The Learning Curve
  Thomas Carothers

From Migrants to Citizens: Membership in a Changing World
  T. Alexander Aleinikoff and Douglas Klusmeyer, Editors

Funding Virtue: Civil Society Aid and Democracy Promotion
  Marina Ottaway and Thomas Carothers, Editors

New Markets, New Opportunities? Economic and Social Mobility
in a Changing World
  Copublished with Brookings Institution Press
  Nancy Birdsall and Carol Graham, Editors

Repairing the Regime: Preventing the Spread of Weapons
of Mass Destruction
  Copublished with Routledge
  Joseph Cirincione, Editor

ASIA PACIFIC AND CIVIL SOCIETY BOOKS FROM
THE JAPAN CENTER FOR INTERNATIONAL EXCHANGE

Asia Pacific Security Outlook 2000
  Richard W. Baker and Charles E. Morrison, Editors

Corporate-NGO Partnership in Asia Pacific
  Tadashi Yamamoto and Kim Gould Ashizawa, Editors

Deciding the Public Good: Governance and Civil Society in Japan
  Yamamoto Tadashi, Editor

East Asian Crisis and Recovery: Issues of Governance and Sustainable
Development
  Chie Siow Yue, Editor

Governance in a Global Age: The Impact of Civil Society
from a Comparative Perspective
  Yamamoto Tadashi, Editor

New Perspectives on U.S.-Japan Relations
  Gerald L. Curtis, Editor

The Third Force

The Rise of Transnational Civil Society

Ann M. Florini
Editor

Japan Center for International Exchange
TOKYO

Carnegie Endowment for International Peace
WASHINGTON, D.C.

Carnegie Endowment for International Peace   Tel. 202-483-7600
1779 Massachusetts Avenue   Fax. 202-483-1840
Washington, D.C. 20036 USA   www.ceip.org

To order, contact Carnegie's distributor:
The Brookings Institution Press   Tel. 800-275-1447 or 202-797-6258
Department 029   Fax. 202-797-2960
Washington, D.C. 20042-0029 USA   E-mail: bibooks@brook.edu

Distributed within Japan and Asia by the Japan Center for International Exchange or
its agents.

Japan Center for International Exchange   Tel. (011) 81-3-3446-7781
4-9-17 Minami Azabu, Minato-ku   Fax. (011) 81-3-3443-7580
Tokyo 160-0047 Japan   www.jcie.or.jp

The views presented in this publication are those of the individual authors and do not
necessarily represent the views of the Carnegie Endowment, the Japan Center for International Exchange, their officers, staff, or trustees.

Printed in the United States of America on acid-free, recycled paper with vegetable-
oil based inks by Automated Graphic Systems, White Plains, Maryland.

Interior design by Jenna Dixon.
Text set in 12/13.5 Wessex, designed by Matthew Butterick, Font Bureau.

Library of Congress Cataloging-in-Publication Data

The third force : the rise of transnational civil society / Ann M. Florini, editor.
    p.   cm.
  Includes bibliographical references and index.
  ISBN 0-87003-180-5 (cloth : acid-free paper) — ISBN 0-87003-179-1 (pbk. : acid-free
paper)
    1. Civil society. 2. Globalization. I. Florini, Ann.
JC337.T45 2000
322.4 – dc21   00-009535

06   05   04   03   02   01   00   5   4   3   2   1   1st Printing 2000

Contents

Foreword vi

Acknowledgements viii

1 What the World Needs Now? 1
   Ann M. Florini and P. J. Simmons

2 A Global Network to Curb Corruption: The Experience
   of Transparency International 17
   Fredrik Galtung

3 Advocates and Activists: Conflicting Approaches
   on Nonproliferation and the Test Ban Treaty 49
   Rebecca Johnson

4 Toward Democratic Governance for Sustainable Development:
   Transnational Civil Society Organizing Around Big Dams 83
   Sanjeev Khagram

5 Transnational Networks and Campaigns for Democracy 115
   Chetan Kumar

6 Building Partnerships toward a Common Goal: Experiences
   of the International Campaign to Ban Landmines 143
   Motoko Mekata

7 The Power of Norms versus the Norms of Power: Transnational
   Civil Society and Human Rights 177
   Thomas Risse

8 Lessons Learned 211
   Ann M. Florini

Annotated Bibliography 241
   Yahya A. Dehqanzada

Index 277

Contributors 293

Japan Center for International Exchange 294
Carnegie Endowment for International Peace 295

Foreword

AS THE WORLD becomes ever more tightly integrated, rapid economic, political, and technological changes create urgent new needs for global rules. Those needs raise pressing questions about who gets to make the rules. A swiftly growing number of coalitions of civil society groups now claim the right to have a say in everything from nuclear arms control negotiations to the operations of multinational corporations. These transnational networks are much in the limelight, alternately portrayed as rock-throwing anarchists disrupting the serious deliberations of governments or as the last remaining hope for global peace and justice. Despite the hype, there has been surprisingly little rigorous analysis of the fundamental issues raised by this growing role of transnational civil society. Are these networks truly powerful, or merely good at attracting attention to themselves? How much of a role are they likely to play in addressing the world's problems in the coming decades? What are their legitimate roles, and what are likely to be their aims?

The Third Force sheds new light on the answers to these questions. Its six case studies compel recognition that these border-spanning networks are a real and enduring force in the international relations of the twenty-first century. That reality will require governments and corporations, the targets of civil society campaigns, to adjust their behavior and their decision-making practices. And, as Ann Florini argues, the networkers themselves need to recognize that their new influence imposes new responsibilities. Above all, those involved in transnational civil society networks must become far more transparent about who they are, what they are doing, why they are doing it, and who is paying for it.

This book grew out of a presentation given by Dr. Florini at a session on civil society and international governance at the 1998 Global ThinkNet Conference, sponsored by the Japan Center for International Exchange (JCIE) in Tokyo. That meeting made it clear that the role of transnational civil society networks in global governance was both important and insufficiently examined, particularly by researchers outside the United States. Accordingly, the JCIE asked Dr. Florini to direct a study that would bring together researchers from a variety of countries. Most of the authors she assembled are both participants in and analysts of the networks they write about, a combination that gives them unusual insight.

The Third Force provides a carefully formulated framework of common questions for each case study, making it possible for the book to uncover broad trends. Its dispassionate analysis reveals not only how useful transnational civil society networks can be but also how difficult it is for those networks to live up to the self-professed ideals that render their power legitimate.

The JCIE and the Carnegie Endowment for International Peace both believe that as globalization changes the identity of policy actors and transforms the processes of international relations, policy research institutes like ours must help policy makers and the public alike understand and respond to the challenges of this new era. *The Third Force* represents a major step forward in that understanding.

The ThinkNet conferences are the centerpiece of the Global ThinkNet project, which the JCIE launched in 1996, with the generous support of the Nippon Foundation, to commemorate its twenty-fifth anniversary. Global ThinkNet aims to strengthen cross-border intellectual networks among research institutions and researchers. Under its auspices, researchers from around the world collaborate on projects related to the themes of globalization, governance, and civil society.

Both of us would like to express our gratitude for the generous support of the Nippon Foundation and the Rockefeller Brothers Fund, without which this project would not have been possible.

TADASHI YAMAMOTO
President, Japan Center
for International Exchange

JESSICA T. MATHEWS
President, Carnegie Endowment
for International Peace

Acknowledgments

AS IS TRUE for all publications, many people whose names do not appear in the contents made valuable contributions to this book. I owe thanks to the enormous range of people I contacted in my extensive search for the ideal case study authors. Cara Carter provided excellent research assistance. Delores Bigby coped cheerfully with multiple revisions of the ever-growing manuscript. Trish Reynolds at Carnegie and Pam Noda at the JCIE skillfully shepherded the manuscript through the complexities of joint publication. Anyone who has spent time at the Carnegie Endowment in recent years knows that one of the institution's major assets is its outstanding library staff, Jennifer Little, Kathleen Daly, and Chris Henley, who found everything needed for both my own research and the annotated bibliography.

I am deeply grateful to the two institutions that published this volume. The JCIE proposed the idea of a multinational study on the role of transnational civil society in global governance, managed all the logistics, and made the project a pleasure. The Carnegie Endowment hosted me throughout this project (and others), providing a most supportive environment. I am particularly grateful to the president of the JCIE, Tadashi Yamamoto, to Hideko Katsumata, executive secretary of the JCIE, to the Carnegie Endowment's president, Jessica Mathews, and to the Endowment's vice president for studies, Thomas Carothers.

My thanks as well to my fellow authors, not only for their written contributions but also for their congeniality. I learned much from them and enjoyed the process greatly.

On behalf of all the authors, we are deeply grateful to the Nippon Foundation for its generous financial support of the project. I also want to extend my thanks to the Rockefeller Brothers Fund for making it possible for me to take on this project.

I

What the World Needs Now?

Ann M. Florini and P. J. Simmons

IN LATE 1999, tens of thousands of people filled the streets of Seattle in one of the most visible manifestations of civil society in recent decades. They had gathered to show their opposition to the World Trade Organization (WTO) and the broader forces of economic integration that it represents. The WTO, which was meeting to set an agenda for a proposed new round of global trade negotiations, found itself under scrutiny as never before. For several days, television news shows around the world displayed protesters being gassed and arrested by the hundreds. Although media reports portrayed the protesters as a combination of American labor unionists who wanted to protect their jobs at the expense of Third World workers and hippies left over from the 1960s, in fact the protesters represented a broad and to some degree transnational coalition of concerns. They objected not only to the WTO's ability to override domestic environmental legislation but also to the very nature of the processes by which governments and corporations are fostering economic integration.

This is not the first time such groups have inserted themselves into global decision making, for good or ill. In recent decades, such stories have filled newspapers and scholarly journals alike.

- Every year, an international nongovernmental organization called Transparency International releases an index ranking the world's countries on how corrupt they are perceived to be.

Although Transparency International only came into existence in 1993, it has galvanized a global movement against corruption.

- Almost since the dawn of the nuclear age, scores of activist groups have campaigned vigorously for a ban on nuclear testing. They argued that a test ban, more than any other measure, could bring nuclear arms races and the spread of nuclear weapons to a screeching halt. In 1996, they got their way when 136 countries signed the Comprehensive Test Ban Treaty.

- For much of the twentieth century, countries around the world have constructed large dams on their rivers to create water supplies and electrical power. But in the past decade, would-be dam builders have found themselves in the crosshairs of a transnational movement protesting the environmental and human costs of these massive projects. Now, governments, the private sector, and transnational civil society have come together to create a World Commission on Dams, potentially setting a precedent for a new style of global problem solving.

- When an obscure guerrilla movement known as the Zapatistas took over four towns in the southern province of Chiapas in 1994, the Mexican government started to respond with force. When nongovernmental activists elsewhere (particularly in the United States) protested, Mexico put its troops on hold.

- In December 1997, 122 countries signed an international treaty to ban land mines, despite the vehement objections of the world's most powerful governments. Standing beside the government delegates were representatives of some 300 nongovernmental organizations, members of the International Campaign to Ban Landmines, without whom the treaty would not exist.

- At the end of the 1990s, former Chilean dictator Augusto Pinochet found himself facing international legal charges based on his alleged violations of human rights in Chile. Nike found that its bottom line suffered dramatically when it was accused of violating the rights of its workers in poor countries. The new standards by which heads of governments and corporations alike are being judged originated and spread due to the determined efforts of a broad network of nongovernmental groups around the world.

Nongovernmental organizations (NGOs), informal associations, and loose coalitions are forming a vast number of connections across national borders and inserting themselves into a wide range of decision-making processes on issues from international security to human rights to the environment. But how significant is this flurry of apparent activity? Is transnational civil society becoming a permanent and powerful contributor to solving the world's problems? And should global problem solving be left to a loose agglomeration of unelected activists?

These questions matter. Transnational civil society is a piece—an increasingly important piece—of the larger problem of global governance. Although the state system that has governed the world for centuries is neither divinely ordained nor easily swept away, in many ways that system is not well suited to addressing the world's growing agenda of border-crossing problems. Even when governments find that their national interests coincide with broad global interests, political will is often hard to muster in the face of dangers that are incremental and long term, and most of the transnational threats to human well-being arise cumulatively rather than as acute crises. Even if states are able to bestir themselves, the transnational agenda is so complex and multifaceted that multiple sources of information and multiple points of intervention are needed. The sheer number of regimes and agreements needed to cope with the wide range of problems demanding governance is overwhelming the resources available to states, which in any case face increasing domestic demands.

And the transnational agenda is becoming more urgent. Thanks to the information revolution, the growing integration of national economies, and the rapidly increasing number of people in the world, human activity is less constrained than ever by national borders. People travel, migrate, communicate, and trade in ever-growing numbers, and the sheer number of economically active people is putting heavy stress on the environmental infrastructure on which everyone depends.

All that integration across borders has important benefits—greater freedom of choice, enhanced economic efficiency—but it also creates (or makes people aware of) problems that threaten human well-being. Such threats include everything from the difficulty of regulating internationally mobile capital to the danger of global environmental change to the corruption of governments and societies around the world. And even when the problems take place squarely within national territories, as in the case of human rights violations or the construction of dams that may devastate local ecosystems and populations, the solutions often draw broadly on the international community.

In short, the world badly needs *someone* to act as the "global conscience," to represent broad public interests that do not readily fall under the purview of individual territorial states or that states have shown themselves wont to ignore. This book sets out to determine whether transnational civil society can, and should, fill the gap between the supply of and the need for global problem solving. Will, and should, transnational civil society play a greatly expanded role in the ever-expanding set of global issues?

To date, a large and growing literature has not made clear whether transnational civil society can provide an appropriate and effective instrument across the board, or whether in the end it will prove to be sound and fury signifying nothing. The literature largely concentrates on other questions. Much of it examines civil society one country at a time or draws comparisons across countries about the status of national civil societies.[1] Relatively few analysts have looked at the networks linking civil society organizations across territorial boundaries, and most of these have examined just one case at a time.[2] Very few studies have compared the various transnational civil society networks to analyze the strengths and weaknesses of this emerging form of transnational collective action.[3] And only a handful have looked systematically at what, if anything, transnational civil society *should* do—at whether, and under what conditions, it is desirable for transnational civil society to play a significant part in making the decisions that shape the future for all of us.[4] (The annotated bibliography in this book lists some of the relevant literature.) This gap badly needs to be filled. Anecdotes and isolated cases cannot answer fundamental questions about the sigificance, sustainability, and desirability of transnational civil society.

This book sets out to fill the gap by comparing six stories. The stories are quite diverse—indeed, they were selected to cover a wide range of issues, to discover what commonalities might lurk beneath the surface. For the most part, they were chosen because at first glance they seem to be success stories. By teasing out what factors might account for success, or at least prominence, it is possible to move on to investigate whether those factors are widely shared. All the cases address the same three basic questions: How powerful is transnational civil society? How sustainable is its influence? How desirable is that influence?

The first case is in many ways the simplest. It is the story of the transnational network to curb corruption, a network that arose with astonishing rapidity in the 1990s to force corruption onto the international agenda. Unlike most cases of transnational civil society, this "network" consists primarily of a single international nongovernmental organization (INGO), Transparency International. Transparency International has created effective links with international organizations and national governments and has systematically cultivated the establishment of national chapters in scores of countries. But the basic story is about what a single man with a powerful idea at the right moment can accomplish through transnational nongovernmental means. Fredrik Galtung, the first professional staff member hired by Transparency International, brings us an insider's account of this remarkable organization.

Rebecca Johnson's chapter addresses a more diverse, and divided, network: the array of groups that campaign for nuclear arms control. As she shows, this motley crew uses very different strategies, from Greenpeace's direct action to the Programme for Promoting Nuclear Nonproliferation's behind-the-scenes meetings of government officials and nongovernmental experts. On occasion, members of the network have found themselves sharply at odds with one another over both tactics and goals. Yet the groups share a common dedication to reducing the risk of nuclear war, and their disparate approaches have proved complementary. Most strikingly, the chapter makes clear that without the active participation of transnational civil society, such fundamental nuclear arms control accords as the Comprehensive Test Ban Treaty and the permanent extension of the Nonproliferation Treaty would never have been signed.

Sanjeev Khagram tells a story that in many ways is the mirror image of Transparency International's top-down approach. In his chapter on the gradual emergence of a global network opposing the construction of large dams, Khagram identifies the origin of the network in multiple *national* civil society campaigns. These campaigns emerged not only in North America and Western Europe but also in Brazil, India, Indonesia, China, and a host of other developing countries. The frequent complaint against transnational civil society—that it overwhelmingly represents the concerns of Northerners who have the time and resources to apply to civil society organizing, rather than the concerns of people in poor countries—clearly does not apply in this case.

Chetan Kumar looks at one of the most controversial of transnational civil society roles: the targeting of specific governments with the aim of changing not just the policies but the very nature of those governments. In case studies on the Zapatista movement in Mexico and the campaign to restore President Aristide to power in Haiti, Kumar grapples with profound questions about the morality and practicality of transnational nongovernmental efforts to influence domestic processes of democratization.

Motoko Mekata recounts the odyssey of perhaps the best known of the recent transnational civil society campaigns: the International Campaign to Ban Landmines. In addition to providing a comprehensive account of the transnational network's activities and impacts, she shows the extent to which the loosely coordinated campaign depended on the quite independent activities of national-level civil society. She provides a particularly detailed insider's account of the Japanese national campaign, which more than most depended for its success on its transnational counterparts.

In the final case study, Thomas Risse explains the complex processes by which transnational civil society has transformed attitudes toward human rights in the second half of the twentieth century. He elucidates the impact transnational civil society has had on setting global human rights standards and changing governmental behavior. And he raises major questions about the future of this large and seemingly well-entrenched sector of transnational civil society.

These quite diverse stories are all variations on a common theme: efforts to solve problems that span borders in the absence of border-spanning governments. This introductory chapter provides a common framework of definitions, questions, and context. Chapter 8 returns to those questions to see what answers have emerged.

The Nature of the Beast

At first glance, it seems odd that transnational civil society should exist at all, much less be able to sway mighty governments and rich corporations. Why should people in disparate parts of the world devote significant amounts of time and energy, for little or no pay, to collaborations with groups with whom they share neither history nor culture? These networks are unlike the other major collectivities in the world. States occupy clearly defined physical territories with the coercive power to extract resources from those territories and their inhabitants, enjoy legal recognition from other states, and can call on powerful sentiments of patriotism to cement the loyalties of their citizens. The various subsidiaries of transnational corporations are tied together by common economic interests and legal obligations.

By contrast, transnational civil society networks—the emerging third force in global politics—tend to aim for broader goals based on their conceptions of what constitutes the public good. They are bound together more by shared values than by self-interest.[5] The values the networks espouse vary tremendously. They range from beliefs in the rights of animals to religious beliefs to beliefs about the inherent superiority of some ethnic groups over others. Some of these values are widely held. Others, particularly the racist views reflected in the hate groups, are repugnant indeed.[6]

We use the somewhat ungainly term "transnational civil society" in preference to other frequently heard lingo (such as "global civil society") to emphasize both the border-crossing nature of the links and the fact that rarely are these ties truly global, in the sense of involving groups and individuals from every part of the world. The Middle East and sub-Saharan Africa in particular are severely underrepresented in transnational nongovernmental coalitions, other than those that address strictly regional and developmental concerns.

The definition of transnational civil society comes in three parts. First, like all civil society, it includes only groups that are *not* governments or profit-seeking private entities.[7] Second, it is transnational— that is, it involves linkages across national borders. Third, as the case studies show, it takes a variety of forms. Sometimes it takes the form of a single INGO with individual members or chapters in several countries, as in the case of Transparency International. In other cases, transnational civil society consists of more informal border-crossing coalitions of organizations and associations, such as the International Campaign to Ban Landmines.

The coalitions overlap with the rapidly growing set of nongovernmental service providers—such as CARE or Médecins sans frontières—that are increasingly familiar from the extensive news coverage of their role in humanitarian disaster relief efforts as well as development projects in poor countries. These service providers have benefited enormously from the increasing tendency of governments and intergovernmental organizations to channel relief and development funds through NGOs rather than to national or local governments.[8] Although there is overlap between the ranks of the nongovernmental service providers, newly flush with government funds, and the members of the advocacy coalitions, the two are not identical, and the fortunes of the latter do not depend on the continued government-provided resources of the former.

The Long Tradition

Although most of the literature on the subject dates from the 1990s, transnational civil society has played a role in global affairs for centuries. Indeed, it may be as old as religion. As one author points out: "Religious communities are among the oldest of the transnational: Sufi orders, Catholic missionaries, Buddhist monks carried word and praxis across vast spaces before those places become nation states or even states. Such religious peripatetics were versions of civil society."[9]

And religious organizations provided the impetus behind the first modern transnational policy campaign: the nineteenth-century campaign to end slavery. Substantial evidence now exists that slavery remained economically viable in most of the places where it was abolished. The practice of slavery ended not because slaveholders found it unprofitable but because growing Protestant movements (especially Quaker, Methodist, and Baptist) found it morally reprehensible, persuaded their religious brethren elsewhere of the cause, and in time enlisted the support of the British government, which used its dominant naval power to constrict trade to slaveholding countries.[10] NGOs dedicated to ending the slave trade date to 1775, with the establishment of the Pennsylvania Society for Promoting the Abolition of Slavery, followed a decade later by the British Society for Effecting the Abolition of the Slave Trade and the French Société des Amis des Noirs.[11] The links among the movements solidified in 1839 with the establishment of the British and Foreign Anti-Slavery Society, in one commentator's view, "the first transnational moral entrepreneur—religious movements aside—to play a significant role in world politics."[12]

Slavery was not the only issue to engage the nascent transnational civil society in the 1800s and early 1900s.[13] Peace groups based in Europe and America lobbied at various international peace conferences. Governments began to use nongovernmental technical experts as delegates to international conferences. A variety of civil society associations formed around trade issues. The International Committee of the Red Cross was formed, the first step in what became the transnational Red Cross and Red Crescent Movement. Such groups as the Institut de Droit International and the International Law Association, both formed in 1873, contributed substantially to the development of international law.[14]

Over the course of the twentieth century (with the exception of the periods covering the two world wars), the rate at which INGOs formed steadily grew. These numbers do not tell the full story of the growth of transnational civil society—they include only formally constituted organizations with members and activities in more than one country.[15] But their numbers do reflect a general trend. By the turn of the century, the rate of formation was about ten a year, although nearly as many dissolved themselves every year. The number increased until World War I, fell to nearly nothing during the war years, then jumped again to about forty a year until war clouds again darkened the horizon. Although only a handful were created during the Second World War, immediately afterward the number jumped to unprecedented levels, starting at about a hundred new international associations a year and increasing ever since, with perhaps only ten to twenty dissolving each year. In other words, formal, transnational NGOs have been accumulating at an unprecedented and increasing rate for fifty years. The Union of International Associations now lists over 15,000 transnationally oriented NGOs.[16] And the growth in informal transnational coalitions and linkages of all sorts is, if anything, outpacing the increase in formal organizations.

Now, coalitions that claim to speak for broad regional and global public interests abound. Hardly an international issue can be found that lacks at least a rudimentary transnational network, and many are highly developed. The Climate Action Network, a 269-organization alliance of national and regional environmentalist nodes, has coalesced around the climate change negotiations.[17] Women's groups have taken advantage of a series of large United Nations conferences to form a thick weave of interconnections.[18] In 1998, some 600 NGOs from around the world linked to put an end to negotiations in the Organization for Economic Cooperation and Development (OECD) on the Multilateral Agreement on Investment.[19] One of the larger networks active in the peace and conflict arena, the Hague Appeal for Peace, held a conference in May 1999 that drew some 10,000 activists, who used the occasion to launch several new campaigns.[20] With all the potential case studies, this could easily have been a very long book indeed.[21]

How Do They Do It?

Standard international relations thinking assumes a hierarchy among the instruments of power: military force ranks highest, then economic resources, then—far down the list, if mentioned at all—such "soft" instruments as moral authority or the power of persuasion.[22] The three types of international actors—states, the private sector, and civil society—vary greatly in their ability to use these instruments. Governments have coercive power, thanks to their control of military forces and the police, and they command economic resources because of their ability to tax. They can, and often do, use control over information to persuade or bamboozle other states, firms, and citizens. Firms lack coercive power but enjoy sometimes substantial economic resources, enabling them to influence governments and the public through everything from campaign contributions to bribes to their ability to provide jobs. And, of course, firms can devote some of their resources to advertising, usually to sell products, but sometimes to sell their views on issues. Civil society groups occasionally command economic resources, but these are usually very limited. By and large, they must rely on softer instruments of power, such as moral authority or the ability to shape how others see their own interests.

In the chapters that follow, the authors show how transnational civil society coalitions have attempted to shape the evolution of international norms—that is, standards about how governments, corporations, and other groups ought to behave.[23] Some of these norms are eventually explicitly codified as treaties, such as many of the human rights standards, the nuclear arms control treaties, the new OECD antibribery convention, or the land-mine treaty. Others may not become treaties but are still widely shared standards of behavior, as is the case for emerging norms about how governments and intergovernmental organizations should treat people who may be displaced by the construction of big dams.

Civil society tries to shape these norms in two ways: directly, by persuading policy makers and business leaders to change their minds about what is the right thing to do—that is, what goal should be pursued—or indirectly, by altering the public's perception of what governments and businesses should be doing. When public pressure is generated, politicians act to please their constituents and businesses must respond to keep investors and consumers happy. Civil society can confer legitimacy on a decision or institution (such as an "eco-label" that gives an environmental seal of approval). It can also threaten to go public with information that is embarrassing or would generate public backlash—a kind of coercion, but one that depends entirely on the ability to persuade the public.

Often, it is nearly impossible to tease out which is driving policy—whether governments and businesses change their policies because of a genuine change of heart or because of a change of calculation about what will look good to the public. Either way, transnational civil society exercises influence through its ability to make someone, policy makers or publics, listen and act. The currency of its power is not force, but credible information and moral authority.

Posing the Questions

This examination of transnational civil society provides more than a set of interesting stories. It provides examples of the variety of governance mechanisms that are emerging to deal with issues with which the nation-state system by itself may be ill equipped to cope.

But the emergence of these mechanisms raises a set of profound questions. How powerful are the transnational networks? Will the trends that hold them together and provide them with power continue? Are the successes of transnational civil society in recent years the result of temporary global upheavals occasioned by, for example, the end of the Cold War, or is the nature of international power truly changing? And most important, what role *should* transnational civil society play as the world struggles to cope with the new global agenda?

The next six chapters provide evidence in detailed case studies of the strength of, and limits to, transnational civil society. Only when there is some basis for evaluating the role of transnational civil society can we have a useful discussion of what that role should be. And opening up a meaningful and detailed debate on that question of "should" is the purpose of this book. Just as societies and their governments have been struggling with the question of what role domestic civil society should have in decision making, the world as a whole must now grapple with the question of the appropriate role of transnational civil society. As globalization proceeds, it will stimulate more transnational civil society formation. And that, in turn, will influence how globalization proceeds. So far, the debate on the role of transnational civil society has been confined largely to polemical broadsides and scholarly journals. It is now time for a broader debate.

Notes

1. CIVICUS, *The New Civic Atlas: Profiles of Civil Society in 60 Countries* (Washington, D.C.: CIVICUS, 1997); CIVICUS, *Citizens: Strengthening Global Civil Society* (Washington, D.C.: CIVICUS, 1994); Estelle James, *The Nonprofit Sector in International Perspective: Studies in Comparative Culture and Policy* (New York: Oxford University Press, 1989); Julie Fisher, *Nongovernments: NGOs and the Political Development of the Third World* (West Hartford, Conn.: Kumarian Press, 1998); Kathleen D. McCarthy, *The Nonprofit Sector in the Global Community: Voices from Many Nations* (San Francisco: Jossey-Bass, 1992); Helmut Anheier and Lester Salamon, eds., *The Nonprofit Sector in the Developing World: A Comparative Analysis* (Baltimore: Johns Hopkins University Press, 1998); Lester M. Salamon and Helmut K. Anheier, *The Emerging Sector: The Nonprofit Sector in Comparative Perspective—An Overview* (Baltimore: Johns Hopkins University Institute for Policy Studies, 1994).

2. There is a vast literature of single-issue case studies. A useful bibliography that includes many types of movements is Sidney Tarrow and Melanie Acostavalle,

"Transnational Politics: A Bibliographic Guide to Recent Research on Transnational Movements and Advocacy Groups," Working Paper, Contentious Politics Series, Lajarsfeld Center at Columbia University, June 1999. This bibliography also provides an extensive listing of relevant theoretical works. In addition, there are several works due out in 2000, such as Peter Newell, *Climate for Change: Non-State Actors and the Global Politics of the Greenhouse* (Cambridge: Cambridge University Press).

3. Steve Charnovitz, "Two Centuries of Participation: NGOs and International Governance," *Michigan Journal of International Law* 18, no. 2 (winter 1997): 183–286; Ann Marie Clark, "Non-Governmental Organizations and Their Influence on International Society," *Journal of International Affairs* 48, no. 2 (winter 1995): 507–25; Margaret E. Keck and Kathryn Sikkink, *Activists Beyond Borders: Advocacy Networks in International Politics* (Ithaca, N.Y.: Cornell University Press, 1998); Thomas G. Weiss and Leon Gordenker, eds., NGOs, *the UN, and Global Governance* (Boulder, Colo.: Lynne Rienner, 1996); Shirin Sinnar, "Mixed Blessing: The Growing Influence of NGOs," *Harvard International Review* 18, no. 1 (winter 1995–96): 54–57; Jackie Smith, Charles Chatfield, and Ron Pagnucco, eds., *Transnational Social Movements and Global Politics: Solidarity Beyond the State* (Syracuse, N.Y.: Syracuse University Press, 1997).

4. John Clark, *Democratizing Development: The Role of Voluntary Organizations* (West Hartford, Conn.: Kumarian Press, 1991); Michael Edwards and David Hulme, eds., *Beyond the Magic Bullet: NGO Performance and Accountability in the Post-War World* (West Hartford, Conn.: Kumarian Press, 1996); David Hulme and Michael Edwards, eds., NGOs, *States and Donors: Too Close for Comfort?* (New York: St. Martin's Press, 1996); Jonathan Fox and L. David Brown, eds., *The Struggle for Accountability: The World Bank, NGOs, and Grassroots Movements* (Cambridge, Mass.: MIT Press, 1998); David C. Korten, *Getting to the 21st Century: Voluntary Action and the Global Agenda* (West Hartford, Conn.: Kumarian Press, 1990); Jessica T. Mathews, "Power Shift," *Foreign Affairs* 76, no. 1 (January 1997): 50–66; P. J. Simmons, "Learning to Live with NGOs," *Foreign Policy* 112 (fall 1998): 82–96; Peter J. Spiro, "New Global Communities: Nongovernmental Organizations in International Decision-Making Institutions," *Washington Quarterly* 18, no. 1 (winter 1995): 45–56.

5. Some cross-border activism is purely self-interested. Many commentators waspishly noted that the labor union leaders demonstrating in Seattle against the WTO showed little concern for working conditions overseas until the removal of trade barriers threatened to allow a flood of cheap imports made by low-paid workers. But such barbs too easily dismiss the vast army of social activists with no discernible selfish interests at stake. Many transnational civil society connections represent more mundane pursuits, such as the many cross-border professional societies and business associations, but such organizations are not the focus of this book. Here we are examining the value-driven organizations and networks.

6. A private monitoring group called Hatewatch monitors the on-line activities of hate groups, which are forming growing transnational connections. See www.hatewatch.org. Another unpleasant set of transnational actors is often incorrectly grouped with transnational civil society: drug traffickers and other ele-

ments of global organized crime. These networks, however, are not civil society groups as this book uses the term. They are pursuing profits, not moral causes.

7. Defining civil society is itself something of a cottage industry. For a useful review of the definitional literature, see Adil Najam, "Understanding the Third Sector: Revisiting the Prince, the Merchant, and the Citizen," *Nonprofit Management and Leadership* 7, no. 2 (winter 1996): 203–19. See also Chris Hann and Elizabeth Dunn, *Civil Society: Challenging Western Models* (New York: Routledge, 1996); Louis D. Hunt, "Civil Society and the Idea of a Commercial Republic," in *The Revival of Civil Society*, ed. Michael G. Schecter (New York: St. Martin's Press, 1999), pp. 11–37.

8. Several of the works described in the annotated bibliography discuss this tendency, known as the New Policy Agenda, and its implications. See, for example, the various works by Michael Edwards.

9. Susanne Hoeber Rudolph, "Introduction: Religion, States, and TCS," in *Transnational Religion and Failing States*, ed. S. H. Rudolph and J. Piscatori (Boulder, Colo.: Westview Press, 1997), p. 1.

10. Presentation by Carl Kaysen at the UCLA Conference on Norms and International Governance, July 17–20, 1997.

11. Charnovitz, "Two Centuries of Participation."

12. Betty Fladeland, *Men and Brothers: Anglo-American Antislavery Cooperation* (1972), p. 258, cited in Charnovitz, "Two Centuries of Participation," p. 192.

13. For short accounts of four early transnational networks, see Keck and Sikkink, *Activists Beyond Borders*, chap. 2.

14. Charnovitz, "Two Centuries of Participation," pp. 191–208.

15. The information in this paragraph is taken from John Boli and George M. Thomas, "World Culture in the World Polity: A Century of International Non-Governmental Organization," *American Sociological Review* 62 (1997): 171–90.

16. Union of International Associations, "International Organizations by Type (Table 1)," in *Yearbook of International Organizations*. www.uia.org//uiastats/stybv196.htm.

17. For information, see www.climatenetwork.org.

18. Keck and Sikkink, *Activists Beyond Borders*, chap. 5.

19. Curtis Runyan, "Action on the Front Lines," *World Watch* November–December 1999, pp. 12–21.

20. The new campaigns include the International Action Network on Small Arms, at www.iansa.org; the International Criminal Court Global Ratification Campaign, at cicc@ciccnow.org; and the Global Ban on Depleted Uranium Weapons, which does not have an independent web site. For information on the Hague Appeal for Peace itself, see www.haguepeace.org.

21. The annotated bibliography lists a number of such case studies, including several edited volumes intended for academic audiences. Although these tend to have a theoretical bent, the case studies are often accessible to a more general audience.

22. Robert O. Keohane and Joseph S. Nye, Jr., "Power and Interdependence in the Information Age," *Foreign Affairs* 77, no. 5 (September–October 1998): 81–94, use the term "soft power" in ways that overlap with its usage here. They discuss the "soft power" available to the United States thanks to its dominance in informa-

tion technology. Like them, we see it as a kind of power that "depends largely on the persuasiveness of the free information that an actor seeks to transmit" (p. 86).

23. A major academic debate is now under way over whether and how norms matter in international relations. Scholars used to focus primarily on military or economic levers of power, ignoring questions of how states and other actors would decide what they wanted to do with that power. A new school of thought called constructivism focuses on questions of how international actors "construct" their interests—that is, how they determine what they want to do and why those goals change. Constructivists point out that structures—those entities with the most military, economic, or other resources—have to interact with agents—people and institutions that shape international norms about what behavior is acceptable and what aspirations are legitimate. In the case of transnational networks of the type analyzed in this book, those agents are nongovernmental actors that are quite consciously attempting to bring about a global political change.

2

A Global Network to Curb Corruption: The Experience of Transparency International

Fredrik Galtung

No country can ignore Transparency International (TI).
—*Economist*, October 30, 1999

IN 1999, AN ARGENTINE group called Poder Ciudadano (Citizen Power) negotiated an integrity pact with the city government of Buenos Aires. Under the agreement, Poder Ciudadano is monitoring a $1.2 billion subway construction project to root out corruption. In other words, a nongovernmental organization (NGO) is now playing a crucial role in ensuring that there is scrupulous compliance with the legal and ethical principles of the procurement procedure, that government and the companies are fully responsible for the actions of their employees, and that there will be greater openness through public hearings and access to all documents and files related to the contract and its implementation.

A decade ago, corruption in such a project would have been taken for granted, not only in Argentina but in an overwhelming number of countries around the world. And certainly the idea that a government might invite an NGO to scrutinize such a project for ethical lapses would have seemed ludicrous. But Poder Cuidadano is not just an Argentine group. It is the Argentine chapter of an international NGO known as Transparency International. In the past decade, the transnational network spearheaded by Transparency International has brought about a sea change in global attitudes toward corruption.[1] How this came about and where the anticorruption movement is heading are the subjects of this chapter.[2]

The Corruption Scene Before
Transparency International

To gauge the impact of this network, it is important to understand the state of affairs prevailing in the early 1990s, before TI was formed. Although corruption had long festered to a greater or lesser degree within most societies, a number of factors combined in the 1990s to bring about what commentators have described as a veritable "corruption eruption" around the world.[3] These factors included the deregulation and privatization of markets in former Soviet bloc countries, the mushrooming of opportunities for international economic transactions between innumerable actors worldwide, and the acceleration and relative democratization of information technologies that can move information and money instantaneously and discreetly around the planet. Together, these conditions created a hothouse for the flourishing of an unprecedented *corruption sans frontières*.[4]

Such corruption has major economic, social, and environmental effects, hurting a wide range of interest groups. The World Bank has named corruption as the single biggest obstacle to economic development in the Third World. Large proportions of donor aid have been fraudulently diverted for personal profit. Developing countries then lose out all over again as foreign investors are deterred by reputations for fiscal mismanagement and corrupt bureaucracy. Members of the business community lament that corruption adds huge margins to their costs. They are concerned, too, that in an increasingly interdependent global economy, corruption constantly threatens to undermine global economic stability (contributing, for instance, to the recent economic collapse in numerous Asian countries). Those committed to improving governance and strengthening the potential of civil society worldwide recognize corruption as a key enemy of good governance. And environmental campaigners know that new regulations to protect the environment are drawing corruption like a magnet, with companies bribing officials to overlook the regulations and grant environmentally harmful contracts. Thus, as TI argues in its mission statement, "corruption is one of the greatest challenges of the contemporary world. It undermines good government, fundamentally distorts public policy, leads to the misallocation of resources, harms the private sector and private sector development, and particularly hurts the poor."

One estimate from the World Bank sets the average cost of bribery among transnational corporations alone at $80 billion per year. Until recently, only one country—the United States—legally prohibited bribe paying by its citizens, with its 1977 Foreign Corrupt Practices Act. According to sources from the U.S. Department of Commerce, American companies lost more than 100 international contracts, valued at $45 billion, in 1994 and 1995 as a result of their inability to bribe. And the U.S. Treasury estimates that U.S. corporations lose $30 billion in contracts every year because of their nonparticipation in bribery.[5] (Of course, their competitors retort that the 1977 act did not actually lead American corporations to stop bribing but rather to bribe more covertly.) A 1999 Commerce Department report found allegations of foreign bribery in fifty-five contracts valued at $37 billion in the first four months of the year. Over a five-year period, bribery is believed to have influenced decisions on 294 commercial contracts worth $145 billion. These reports are characterized as the "tip of the iceberg."[6] And significantly, about half the corruption complaints concern international defense procurement.

Before TI, little progress was made in combating corruption. Indeed, many people did not see it as a significant problem. Aside from the Americans, other transnational corporations tended to oppose the imposition of international—let alone unilateral—standards and regulations against (their) corruption. The International Chamber of Commerce's 1977 "Rules of Conduct to Combat Extortion and Bribery" were widely recognized as a toothless and unenforceable instrument. As late as 1994, on a BBC World Service program, Lord Young (then chairman of Cable & Wireless and former minister for trade and industry) stated, "When you are talking about kickbacks, you're talking about something that's illegal in [the United Kingdom], and of course, you wouldn't dream of doing it here. But there are parts of the world

I've been to where we all know it happens. And if you want to be in business you have to do [it]." Similarly, Father Lay, a leading German theologian and management consultant on business ethics, went so far as to state in the same year that the only "moral issue pertaining to corruption in international trade is jobs," by which he presumably meant the potential loss of jobs—in particular, German jobs—that might ensue from corruption exposure and prosecution.

As the 1990s progressed, most European countries continued to allow for the tax deductibility of bribes as business expenses. This was done on the basis of a tacitly agreed sliding scale, according to which exporters could pay up to 15 percent in tax-deductible illicit commissions in high growth–high corruption countries and up to 3 percent even for bribery expenses incurred inside the European Union.[7]

Until very recently, social scientists had failed to assess the damage done by corruption. Some economists have long entertained a distinction between supposedly "good" and "bad" corruption, "good" corruption being, for instance, bribe paying that would cut red tape in public administration and speed up the process of acquiring permits and paperwork. Underlying this "grease-is-positive"[8] hypothesis is the notion that corruption allows supply and demand to operate in the public sphere to the benefit of the highest bidder. But in fact, experience shows that this systematically increases the costs of public procurement.[9] Meanwhile, other leading economists were making it clear that, in their view, the solution to systemic corruption at the interface of the public and the private sectors was simple. Gary Becker argued that "the only way to reduce corruption permanently is to drastically cut back government's role in the economy."[10] In other words, governments should privatize state holdings and public services. But the experience of many countries over the past few years indicates that the privatization process can itself be a significant source of corruption.[11] In one particularly telling example, after a coup in Nigeria, the military rulers used the cover of a war on corruption to "speed up the privatization of the state companies, whose profitable shares could be sold to loyal servants of the new regime."[12]

Most social scientists simply ignored the subject. Robert Putnam's 1993 book *Making Democracy Work*, the outcome of a twenty-year study of the relative effectiveness of Italian public institutions, is one of the decade's most influential works in political science. Yet it contains only minor references to corruption. No serious observer of the Italian state system could now overlook the system of networks and values that so marks the country's political economy.[13] Similarly, as late as 1993, the World Bank published *Governance*, a treatise on the four constitutive elements of "good governance": (1) public-sector management, (2) accountability, (3) the legal framework for development, and (4) information and transparency.[14] However, the document barely mentions corruption, despite the fact that corruption is actually a key symptom of the failure of each of these governance dimensions and is a constant variable affecting governance in general.

Tellingly, an internal memorandum circulated in the World Bank around this time referred to corruption as the "c" word; this was symptomatic of the taboo both within the Bank and in much of the multilateral development community surrounding the corruption issue at the time. The taboo becomes more understandable when we consider that even today, the five largest national clients of the World Bank are still ranked by TI and other agencies as being among the most corrupt countries in the world.

It would be misleading to argue that TI grew on ground that was entirely infertile. At the same time that corruption was getting worse, it was also becoming politically easier to address. Before the fall of the Berlin Wall, for instance, tyrants on every continent were shored up by Western governments anxious to secure and retain support for their own geopolitical agendas. Much of this support was channeled through international organizations. But with the Cold War imperative gone, the scope for action against corrupt governments has greatly widened. Systemic corruption has at last come to be understood as a major impediment to development and to the legitimacy of democratic institutions. And U.S.-based corporations, whose hands have been tied—at least officially—since the 1977 anticorruption act, would for that very reason like to see other countries being similarly constrained, making it a bribe-free, level playing field.

One significant social factor contributing to TI's early recognition was the popular movement against corruption in so many countries since the late 1980s. "People power" recently contributed to bringing down corrupt rulers in the Philippines; in Bangladesh, protesters choked the streets to Dhaka to force down President Ershad. Meanwhile, in Brazil, thousands of "painted faces" took to the streets and deposed

President Collor.[15] Throughout 1992 and 1993, significant corruption scandals reached the highest political echelons in countries as diverse as Belgium, Spain, Italy, Japan, France, and Russia, making it clear that corruption was not a problem limited to developing countries alone. These scandals effectively exploded any myths about the moral superiority of advanced industrialized countries—or indeed democracies—and helped demonstrate that the North could no longer preach from a position of supposed virtue. More importantly, these problems made it clear that corruption was not merely a necessary, albeit difficult, stage in state formation and capital accumulation that countries pass through on the road to modernization.

Along with the end of the Cold War, the new wave of democratizations provided an ideal moment to challenge corruption. In addition, without its powerful traditional opponent, the United States now enjoyed more leverage to influence the agenda in international forums such as the Organization for Economic Cooperation and Development (OECD) and the Organization of American States (OAS) and to press for regional anticorruption conventions worldwide.[16] U.S. business interests were, of course, keen to seize this opportunity to have other countries judicially bound not to bribe.

The Genesis of Transparency International

In 1990, World Bank representatives stationed in Africa met in Swaziland to discuss the long-term-perspective study on improving governance as a condition for economic development.[17] Peter Eigen was then the regional director for East Africa, based in Nairobi. Eigen was not particularly interested in corruption per se, but he had witnessed firsthand, through more than two decades of development work, the devastating impact of corruption, and he was convinced that corruption had to be tackled for meaningful and sustainable development to occur. The response among the Bank's representatives in Africa—and above all from the political leaders in the region—was enthusiastic. It was agreed that the time had come to develop an anticorruption agenda within the World Bank.

At the Bank's Washington headquarters, however, doubts quickly emerged. The Bank's legal department was implacably opposed, repeatedly citing the Bank's articles of confederation as prohibiting it from being involved in a member government's political affairs and claiming that corruption was therefore beyond the Bank's legal mandate. This viewpoint dominated senior and middle management circles. In spite of encouragement from the field generated by staff members' experiences, from certain individuals within World Bank headquarters, and from some (though by no means all) political leaders in the African region, many of the Bank's managers felt that tackling corruption would interfere with the Bank charter's "requirement" to abstain from "political" considerations in lending decisions and was therefore not an option.

Frustrated by the Bank's unwillingness to change from within, Eigen took early retirement and set out on an arduous odyssey to concretize the anticorruption concepts floated in Swaziland. With support from the German technical assistance agency (GTZ), which had encountered corruption in its own development assistance projects and was anxious to confront what seemed to be a growing menace, Eigen crisscrossed the world, holding a seemingly endless succession of small meetings with those who expressed interest and drumming up support for the enterprise. Eigen met with business executives from major and medium-sized companies, development officials, journalists, academics, corporate investigators, and political leaders in all major regions of the world.

A number of Eigen's friends and colleagues supported the idea of creating a structure independent of the constraints of an intergovernmental framework. They formed a working group that met at regular intervals throughout 1991–92—first in Eschborn (near Frankfurt), then in Kampala, London, Washington, D.C., and finally the Hague. By the end of 1992, a substantial group of supporters formed Transparency International's initial board of directors and advisory council, including such disparate figures as Nobel laureate Oscar Arias, President Olusegun Obasanjo of Nigeria, and Kamal Hossain, a prominent human rights lawyer from Bangladesh and the country's former minister of justice and foreign affairs. (The original group has been considerably expanded since then to include former presidents of Germany, the

United States, and Botswana; business leaders; and the heads of a number of prominent NGOs.)

The founders thought that to safeguard the independence of the organization, care should be taken to avoid becoming overly dependent on funding from any one source or any one category of sources. Particular effort was made not to be too dependent on funding from the public sector. But as the annual accounts show, TI receives significant grants from several governmental and institutional sources. Its fund-raising in the private sector has been slower than expected and presently stands at about 10 percent of its budget. The funding comes from more than a dozen countries.[18]

It was clear from the outset that TI would be a one-issue nonprofit organization aimed at curbing corruption both in the South and in the formerly communist countries in transition in Eastern and Central Europe and the former Soviet Union. Although TI recognized that corruption is found everywhere, many of those who founded the organization were most concerned with curbing its most flagrant damage. As one leading TI figure put it, while "countries of the North may be able to 'afford' the luxury of corruption, those elsewhere cannot."[19]

In addition to working in countries where internal systemic corruption was prevalent, TI would focus on countries in the North whose business communities were fueling corruption by bribing to obtain export orders. It was felt that this sort of international "grand corruption" had the most devastating impact on the economic and social development of countries in the South and in transition. Furthermore, this international corruption was taking place in a legal vacuum, since only one country—the United States—had criminalized bribery by its multinationals abroad, and international mutual judicial assistance arrangements were not geared toward indicting leading political figures.[20]

Finally, TI's founders decided that international corruption, whatever its source, was a legitimate agenda for an international NGO, but that petty corruption within countries remained an issue that was best left to local institutions. Therefore, TI's motto in the first few years described the organization as "the coalition against corruption in international business transactions."

But precisely how these ambitions were to be realized was unclear. Initially, some supporters advocated an organization devoted to exposing cases of corruption throughout the world, much like Amnesty International does for human rights abuses. But Ian Martin, Amnesty's former secretary-general, was among those who convincingly argued that this model would not suit TI: a muckraking role would be incompatible with TI's resolve to build coalitions to reform corrupt systems. One could not, for example, seek to work with the government and private sector in strengthening the procurement system of a country while at the same time exposing the corrupt practices of those same companies and public officials. Nor could TI claim any obvious competitive advantage at the task of publicizing corruption, which is more legitimately the concern of investigative journalists.[21] And such a role would entail considerable personal risk and the threat of ongoing libel actions.

In any case, the governments most amenable to the TI approach were likely to be those least implicated in corruption. Resources would have a greater impact when directed at countries where structural anticorruption measures would be more readily accepted, rather than wasting resources on pursuing governments at the top of the corruption league who demonstrated no sign of quickly mending their ways. It became clear that the TI approach would need to be evolutionary and focused on reforming systems. To this end, the name Transparency International was decided on, in preference to earlier (and perhaps for many, more alarming) names such as the International Business Monitor.[22]

Another cornerstone of TI's working consensus was that although corruption is undoubtedly a moral issue, a sufficiently broad coalition of interests could be built only around the social, political, and economic costs and drawbacks of corruption. The issue simply could not be convincingly sold to a sufficiently wide range of interests on moral grounds alone. Instead, different messages of self-interest would need to be generated.

In May 1993, TI held its launch conference in Berlin, with over seventy participants from all inhabited continents. They included people from the three sectors that are the core international stakeholders in this anticorruption process: national governments in the South, the international development community, and transnational corporations (TNCs).[23] Among the conference's participants from the South were Olusegun Obasanjo; Oscar Arias; Festus Mogae, now the president of

Botswana; Ronald MacLean Abaroa, then foreign minister of Bolivia; Alberto Dahik, then vice president of Ecuador; and Enoch Dumbutshena, a former chief justice of Zimbabwe. Numerous bilateral and multilateral donors were represented, including Germany, the Netherlands, the United Kingdom, and France. Representatives of the World Bank and the United Nations Development Programme (UNDP) also attended; private-sector participation included companies such as General Electric and Boeing.

Transparency International's Anticorruption Strategy

In the years since TI came into existence, the anticorruption scene has changed beyond recognition. From being a taboo topic in international circles, corruption has now become a major focus of attention and the subject of international treaties. The task of effecting and maintaining these changes has required a multistranded strategy:

1. Collecting, analyzing, and disseminating information to raise public awareness about the damaging impact of corruption on human and economic development (especially in low-income countries).

2. Building national, regional, and global coalitions that embrace the state, civil society, and the private sector to fight domestic and international corruption.

3. Coordinating and supporting national chapters to implement this mission.

Raising Public Awareness

TI's primary goal in terms of awareness-raising was to crack the taboo surrounding open discussion of corruption. This taboo was, of course, rooted in both the bribe payers' and the bribe takers' fear of exposure, scandal, prosecution, bad public relations, and loss of income (both legitimate and illicit), contracts, and jobs. It was more subtly rooted, too, in old distortions caused by the Cold War, because each side in that ideological struggle had tolerated misbehavior by its client states and allies. The taboo had even finer roots in the feeling that the North could not discuss corruption without seeming morally superior (as many Northerners initially thought they were) and in the feeling that the South and East were under attack. So TI had the task of pointing out that the leading exporters, for instance, from Europe, were likely to be just as corrupt as anyone else. Certainly their institutional integrity systems were older and perhaps in better working order, so that internally, corruption was viewed as a high-risk, low-profit undertaking. But externally, their governments connived in the corruption of politicians and officials in the South—that is, in the active "export" of bribery—by giving tax deductions for bribery, by refusing to criminalize corrupt conduct in their citizens' dealings abroad, and by providing advice and support in corruption matters through the good offices of diplomats stationed in their missions abroad. At the same time, public opinion in the North had to be alerted to the fact that taxes were not only paying for official overseas aid programs but also subsidizing bribery for corruptly obtained contracts. This, too, was potentially difficult territory for TI, as it would have been all too easy for such efforts to fuel the anti-aid lobby, precisely the opposite of what TI was trying to achieve.

The media have assisted TI greatly in raising public awareness. The extent of press coverage for TI's agenda has been remarkable from the beginning. Hardly a day passes without reference to the organization somewhere in the media. Of course, corruption is in many ways a media-friendly topic, with its atmosphere of subterfuge, scandal, and colorful exposés, and the public-oriented aspect of TI's campaign has made maximum use of the righteous social condemnation the media can arouse around specific scandals. But on the downside, media attention has been so prolific that at times TI's appearances in the media (and thus expectations of it in the public eye) have been running well ahead of its actual capacity in terms of funding, human resources, and practical powers.

TI's most effective public awareness tool by far has been the TI Corruption Perceptions Index (CPI).[24] The CPI is a compilation of professional polls and surveys that captures the perception of thousands of international business leaders, risk analysts, and business journalists on the relative degree of corruption in almost 100 countries (figures for 1999). Countries are included in the CPI if they are covered by at least four polls, and their scores are averaged on a scale of zero to ten, where zero is entirely corrupt and ten is a perfectly clean state. In the 1999 CPI, covering ninety-nine countries, Cameroon ranked as the most corrupt, and Denmark as the least corrupt.

There is widespread recognition that the CPI is perhaps the most useful indicator of corruption available today, and there are few scholarly publications on corruption that do not cite it or use it in some manner. However, the impact of the CPI goes well beyond the academic world. It extends into the international media and reappears, for instance, in jokes made by taxi drivers in Pakistan. Jeff Stein quotes his Pakistani driver in an article on corruption in Pakistan:

> "You know," asked Ahmad, swerving around a crater that could have swallowed his little taxi, "how Pakistan was No. 2 in the world in corruption?"
>
> I said that I'd heard something about it. Pakistan had been ranked second only to Nigeria in a 1996 "global corruption index" by an outfit called Transparency International.
>
> "Actually," Ahmad went on, "we were No. 1. But we bribed the Nigerians to take first place."[25]

Shortly after publication of the 1996 CPI, opposition members of Pakistan's parliament confronted then prime minister Benazir Bhutto with the results of the survey. She erupted angrily, claiming that hers was the "most honest administration in Pakistan's history." Street demonstrations followed, and only days later, she was dismissed from office by a president whose decision had reportedly been influenced by response to the CPI. Bhutto lost the ensuing election in a landslide.

Similarly, in Cameroon, the government initially reacted strongly against the country's poor showing in the 1998 CPI. It responded with a national press campaign to publicize the work it had been doing against corruption in recent years. However, the overwhelming response within the country's media and business community seemed to be one of relief that the extent of corruption could finally begin to be addressed openly.[26] And a couple of months after the release of the 1998 index, TI received a letter of invitation from the president asking for assistance in strengthening Cameroon's corruption-control efforts.

These examples from Pakistan and Cameroon are indicative of the influence the CPI can have. One former South American president was so incensed at his country's poor score in the CPI that he threatened to mount a legal action against TI, claiming that the CPI had a negative effect on foreign direct investment and even on aid. Even a country's absence from the CPI can now be a source of controversy. For instance, the fact that Ecuador was excluded from the CPI was taken as a sign that the country is so corrupt that it does not deserve to be included. And in Kenya, the government improbably claimed that the country's absence from the CPI must mean a clean bill of health for its own anticorruption program.

Because of this considerable impact, TI is under pressure to improve and expand on the CPI's original methodology. At best, however, this sort of survey can measure only two things: trends over time and relative positions vis-à-vis other countries. It does not capture the absolute amount of corruption in any one country, nor does it go into much detail.

One of the first criticisms of the CPI when it was first published in 1995 was that it illustrated only one side of the international corruption equation: the receiving end. It says nothing about the bribe payers. The ranks of corruption-prone countries are overwhelmingly filled with those that are very poor. The countries with low levels of corruption are all advanced and industrialized. Yet one of the founding principles of TI was to highlight the international dimension of corruption, addressing it as a shared problem of both the bribe payer and the bribe taker.

A ranking of the propensity to pay bribes among leading exporting countries was urgently needed. The problem TI faced was the lack of any empirical evidence for such a ranking. Whereas numerous companies regularly provide data on corruption among public officials, so far no one has published a ranking of bribe payers. A "poll of polls" approach was therefore not an option for the BPI—the Bribe Payers Index. Conducting a new survey on this sensitive topic would have to be done from a clean slate by developing a sample questionnaire and using focus groups and pilot testing—and finding the necessary funding for a major international survey. Only in 1999 was TI able to bring

the necessary resources together. The 1999 BPI covers the top nine-
teen exporting countries, from Australia to the United States—a logical cutoff point, since it excludes countries that largely export com-
modities. About 90 percent of the respondents are from the emerging
or developing world.

Forging Coalitions Against Domestic and International Corruption

It was clear from the beginning that the coalition-building approach
would be at the center of TI's strategy. To change such deeply entrenched
practices would require the support of businesses, governments, intergovernmental organizations, and other NGOs. A core element of TI's
institutional strategy has been to build what its chairman, Peter Eigen,
calls "natural coalitions of interests."[27] This emphasis on coalitions
reflects TI's conviction that anticorruption programs will succeed
only if they have broad-based support, and only if a wide cross section
of civil society recognizes specific reasons (beyond the general public
good) for curbing corruption. Those reasons are many and varied.
Corruption stunts and corrodes the protection of human rights, the
enforcement of property rights (which are essential for business), the
development of professional standards (for instance, in law, accounting, and engineering), the protection of children against exploitation,
and environmental protection. Hence, the diverse appeal of the anticorruption movement means that it can bring together actors who are
normally strangers. TI's wider goal, shared today by many who are
working on behalf of NGOs, advocacy, and improved governance, is to
form coalitions of the state, civil society, and the private sector.

Business. From its discussions with sympathetic business leaders,
TI knew that there was a significant business lobby ready to start
pushing corporate conduct toward an anticorruption culture with
sharp distinctions between public duty and private gain. Crucially,
this collective culture would be supported only if corruption could be
controlled without conceding competitive advantage to business ri-
vals. The businesspeople did not trust their competitors, who were
imprisoned with them by the snares of corruption. Yet unless they all
cooperated, none of them would escape from the corruption scenario.

The rules must change for everyone and all at once, so as to avoid the sort of unilateral action U.S. companies had complained of since the passage of anticorruption legislation back in 1977.

Another contributing factor to the private sector's gradual willingness to take up the anticorruption crusade has been the growing interest in business ethics, with a proliferation of research centers, publications, seminars, and business networks worldwide, but particularly in the United States, newly devoted to the evolution and application of ethics. This drive toward ethics in public life certainly coincides with TI's own motivation, but TI tends to recommend the pragmatic benefits of anticorruption measures rather than calling for moral sacrifices. In any case, this dual, pragmatic perspective seems to underpin most of the business ethics movement too, with the principal argument being that in the long run, ethics are good for business, rather than a constraint on it.

Government. TI scored its first major triumph when a number of TI national chapters in the Americas, working with then-chair of the TI advisory council, vice president of Ecuador Alberto Dahik, lobbied to place the issue of corruption on the agenda for the intergovernmental Summit of the Americas, held in Miami in 1994. It was important that the voice of the South was heard to be behind such a move, because there was a common perception in some quarters that this topic was largely being driven by U.S.-based interests.

In an official communiqué, over thirty elected heads of state and government leaders from countries as diverse as Colombia and Canada, the United States and Uruguay, unanimously agreed that corruption was a problem in all their countries and required concerted action at both the national and international levels. This was a landmark declaration, representing the first time that leaders from both South and North had clearly joined to lay the groundwork for a regional convention. Furthermore, their declaration specifically addressed the need to incorporate civil society into any anticorruption effort. Thus the taboo around the "c" word was finally shattered in Miami.

The next task of TI was to lobby the Paris-based OECD. TI knew that mechanisms emerging from the OECD had the potential to curb the export of international corruption, as OECD members were the source of most of the world's bribes. These mechanisms could also be extended to include non-OECD countries once the process was ratified.

TI had a ready-made governmental partner for this effort. When the U.S. Congress amended the Foreign Corrupt Practices Act in 1988, it countered critics of the legislation by encouraging the U.S. government to call on the OECD to prohibit its member countries from bribing foreign officials. At the beginning of the Clinton administration, corruption reform became a high priority within the executive branch as well. Dan Tarullo, assistant secretary of state for economics and business affairs from 1993, became actively involved and was strongly supported by Secretary of State Warren Christopher. Their combined efforts led to the adoption of the first OECD recommendation on corruption at the May 1994 ministerial meeting.

Because this U.S. diplomatic initiative coincided with the launch of the TI movement, TI lobbied for the proposed initiative, with TI chapters in OECD countries such as Australia, Belgium, Britain, Canada, Denmark, France, and the United States maintaining a dialogue both with their own governments and with missions at the OECD. Through its network of national chapters in key OECD member countries that lobbied their governments at opportune moments, TI played a role in advancing the process. The result was that in November 1997, the twenty-nine industrialized members of the OECD, along with five additional non-OECD countries, finally completed a treaty requiring all signatories to ban overseas bribery, going well beyond the original objective of ending the tax deductibility of bribes paid abroad. Editorials in the *New York Times*, *Washington Post*, and *International Herald Tribune*, for instance, credited TI for its contribution.[28]

Meanwhile, TI-Brussels was instrumental in encouraging the European Commission to issue directives against intra–European Community transborder corruption, encompassing areas previously outside the bounds of legal prosecution. TI-Brussels is a national chapter for Belgium and also has a pivotal role within the European Union (EU), which is headquartered in Brussels. It prepared and circulated a detailed discussion document that outlined initiatives the EU could develop in ways consistent with both TI's and the EU's own general mandates. The presence of senior retired EU officials in the TI-Brussels chapter gave this paper particular weight and helped to ensure that it would receive serious attention at the highest levels.

Such regionalization of international corruption control is not merely a pragmatic compromise between unilateral action and a global convention. Rather, regional controls set the stage for development of appropriate instruments and jurisprudence within a smaller group of countries, a necessary building block if international cooperation is to work.

International Financial Institutions. Meanwhile, TI was also convincing the World Bank and the International Monetary Fund (IMF) to adopt more assertive postures against corruption. "Brown bag" lunches organized around the issue at the World Bank in Washington from 1993 onward consistently drew crowds that extended down the corridors outside. While these meetings went on at the core of the Bank, TI was creating a partnership out in the field with the Economic Development Institute (EDI) of the World Bank. For instance, Petter Langseth had been the World Bank adviser for civil service reform in Uganda in the early 1990s and had excellent contacts both inside and outside the Ugandan government. TI's 1995 work in Uganda and Tanzania quickly attracted his interest, and since then, the EDI has been able to magnify the scope and impact of TI's in-country work.

For example, the EDI published the proceedings of the TI-organized first Arusha National Integrity Workshop, held in Tanzania in 1995. This book included the integrity pledge adopted by Benjamin Mkapa when he was elected president of Tanzania a month after the workshop. In addition, the EDI published, translated, and widely disseminated the TI publication *National Integrity Systems: The TI Source Book*, and the book has assumed a central role in much of TI's and the EDI's in-country work. Within the EDI, Langseth was able to demonstrate to skeptics in the World Bank that it was possible to become engaged in anticorruption work without courting controversy, provided the work was implemented with a careful partner NGO like TI.

Then James Wolfensohn's 1996 appointment as the World Bank's president brought new opportunities. Whereas the EDI was doing experimental work out in the field, Wolfensohn was determined to mainstream anticorruption values into the core of the Bank's activities. During his first year in office, he invited a TI group to Washington to conduct a half-day seminar on corruption for him and his senior staff. As a result, TI was engaged on a consultancy basis to assist the World Bank internally in developing its own new strategy against corruption. Several TI national chapters now work actively with the World Bank in the Bank's member countries, and there is a relatively free flow of information between the international financial institutions and TI.

Individuals. This international coalition of interests against corruption would not have been possible without individual leadership and commitment. For this, TI has relied heavily on and benefited enormously from a large network of voluntary supporters. This has instilled a unique culture that places it quite clearly in the NGO community, as distinct from multilateral organizations or private-sector consultancies.

This voluntary commitment starts with Peter Eigen, who has worked as a full-time "volunteer" chairman of the organization from the beginning. It includes, too, an activist and unpaid board of directors comprising thirteen people from all continents, a number of them contributing a substantial part of their workdays to TI's ongoing activities. TI also has the volunteer services of two "support groups," one based in Washington, D.C., and the other in London.

The involvement of these high-level professionals, and the access that they, in turn, provide to key decision makers, undoubtedly makes TI more powerful than many traditional advocacy groups. To this end, TI has formed in many countries small, expert working parties of lawyers and accountants who are dedicated to developing approaches that abolish the tax deductibility of bribes and criminalize foreign bribery.

Academics also contribute actively to TI's work in research and dissemination. TI consults a steering committee of leading academics and professionals for its work on the annual corruption indices. For instance, a group of more than thirty academics from over twenty countries contributes to the TI Council on Governance Research.

This international network of skilled, specialized volunteers helps explain how TI was able to operate during its first four years with only a minimal professional capacity in its Berlin office. Remarkably, it was not until 1997 that TI grew to four senior staff members, in addition to eight program officers from six countries. But by 1999, the international secretariat alone had a staff of almost forty professionals.

In short, TI has become the centerpiece of a vigorous transnational coalition. Perhaps the most telling expression of TI's leadership in the international anticorruption sphere has been its role as the secretariat for the Council of the International Anti-Corruption Conference (IACC). The IACC has been held biannually since it was started by the Hong Kong Independent Commission Against Corruption in the 1980s. It was originally the main international meeting for public officials engaged in corruption and fraud control, but it has now expanded to embrace multilateral organizations, the private sector, academia, and NGOs. At the 1995 IACC in Beijing, TI was invited to act as facilitator. Under TI's stewardship, the conference grew in breadth and depth to include 1,200 participants from over ninety countries at its 1997 gathering in Lima (the first meeting at which TI played this facilitating role). On that occasion, the "Lima Declaration" was issued, setting out the actions and responsibilities that need to be undertaken in the coming years. The ninth IACC was held in Durban, South Africa, in 1999, with contributions, for the first time, from the heads of the United Nations, World Bank, OECD, and Interpol; numerous heads of state and chief executive officers; and over 1,300 participants from more than 100 countries.

Building Effective National Chapters

Although popular protest against corruption in individual countries became more common as public awareness grew and expressed itself during the early 1990s, there were few organized anticorruption groups and strategies at national levels. Without such national-level activism, education, and self-regulation, anticorruption efforts were sure to fail. So TI created the web of national chapters that has become the backbone of TI's activities. They define TI both as an international NGO and as an entity entirely distinct from a multilateral body. They embed TI's agenda clearly and coherently into the civil society of over seventy countries worldwide, and it is they who will ensure the sustainability of TI over the long term.

The Berlin secretariat includes a growing team of paid management and staff whose main task is to support the work of the national chapters and to coordinate the mass of anticorruption information that TI processes and produces. This includes the maintenance of an electronic database; an intensive web site carrying a wealth of anticorruption information, as well as links to national chapters; and the publication of the TI *Guidelines*, *Source Book*, CPI, and BPI, as well as other documents and newsletters conveying TI's philosophy, goals, strategies, and challenges.

As a result of extensive media coverage from the beginning, TI's secretariat in Berlin received hundreds of letters and faxes in its first year alone, with inquiries about the possibility of forming affiliated national chapters. The notion of working in specific countries through national chapters was part of TI's original strategy. What no one could have predicted was the overwhelming response this initiative would receive. TI's ready response to these requests meant that by the end of 1999, it had established a network of almost eighty national chapters worldwide.

TI's national chapters draw on people from all segments of professional society. They tend not to be grassroots organizations. In Belgium, for instance, the chairman of the national chapter is Baron Jean Godeaux, former president of the central bank. In Benin, it was the recently deceased Monsignor de Souza, the archbishop of Cotonou; in Malawi, an Anglican bishop, the Right Reverend Bvumbwe, heads the chapter. In Brazil, Canada, Egypt, Germany, Poland, New Zealand, Russia, Singapore, and South Korea, university academics lead the chapters, while chapters in Colombia, the Gambia, Mali, and Panama are led by newspaper editors and publishers.

In numerous countries (Denmark, Hungary, Italy, Kenya, Malaysia, Mauritius, Paraguay, Tanzania, Uganda, the United Kingdom, the United States, and others), the initiative has been taken by members of the private sector, representing large, medium, and small companies. Current and former public officials have also taken leadership positions in the TI national chapters of countries such as Bolivia, Ecuador, France, Jamaica, Namibia, Papua New Guinea, Peru, Zambia, and others. And in countries such as Argentina, Pakistan, Panama, and Venezuela, existing NGOs with anticorruption agendas have been accredited as TI national chapters.

In the taxonomy of national chapters used in TI's annual report, three distinctions are made: those chapters that have been formally accredited by the TI board of directors, those that are in formation, and those countries where there is a TI contact person but an insufficient basis to start a chapter-forming process. Of the ninety to a hundred chapters currently accredited or in the process of being formed, about thirty are already effectively engaged in their own anticorruption activities.[29]

The diversity of people worldwide who are engaged in or calling for the formation of national chapters indicates that TI has been largely demand driven. TI has not followed a blueprint for the formation of local chapters, preferring to await local expressions of interest. Importantly, TI's national chapters are wholly sui generis and develop their programs based on their own perceptions of their needs and possibilities. Two restricting principles, however, are articulated in TI's *Guide-*

lines for National Chapters. First, TI national chapters must be politically nonpartisan. Prominent members of the opposition or the governing political party cannot occupy leadership or board-level positions in the national chapter. In Ecuador, TI learned the hard way what mistakes can ensue if this is not taken seriously enough.

The founding chairman of TI's advisory council was the former vice president of Ecuador, Alberto Dahik. He took personal initiative in bringing together prominent members of the Ecuadoran establishment to form a national chapter. But irrespective of his actual policies, civil society groups in the country were justifiably skeptical about this national chapter's independence from the government. Then Dahik was accused of bribing members of parliament using a secret slush fund. In fact, this practice of using bribery to assist the passage of new legislation was an unfortunate, although commonplace, practice of long standing. Ironically, the crucial piece of legislation that Dahik was trying to get passed was antibribery legislation. When pursued by the judiciary, Dahik left Ecuador and sought political asylum in Costa Rica, immediately resigning his post with TI and expressing concern that the events might reflect adversely on the organization.

TI learned two lessons from this experience. First, active politicians should not be members of TI's international board or advisory council. Second, national chapters must be perceived to be and actually be independent of the governing party and politicians.

The second restriction that TI imposes on its national chapters is that they do not "undertake investigations of individual allegations of corruption." As noted earlier, the pursuit of such specific instances could undermine TI's more important overall efforts to build coalitions that can strengthen anticorruption systems.

With these two caveats, national chapters are free to develop any activities that might contribute to the anticorruption movement's objectives. This balance of firm guidelines and decentralized autonomy has empowered national chapters to improvise a wide range of strategies that are effective within their own specific cultures. Strategies have included:

- Commissioning a touring street theater to take anticorruption messages to rural areas, as in the Ugandan national chapter.

- Organizing and participating in national integrity work-shops, as in the Indian, Malaysian, Malawian, Tanzanian, and Ugandan chapters.

- Adapting the TI *Source Book* on national integrity systems to local circumstances and jurisprudence, as in the Latin American chapters and in Uganda.

- Organizing national integrity surveys and publicizing the re-sults, as in Bangladesh, Denmark, Tanzania, and Uganda.

- Providing training programs for investigative journalists to strengthen the role of the media in containing corruption, as in Russia, Tanzania, Uganda, and Zimbabwe.

- Campaigning for leading politicians to sign specific anticor-ruption pledges during electioneering periods, with built-in follow-up mechanisms, as in Argentina, Papua New Guinea, and Tanzania.

- Promoting a national competition for schoolchildren to write essays on the dynamics of bribes and cheating, as in Argen-tina.[30]

In some cases, the anticorruption movement is empowering civil society to call for transparency and accountability from their elected representatives. Recently, for instance, the villagers of rural Rajasthan organized a community hearing that revealed webs of corruption among their public servants. Commenting insightfully on the deeper poten-tials of this sort of civic action, *Frontline* magazine pointed out that "apart from being a practical weapon to eradicate corruption at the vil-lage level, the public hearing is a creative exercise in government for the people by the people. It is a small but significant step towards the transition from representative to participative democracy."[31]

However, even the national chapters of TI are primarily a lobbying force not of the grassroots but of elites[32]—that is, of professional, spe-cialized and highly placed individuals in "insider" contexts. Because of its emphasis on institutional change rather than scandalous exposures, TI may well promote "top-down" leadership over grassroots mobilization.

In general, TI's national chapters in the North have tended to focus on the sort of transnational corruption at which Northern countries seem particularly adept, while chapters in the South tend to work on combating corruption at national and local levels. However, cooperation is fostered among chapters across all levels. Chapters in developed countries, for instance, often assist new chapters in developing countries, which in turn form their own alliances with other NGOs, such as churches and human rights organizations, whose goals overlap with theirs. National chapters also initiate their own regional alliances, as did the chapters in Latin America and the Caribbean in 1996 when they formed a regional chapter together.

Multilateral organizations are increasingly keen to enlist the support of TI's national chapters. The World Bank is forging partnerships with national chapters in Tanzania, Uganda, Mauritius, and Bolivia. This reaching out for alliances with TI's chapters reflects the realization that civil society has an indispensable and creative role to play in the development, implementation, and monitoring of national anticorruption strategies. The UNDP has also worked with several of the national chapters and is developing a broader strategy together with the TI movement.

In some cases, multilateral donors admit that cooperation with a recognized local NGO brings them a legitimacy they would not have on their own. In the best of cases, national chapters can provide "local knowledge" that an international organization, whether governmental or nongovernmental, would lack. However, cooperation with local infrastructures is not without its difficulties. In Zimbabwe, for instance, an anticorruption workshop was held for the police fraud squad. But it emerged that members of the squad were unable to read balance sheets and did not know what the term "debit" meant. Assuming that funds could be organized, an apparently logical response might be to provide some form of basic accounts training for these inspectors. But the police commissioner objected, pointing out that if his officers were trained in accounting, they would immediately leave the police force for better pay in the private sector. Under these sorts of enmeshed local circumstances, there can be no ready-made foreign solutions. The solutions have to be evolved locally.

Although TI's national chapters have been spreading around the globe, many are new and relatively fragile. In some countries, they operate in environments that are traditionally alien to the very notion of civil society asserting its values and operating freely. But in others, the creation of new NGOs has become something of a cottage industry, attracting unscrupulous individuals with self-serving agendas.

Some opportunistic individuals have seized on the donor community's current interest in governance and corruption by claiming to represent accredited national chapters. In Burkina Faso, for instance, an NGO calling itself Faso Transparence wrote to bilateral and multilateral donors based in the country claiming to be the TI national chapter. After a TI staffer had visited the country to attend a regional conference, representatives of Faso Transparence also claimed that they had been with him to see the prime minister, when he had in fact met neither them nor the prime minister. A representative of one of the donors checked with the head office and was (correctly) assured that the TI secretariat in Berlin did receive support from that donor. Unfortunately, the donor assumed from this information that the so-called national chapter in Burkina Faso could also be trusted and did not check the credentials of Faso Transparence with the TI head office in Berlin.

Regrettably, similar scenarios have occurred in some other countries, but luckily, only in Zambia has an actual government connived to establish a "stooge" national chapter. Fortunately, news of this fraudulence reached Berlin, and the donor community was quickly alerted. In all, these lessons indicate that in addition to anticorruption coalition building, better coordination between the various funding agencies is important.

Because the movement has spread so rapidly, it has been crucial to maintain quality control over national chapters while also providing them with an active and sustained support system. To this end, there is an active certification process that involves careful and discreet examination of the credentials of the chairperson, in particular, of a new national chapter—not only to check his or her good standing but also to ensure that the rules of nonpartisanship and the prohibition against investigations and exposures are being followed. A process that TI recently introduced requires national chapters to meet additional criteria. They are initially affiliated for only two years, as a form of probation; for their affiliation to be kept "alive," they must meet continuing performance targets, including providing to the secretariat audited annual accounts and a work plan. But because each national chapter is sui juris and an independent organ of civil society, there are limits to the control a central secretariat can exercise.

The Globalization of Corruption Control

Spanish sociologist José Maria Tortosa has observed that to analyze corruption in any country, one has to understand the world system in which it functions.[33] Corruption can no longer be simply a local issue. In recent years, there has seemed to be an international dimension to most cases of grand corruption. Such cases might involve, for instance, a transnational corporation or a corrupt politician going abroad to seek refuge from prosecution or, most common of all, the proceeds of corruption being secreted into numbered accounts at foreign destinations.

Nonetheless, despite these international implications, until TI, most anticorruption activity and a substantial part of the literature on corruption focused almost exclusively on the use of national measures to control a national or local problem. But TI has initiated—and in many instances, led—moves to internationalize efforts to curb corruption. In the years since its launch conference, TI has been widely recognized for its leadership in influencing and setting the agenda for corruption reform. It has played a considerable role in raising public, governmental, and private-sector awareness of the importance of corruption control and in influencing intergovernmental organizations and the drafting of conventions. National chapters have been formed or are in the process of formation in over seventy countries, and programs have been undertaken in more than two dozen countries. Interestingly, TI did not gain this position by producing cutting-edge academic research in the field, but rather by pragmatically providing a creative, diverse, widespread, and legitimizing framework in which to address the need for corruption control.

So why has TI been so unexpectedly successful, with its work mushrooming in the space of seven years to proportions one might expect from an NGO of thirty years' standing? Three factors predominate. First, the time was ripe for such an initiative. Second, TI was from the outset a network of worldwide experts and highly placed "insiders," as opposed to a grassroots protest movement. And third, TI (perhaps precisely *because* of being so specialized) has been particularly careful about handling the delicate politics and dynamics involved in being a lobbying NGO.

One of TI's most significant contributions has probably been to identify and assert the role of civil society—in a broad sense—as the missing factor in previous efforts to contain corruption. By challenging the monopoly previously claimed for governments and international agencies, TI has forced a rethinking on the part of many actors. The interests that the anticorruption movement bridges are tremendously broad based, ranging from leading U.S. corporations to grassroots village movements in India. Institutionally, TI works closely with the World Bank while actively supporting grassroots social movements in Uganda. Such a breadth of coalitions could be carried only by an international NGO. But this particular NGO has also had the challenging job of breaking through an international taboo and openly stating that its primary commitment is to the interests of developing and transitional economies.

So what are TI's successes to date, and what challenges face it now? Its campaign is widely acknowledged to have been successful in its aims to raise public awareness; change attitudinal norms toward corruption; form global, networked coalitions of activism; foster indigenous anticorruption campaigns in individual countries; and get an international treaty against corruption signed (by twenty-six OECD countries and six others). One independent academic case study on TI's part in shifting norms around corruption in the 1990s describes a "profound normative change" that has, in fact, radically reduced the tolerance of corruption.[34] The study points to TI as an "important and effective educator" and a "vital transnational coordinator" in these "changes in the global normative context." TI has already broadened its agenda from its relatively narrow initial focus on international bribery. Inspired by the demands of its national chapters, the 1997 mission statement described the purpose of the organization as being "to curb corruption by mobilizing a global coalition to promote and strengthen international and national integrity systems."

Some of TI's early strategic choices, such as its noninvestigative, nonconflictual, collaborative, yet zero-tolerance approaches, have been vindicated over time and may partly explain its success. One academic case study on TI's strategic effectiveness as an NGO concludes that a key element in TI's success has been its decision to "change underlying structures—the legal and institutional framework—instead of exposing single cases."[35]

But several important challenges still face TI. First, the ratification of an international convention is, after all, only an early step in the criminalization and elimination of corrupt practices. Implementing, monitoring, and policing the convention lie ahead. TI national chapters in the North will need to ensure that their national legislatures codify and actually enforce the terms of the convention, genuinely making the necessary changes in their national criminal legislation. National chapters in the South, especially in rapidly developing regions, will also be lobbying their governments to adhere to the convention, which has a specific outreach intention toward non-OECD countries. Several Latin American governments that are not members of the OECD are already signatories to the convention. And in addition to the convention, the OECD is considering equally important "soft law" measures to bring taxation and auditing practices into line with anticorruption values.

A second challenge facing the campaign is that it must now turn closer attention to certain sectors of the business community that are less willing to challenge corruption. TI is actively lobbying the World Trade Organization, the only major international regulatory institution that remains reluctant to tackle corruption. In terms of particular business sectors, the arms trade is well known to be the leading offender by a wide margin. Yet a protective taboo still shrouds discussions of this particular zone of corruption.

A third challenge that faces TI is the need to simply sustain itself and its level of achievement. The first phase of the campaign—achieving widespread consensus on the existence and importance of the problem—has been completed, with results beyond all expectations. However, the very extent of this success, if not met with adequate second-phase resources, could become a problem in itself. To continue supporting this mushrooming worldwide network, TI will require new resources, consisting of both funding and knowledge.

The need for funding and for paid, stable human resources is a constant for NGOs in general. But TI, with its worldwide catchment area and its almost eighty national chapters crying out for all sorts of expertise and advice, has an equally great need for specialist knowledge, renewed theoretical frameworks, and updated methodologies. This will mean a deeper interaction between the anticorruption movement and the academic experts and institutions that can study, theorize, educate, and inform about the complex dynamics facing transnational NGOs in the twenty-first century.

In pragmatic terms, there is an urgent need for universities to begin offering a specific syllabus and modules of theory and training on good governance and anticorruption measures, so that professionals from the public and private sectors and from NGOs worldwide can meet, discuss, learn, and train within such programs. A couple of farsighted universities are already stepping forward to meet this worldwide need, and TI is preparing its own plans for such academic partnerships as well.

The broad challenge will be to turn the momentum generated in the past seven years into concrete successes to match the new global anticorruption rhetoric. It is far too early to know whether the transnational network anchored by TI is up to the task. The scale of bribery worldwide has escalated so fast in the past fifteen years or so that a 1997 article in the *Financial Times* could describe the going rate as having "soared" from 10 to 30 percent.[36] The article's catchy title—"Goodbye Mr. 10%"— used to describe the power of the anticorruption movement, was certainly amusing. But further on, the article also wittily highlighted the challenge facing that movement. It pointed out that the 1990s climate was so propitious for corruption that while TI was encouraging everyone to say goodbye to "Mr. 10%," other circumstances might be offering "Mr. 30%" opportunities to come in through the back door.

Notes

1. The organizational structure of TI involves a board of ten to fifteen directors, with a chairperson and two vice-chairs who legally act for the organization. They are assisted by an elected advisory council consisting of international experts from different geographic and professional areas. The board of directors and the advisory council both work for TI on an unpaid, voluntary basis, and they oversee the work of both the central secretariat in Berlin and more than seventy national chapters worldwide.

2. For this assessment of TI's activities and effectiveness, it would be ideal to draw on a critical secondary literature on TI. Unfortunately, although TI has been cited in innumerable articles and books on corruption, only one aspect of TI's work—the annual Corruption Perceptions Index—has been subject to critical review. Therefore, outsiders are invited to analyze other dimensions of TI's work, and the final section of the chapter points out some of the specific areas that most need renewed theoretical models and critiquing in the years ahead.

3. Moisés Naím, "The Corruption Eruption," *Brown Journal of World Affairs* 2 (1995): 245–61.

4. "Corruption—Le Classement Mondial," *Le Nouvel Observateur*, July 16, 1998, p. 4.

5. Hongying Wang, James Rosenau, et al., "Contesting Corruption Globally: Exploring a Normative Transformation," paper presented at the Conference on International Institutions: Global Processes—Domestic Consequences, Duke University, Durham, N.C., 1999, p. 15.

6. "Defense Deals Pervaded by Bribery, Says US," *Financial Times*, July 7, 1999, p. 6.

7. Based on conversations with European exporters, in particular French arms exporters. See also *Le Monde*, March 17, 1995.

8. Daniel Kaufmann, "Corruption: The Facts," *Foreign Policy* (1997): 114–27.

9. Kaufmann, "Corruption."

10. Gary S. Becker, "If You Want to Cut Corruption, Cut Big Government," *Business Week*, December 11, 1995, p. 10.

11. Susan Rose-Ackerman, "The Political Economy of Corruption: Causes and Consequences," *Viewpoint*, World Bank Note 74 (April 1996).

12. R. T. Naylor, *Hot Money and the Politics of Debt* (Montreal: Black Rose Books, 1994), p. 361.

13. Sidney Tarrow, "Making Social Science Work Across Space and Time: A Critical Reflection on Robert Putnam's *Making Democracy Work*," *American Political Science Review* 90 (1996): 389–97.

14. World Bank, *Governance: The World Bank's Experience* (Washington, D.C.: World Bank, 1994).

15. This process of civil action continued. For instance, during the Supreme Court hearings of President Pérez, the housewives of Caracas beat their pots and pans every evening in protest because they feared the trial was rigged. And when the Mani Pulite judges in Milan were going to have their authority undermined by the very politicians they were investigating, some of the largest demonstrations in Italy's postwar history came to their support. Highlighting, albeit unwittingly, the sort of global coalitions TI seeks to foster, an article in the *Economist* remarked, on an ironic note, how unusual it was that these mass protests against corruption meant that for once, protesters in the streets of Jakarta and Harare were on the same side as the International Monetary Fund. However, the article went on to stir the debate about the anticorruption movement's attitude toward the more ordinary inequalities of capitalism—inequalities produced not by corruption but by legitimized, "corruption-free" economic practice. As the article laconically put it, "angry demonstrators rarely distinguish between the inequalities created by an honest system, and those perpetuated by corruption" (*Economist*, January 16, 1999, p. 27).

16. The change in climate was timely. For some years, there had been strong dissatisfaction on the part of corporate America with the Foreign Corrupt Practices Act, and successive administrations had been lobbied to repeal the legislation on the grounds that no one else had such a law and it was imposing a competitive disadvantage on U.S. exporters. To their credit, the Reagan, Bush, and Clinton administrations all resisted this pressure, opting instead for a policy to "export" the act and level the playing field that way. Just what the present situation would be if the United States had opted for repeal of the Foreign Corrupt Practices Act is food for thought, particularly for those who believe that the United States has pushed too hard in international fora on this issue.

17. World Bank, *Sub-Saharan Africa: From Crisis to Sustainable Growth* (Washington, D.C.: World Bank, 1989).

18. Reflecting a considerable growth in activities and institutional support, TI's budget had increased substantially: expenses totaled $570,000 in 1995, $730,000 in 1996, and $1.1 million in 1997. In 1998, the budget was over $2.5 million, and it almost doubled again in 1999.

19. Jeremy Pope, "Strengthening the Role of Civil Society and the Private Sector in Fighting Corruption," unpublished paper, 1998.

20. Most international mutual legal assistance treaties contain a "political exemption" clause that can be used to block the provision of assistance when it is claimed that a case is being pursued for political reasons. Because a fallen politician in exile is almost invariably not of the same political persuasion as those seeking to extradite him or her or to confiscate assets, the arrangements (designed for more ordinary crimes) were generally ineffective. Allied to this, the insistence on bank secrecy in such havens as Switzerland posed insuperable barriers to investigators seeking to trace assets internationally.

21. Curiously, it was journalists who criticized TI for adopting a noninvestigative approach. However, these critics generally came to understand the legitimacy of the approach, and a number have joined the TI movement. Membership in TI does not, of course, impose fetters on individual actions.

22. A further indication that the time was ripe for action was the United Nations Development Programme's 1992 *Human Development Report*, which called for the creation of an "Honesty International" to fight corruption.

23. In early 1993, there was only a handful of national NGOs active in this area, but they now constitute the fourth party in this process.

24. I joined the organization as its first staff member in 1993. In addition to country-specific work in more than thirty countries in Europe, Latin America, and Africa, I have been in charge of coordinating the international steering committee of experts that advises TI on the CPI and BPI.

25. Jeff Stein, *International Herald Tribune*, September 12, 1997, p. 15.

26. See articles from *La nouvelle expression* (September 28, 1998) and *Le Messager* (September 25, 1998).

27. One independent academic study observes that "a profoundly co-operative approach . . . constitutes a kind of hallmark of TI" (Werner Van Ham, "Transparency International—The International NGO Against Corruption: Strategic Positions Achieved and Challenges Ahead [A Case Study]," MBA diss., Anglia University, England, 1998, p. 18).

28. *Washington Post*, November 28, 1997, and *International Herald Tribune*, December 2, 1997.

29. By comparison, Greenpeace and Amnesty International, two more well established and older international NGOs, have thirty-three and approximately fifty national sections, respectively. Their membership is far more substantial because they are mass-membership organizations, which TI is unlikely to ever become. In 1998, Greenpeace UK alone had almost 200,000 members, and Amnesty International (UK) had over 140,000 members. By comparison, TI's membership is minimal.

30. More detailed descriptions and case studies of TI national chapter activities can be found on TI's web site, www.transparency.de.

31. *Frontline*, March 6, 1998, p. 103.

32. Wang and Rosenau, "Contesting Corruption Globally."

33. José Maria Tortosa, *Corrupcion* (Barcelona: Icaria, 1995).

34. Wang and Rosenau, "Contesting Corruption Globally."

35. Van Ham, "Transparency International," p. 30.

36. John Mason and Guy de Jonquires, "Goodbye Mr. 10%," *Financial Times*, July 22, 1997, p. 15.

3

Advocates and Activists: Conflicting Approaches on Nonproliferation and the Test Ban Treaty

Rebecca Johnson

> Over the past 25 years non-governmental organizations have performed valuable services for the Non-Proliferation Treaty—in encouragement, ideas, public support and advocacy of further progress towards the goals of the Treaty. I should like to pay them a sincere tribute for their dedication.
>
> —Jayantha Dhanapala, May 13, 1995

IT WAS JUST PAST MIDNIGHT in New York on May 13, 1995. Diplomats from the 178 countries that were party to the 1968 Treaty on the Non-Proliferation of Nuclear Weapons (NPT) had agreed on a package of decisions to strengthen and extend the treaty indefinitely. More than 700 representatives from 195 nongovernmental organizations (NGOs) had spent the previous four weeks attending the conference at which the treaty was evaluated and renewed, the culmination of years of work for some of them. When the conference president, Jayantha Dhanapala, closed with his tribute to NGOs, he was paying a well-deserved compliment, albeit one that many governments would have begrudged. Governments may not like having civil society involved in national security issues, but progress toward nuclear arms control seems more and more to require its participation. Without it, there might well have been no agreement on extending and strengthening the NPT, the cornerstone of efforts to prevent the spread of nuclear weapons. Similarly, when the Comprehensive Test Ban Treaty (CTBT) was concluded and opened for signature in September 1996, U.S. President Bill Clinton described it as "the longest sought, hardest fought prize in arms control history."[1] He was right, but he failed to mention that most of the pushing came not from governments but from civil society. From the 1950s onward, the protests and advice of transnational civil society, in the shape of doctors, antinuclear activists, women's groups, and scientist-advocates, maintained the pressure that eventually led governments to achieve a complete ban.

This chapter tells the story of civil society's role in both the NPT extension and the test ban negotiations. It is a single story because the two treaties are deeply intertwined. The NPT, which aims to stop countries from acquiring nuclear weapons, has always rested on an uneasy bargain. Signatories without nuclear weapons agree to renounce them, and signatories with nuclear weapons agree to provide assistance to nonmilitary nuclear programs and to seek complete nuclear disarmament. The NPT also made explicit reference in its preamble to the objective of ending all nuclear testing, viewed as a fundamental step the nuclear states should take toward fulfilling their disarmament obligation. It is hard to begin or sustain a nuclear arms race if the countries involved cannot test new designs to make sure they work as expected. The NPT, which entered into force in 1970, was not designed as a permanent treaty, but instead required a decision on renewal after twenty-five years. The failure of the weapons states to conclude a comprehensive test ban became a major point of contention in the debate over extension of the NPT. Although few argued that the NPT should be allowed to lapse altogether, debate raged over whether it should be made permanent or should come up for reconsideration after another fixed period, perhaps twenty-five years or as little as five years. Some viewed a long extension as necessary for stability, while others thought that a shorter, conditional extension would act as a better lever for nuclear disarmament.

Civil society divided as sharply as did governments over this issue. Some NGOs regarded the NPT as the indispensable basis for promoting arms control and nonproliferation. Others viewed the treaty as a flawed and discriminatory instrument that validates the possession of nuclear weapons by a chosen few and continues to promote nuclear energy, which many—but not all—disarmament NGOs also oppose.

As an activist turned analyst whose regular reports for the newly formed Acronym Consortium served as a major source of information for civil society (and for many governments) on both the NPT and the CTBT negotiations, I sometimes found myself caught between these strongly held views.[2] I missed Dhanapala's tribute to the NGOs because I was in the corridor outside the United Nations General Assembly, locked in furious argument with the convenor of the Campaign for the NPT, a coalition of eighteen Washington-based NGOs that had pushed hard for indefinite extension. He considered my reporting of the indefinite extension decision to have been insufficiently celebratory. Two hours later, I was at a friend's home sharing food with a group of grassroots activists, including Daniel Ellsberg, who was just breaking the twenty-eight-day fast he had kept through the conference "to express with moral urgency a demand for recommitment ... to the abolition of nuclear weapons."[3] I was exhausted, as writing daily analyses had meant long weeks of eighteen-hour days. While one friend tried to give me a relaxing shoulder massage, another—a prominent member of the newly formed abolition caucus—harangued me for not describing the NPT outcome as a huge defeat.

That night epitomized the conflicts and contradictions that characterize NGO work on nuclear nonproliferation and disarmament. There is a complicated history of rivalry and distrust among various groups working on these issues. NGOs managed to unite around the goal of achieving the strongest CTBT that was politically achievable, though there were serious differences of definition and strategy and some disagreement about the effectiveness of the finalized treaty. In the case of the NPT, there has been less common ground. NGOs have long been divided about the treaty's value, effectiveness, and extension.

The transnational civil society actors involved with these treaties encompassed a considerable range of organizations. Some represented a large membership, such as International Physicians for the Prevention of Nuclear War (IPPNW). Some were really just one or two dynamic individuals, such as Ellsberg's Manhattan Project II, which was based on the premise that nuclear disarmament would take the kind of priority, resources, and intellectual brilliance that had built the weapons in the first place. Some organizations were small research or policy institutes; others comprised a handful of people based near nuclear production sites or laboratories, such as the Western States Legal Foundation or the Los Alamos Study Group. Some involved international networks with members in many countries but with small organizational bases, such as Parliamentarians for Global Action or the German-centered International Network of Scientists and Engineers Against Proliferation. Some were hierarchical, like Greenpeace; others, such as Britain's Campaign for Nuclear Disarmament (CND), mirrored a trade union or political party, with established democratic procedures involving a broad-based membership. A number of the conference participants represented only themselves, with no observable organizational links, and some purported to speak for large numbers but lacked any apparent mechanism for accountable representation.

This plethora of organizations breaks down into three types, although there are inevitably overlaps:

1. Elite, principally nongovernmental experts, academics, and professionals, such as the Programme for Promoting Nuclear Non-Proliferation (PPNN), the Monterey Institute for International Studies, the Verification Technology Information Centre (VERTIC), and most of the individual organizations in the Campaign for the NPT. Typically, such elites use their expert knowledge and professional status as a "respectable" lobbying tool and aim to affect policy and influence governments by information and the logic of their arguments. They may be committed to the abolition of nuclear weapons, to arms control, or just to a specific measure, but in general, they tend to promote limited, practical, incremental demands and policy initiatives that are perceived by governments as pragmatic steps that can be realized in the short to medium term. Even those that are nationally focused are likely to network internationally, by means of e-mail and conferences.

2. Public movement campaigns, with a grassroots membership and skilled organizers, who may be voluntary or paid. Examples of international public movement campaigns include IPPNW and Greenpeace, but there are also nationally based

public movement campaigns, such as Peace Action in the United States, CND, Mouvement de la Paix in France, and both Gensuikin and Gensuikyo in Japan. Some religious or church-based networks also contribute to public movement campaigning on nuclear disarmament. The typical tools of public mobilization include petitions, meetings, demonstrations, and use of the Internet and letter writing to raise public awareness, exchange information and ideas, obtain media coverage, and exert pressure on local and national political decision making.

3. Nonviolent direct action, which can be used as an organized tactic, as Greenpeace does, or arise from grassroots campaigns with fluid participation. Such actions can generate dramatic headlines, such as "Greenham Girl Halts Nuclear Blast 7 Minutes from Death,"[4] following a four-person hike to ground zero at the Nevada test site in 1990, or "Mass Break-in at the Palace,"[5] after thirteen women entered Buckingham Palace to protest British nuclear testing in July 1993. The American Peace Test (now Shundahai Network) has for many years coordinated mass trespasses at the Nevada test site.

This case study on the CTBT and the NPT extension decision demonstrates that transnational civil society played a significant role in influencing the decision making of some governments, but by means of multiple interventions rather than a coordinated strategy. Different types of groups played different roles, often disagreeing sharply over strategies and tactics. The case study also illustrates how ambiguous the role of transnational civil society can sometimes be. With regard to the NPT extension, there was no consensus among governments or civil society actors on the desired outcome, and there have been conflicting assessments of the implications of the decisions made in 1995. It is therefore impossible to make a straightforward judgment regarding the success or failure of transnational civil society's role. In the case of the CTBT, the existence of the treaty is clearly a success, but a limited one unless it actually comes into force—a prospect that at time of writing looks remote.

The Origins of Civil Society's Role

Transnational civil society's involvement in nuclear issues dates back nearly to the beginning of the nuclear age. The first antinuclear protesters were established peace advocates and women's groups; they were joined by scientists and doctors concerned about the growing nuclear arms race and the adverse health effects from atmospheric tests.[6] By 1957, when Britain joined the U.S.-Soviet arms race by conducting its first hydrogen bomb test, nuclear testing had become "a burning public issue."[7] New antinuclear groups formed during the late 1950s, stepping up pressure for a test ban until the United States, the USSR, and Britain (the three countries then conducting tests) began negotiating what eventually became the 1963 Treaty Banning Nuclear Weapon Tests in the Atmosphere, in Outer Space and Under Water (also known as the Partial Test Ban Treaty, or PTBT).

The measure, which ended the public health and environmental threat from atmospheric testing but permitted underground nuclear testing, represented both victory and defeat for test ban advocates. Although most of the NGOs had called unequivocally for a CTBT, their main public and political appeal had focused on the health risks from radioactive fallout. By eliminating the mushroom clouds, the PTBT also removed the visible reminder of the nuclear arms race. After 1963, nuclear testing continued out of sight, still fueling the qualitative arms race with new, advanced, and modernized weapons systems. Although the PTBT enshrined in its preamble a commitment to seek the comprehensive "discontinuance of all test explosions of nuclear weapons for all time," once the tests had disappeared underground, much of the driving force to achieve a total ban was dissipated.

The antecedents of the NPT were rather different, less a response to civil society pressures than a product of government assessments. Initiated by Ireland in 1958, the NPT was pushed by the major powers from 1965, after they recognized that the value of their own nuclear forces would diminish if many others acquired the capabilities. Italy and others, unsure of the effectiveness of nonproliferation, insisted that the treaty's duration be set at only twenty-five years, with a decision to be made in 1995 about the length of its extension and with interim review conferences among the treaty parties every five years. The 1995 Review and Extension Conference of the NPT was hence crucial to the future of the nonproliferation regime. And its outcome was in doubt, with parties divided over whether the treaty should be extended indefinitely and unconditionally or extended for a more limited period, with further renewal contingent on progress toward full implementation.

The Major Players

All the NGOs working on a CTBT shared the goal of a strong and comprehensive treaty, though there were divisions over definitions, strategies, and tactics and disagreements over what compromises might be necessary in order to reach a politically viable treaty. The main target governments were obvious: the five nuclear weapon states (N-5)— Britain, China, France, Russia, and the United States—and the three nuclear-capable countries—India, Israel, and Pakistan, which were not members of the NPT and so had no other treaty constraints on nuclear acquisition and development. A wider group of targets for information and advice were the thirty-seven negotiating delegations in the Conference on Disarmament.[8] Civil society strategists found it fruitful to work with the more active delegations to seek constructive solutions to strengthen provisions or move obdurate positions. These included Australia, Brazil, Canada, the Netherlands, Germany, Japan, Mexico, Indonesia, Iran, and Egypt.

After the half success of the PTBT, civil society's efforts to achieve a comprehensive test ban went through three stages. The period from 1963 to 1989 constituted the "wilderness years," when direct action, sometimes combined with diplomatic strategies, tried to keep the issue alive in the public and political consciousness. Arms control experts and former diplomats maintained a level of interest, contributing to the tripartite testing talks among Britain, the United States, and the USSR from 1979 to 1981, but political conditions were not conducive to positive policy developments on nuclear issues. The key international actors were Greenpeace, which created dramatic actions and images to back up its political lobbying; IPPNW, founded by American and

Russian physicians at the height of the 1980s crisis over the deployment of "Euromissiles"; and the Nevada-Semipalatinsk Movement, the first genuinely indigenous emergence of antinuclear activism in Soviet civil society. During this time, there were also ongoing grassroots protests at the test sites, including American Peace Test, which worked with the Western Shoshone Nation in Nevada; the Greenham and Aldermaston women's camps in Britain; and the Tahiti-based antinuclear NGO Hiti Tau, closely associated with the main Polynesian independence party, Tavini Huiraatira. Additionally, the nongovernmental Natural Resources Defense Council in the United States developed groundbreaking joint initiatives on test site monitoring with Soviet scientists during the 1980s. NGOs also worked closely with governments on diplomatic strategies to exert pressure through the fourth review conference of the NPT in 1990 and to call for an amendment conference to explore converting the PTBT into a comprehensive ban. Although these initiatives were taken forward by governments, principally Mexico, Sweden, and Indonesia, transnational civil society played an important role in generating the ideas and providing support and information—most importantly, Parliamentarians for Global Action, Greenpeace, and the U.S. Test Ban Coalition (which subsequently dissolved). Despite the growing campaigns and heightened public awareness, however, little demonstrable progress was made during the wilderness years.

The period from 1990 to 1993 constituted the prenegotiation phase. During these years, political-diplomatic initiatives from NGOs, backed up with direct action, were influential in achieving unilaterally declared moratoria on testing first by the Soviet Union[9] and then by France and the United States, creating the conditions for negotiations to begin. The target date of achieving a CTBT by September 1996 was set by the U.S. Congress, which, thanks largely to legislative strategies pursued by Washington-based NGOs, had imposed the initial nine-month U.S. moratorium over the opposition of a hostile Republican president, George Bush. When this moratorium, which had begun in September 1992, came up for consideration in 1993, U.S. and British NGOs played a significant role in persuading the new Clinton administration to withstand the heavy pressure from the British government and the Pentagon not to renew and to allow some planned tests to go ahead at the Nevada test site. Clinton's extension of the moratorium and his commitment to the target of concluding a CTBT by September 1996 were crucial to the success of the negotiations.

From 1994 to 1996, formal negotiations were under way, leading to the signing of the treaty in September 1996. Although governments conducted the negotiations, a complex interplay of public movement pressure, legislative tactics, and citizens actions helped maintain momentum for the treaty and bring about key decisions, including the zero yield agreement. A few U.S.-based NGOs focused more on the inadequacies of the emerging test ban, especially the stockpile-reinforcing laboratory programs that would receive increased funding, but their concerns were peripheral to the outcome. Almost all existing antinuclear NGOs had the CTBT prominently on their agendas at this time, but few played significant roles beyond exhortation until France resumed nuclear testing in 1995, sparking public demonstrations and boycotts around the world.

Unlike the test ban, the NPT was not an issue that readily lent itself to public mobilization. The details of its provisions, implementation, and extension options engaged primarily the arms control academics and professionals. Viewing the NPT as largely an instrument of the nuclear status quo, many antinuclear NGOs ignored the forthcoming extension decision until 1994, when the conference was almost upon them. The majority of these NGOs opposed indefinite extension. Some advocated a short extension: CND, for example, argued for ten years, conditional upon agreement to negotiate a global treaty to ban nuclear weapons.[10] A sizable group, which included some major funders such as the W. Alton Jones and Rockefeller Foundations, was concerned that any weakening of the NPT could destroy the chances of further nuclear arms control, including the CTBT. Support for indefinite extension from key U.S. funders was instrumental in forming the Campaign for the NPT in late 1993 and in persuading some of the Campaign's eighteen U.S.-based organizations and institutes to back indefinite extension rather than an alternative long duration or renewable option.[11] Not all the NGOs focused on the extension options; some worked for an overall constructive outcome that would strengthen the nonproliferation regime and prospects for nuclear disarmament together.

Governments were players as well as targets for pressure and information from transnational civil society. As with the CTBT, the primary targets for messages about the need for better progress on nuclear disarmament were the N-5 nuclear powers, four of which were push-ing for indefinite, unconditional extension.[12] Nonaligned states that had not yet committed to a specific extension decision were targeted by both the Campaign for the NPT and other NGOs that lobbied for or against indefinite extension.

In the space available, it would be impossible to do justice to the va-riety of roles, strategies, and actions pursued by the many NGOs that worked on test ban and nonproliferation issues between 1985 and 1996. The following sections consider four distinct approaches that are rep-resentative of different strategies and levels of impact: the high-profile campaigning by Greenpeace in the early years of the CTBT; grassroots activists and public movement campaigning, giving rise to the Abolition Caucus in 1995; elites and arms controllers, as illustrated by most of the groups constituting the Washington-based Campaign for the NPT; and the low-profile facilitation of ideas and contacts, as ex-emplified by PPNN and the Monterey Institute.

High-Profile Direct Action: The Greenpeace Story

Probably the best-known NGO in the antinuclear field is Greenpeace, which was born in 1971 when a small group of Canadians and expatriate Americans living in Vancouver decided to sail a "rustbucket of a fishing boat" to the Aleutian island of Amchitka, off Alaska, to protest U.S. testing.[13] Soon after, Greenpeace sailors challenged the exclusion zone around the French nuclear test sites in the South Pacific. Over the next decade, the "boy's sailing club with a conscience"[14] grew into the multi-million-dollar Greenpeace International, with several ships, impres-sive offices, and semiautonomous branches across Europe, America, and the Pacific. Although Greenpeace worked on a variety of environ-mental issues, its signature campaigns were against nuclear testing and the slaughter of whales and seals, and its signature tactic was David-and-Goliath confrontation using boats. At that time, Green-peace regarded itself as a public movement campaign, but it relied on its members for fund-raising rather than direct campaigning. Its ac-tions were highly centralized and controlled. As its reputation grew,

Greenpeace also hired specialists as consultants or researchers and sought to utilize elite strategies, making itself an expert in key areas.

By 1985, the Greenpeace antinuclear strategy used two principal tactics: lobbying and direct action. Greenpeace was one of the first organizations to see the leverage potential in the NPT. But it was direct action that had a wholly unexpected and enormous payoff, for tragic reasons. On July 10, 1985, the Greenpeace flagship *Rainbow Warrior* was bombed in Auckland Harbor, just as it was about to join an antinuclear flotilla to protest French nuclear testing at Moruroa, in the South Pacific. The boat sank, killing a photographer on board, Fernando Perreira. After initial confusion, the perpetrators were discovered to be French secret service agents, intent on preventing any disruption of France's nuclear testing program. As the victim of a government-sponsored act of terrorism, Greenpeace found that its moral authority with the international public soared.

Despite the tragedy, Greenpeace was determined to carry on with its lobbying campaign at least, sending a team to Geneva to push for a CTBT by lobbying delegates to the third NPT review conference. Greenpeace wanted the NPT parties to withhold agreement on any decisions until the nuclear weapon states committed themselves to open negotiations on a CTBT, as called for in the NPT's preamble. Despite putting its best people in, equipped with professionally presented informational material well beyond the level usually associated with NGOs at that time, Greenpeace was unsuccessful. One important lesson the organization learned was that to affect diplomatic positions, civil society must exert pressure well in advance on the governments and officials who will make the decisions and issue instructions; diplomats at international meetings have relatively little room to maneuver. Five years later, Mexico, with low-profile support from NGOs such as Parliamentarians for Global Action and Greenpeace, blocked adoption of a final document at the 1990 review conference by utilizing the strategy of linking continued acceptance of the NPT with achievement of a CTBT.[15]

After two years of inactivity on nuclear issues following the sinking of its flagship, Greenpeace sought to reframe its strategy. Its reinvigorated test ban campaign aimed to make visible the continuation of underground nuclear testing by *all* the nuclear powers, using direct actions at the U.S., British, Soviet, and French sites.[16] Much less was known about China's test site at Lop Nor in Xinjiang province, so Greenpeace commissioned research and satellite pictures, with a view to a possible future campaign.[17]

In October 1990, the MV Greenpeace was intercepted by the KGB after sending an inflatable dinghy with four campaigners and radiation detectors to the Soviet test site at Novaya Zemlya, where high levels of radioactivity were measured at abandoned nuclear test shafts. The ship and its crew were detained for a week, causing massive worldwide publicity. Moscow's mayor, Boris Yeltsin, publicly called on President Gorbachev to end nuclear testing. On October 18, 1990, after deporting the Greenpeace crew, the Soviet Union belatedly carried out its planned nuclear explosion at Novaya Zemlya, facing widespread criticism. That turned out to be the last Soviet test. One year later, on October 5, 1991, President Gorbachev announced a unilateral moratorium on Soviet testing. This was the first major breakthrough and was largely the result of antinuclear organizing by Kazakh nationalists, especially the Nevada-Semipalatinsk Movement described later, although Greenpeace's embarrassing spotlight undoubtedly influenced the timing.

Greenpeace swiftly followed the Novaya Zemlya events with simultaneous actions in London and Nevada to draw attention to a planned British test. In London, a team of climbers hung a huge banner from Tower Bridge, proclaiming "Stop UK Nuclear Tests."[18] At the same time, Greenpeace sent four activists, including three British women (formerly of the Greenham Common Women's Peace Camp) to the Nevada test site. After hiking for three days, they reached the ground-zero location of the planned explosion, which was halted only minutes before detonation. The highly publicized action and subsequent arrests caused great embarrassment to U.S. and British authorities and gained widespread attention, as both actions were covered extensively in the British tabloid press and political dailies, as well as by some American and international media.[19]

A month later, Greenpeace returned to the French test site at Moruroa with the new Rainbow Warrior, after preparing the ground with scientific studies and a book testifying to the harm caused by the tests.[20] Members of the crew were arrested for breaching the twelve-mile exclusion zone but managed to smuggle out some samples of lagoon water containing flora and fauna. The arrests and subsequent deportations received significant media coverage, including in France. Analysis of the samples, which Greenpeace published in September 1991, revealed the presence of radioactive plutonium and cesium. The contamination was publicized, together with further requests and resolutions in the European Parliament calling for conditions at the French test site to be independently investigated. After being ignored by the government, Greenpeace hung a large banner from the Arc de Triomphe in Paris proclaiming *"non aux essais"* (no to nuclear tests) and returned to the Pacific test site in early 1992. By focusing on the science and the "soft" health and environmental effects of testing rather than confronting the weapons issue directly, Greenpeace appealed to a growing French interest in environmentalism and was thus successful in getting more sympathetic press coverage than ever before. In April 1992, to the surprise of many, France joined Russia in declaring a unilateral moratorium on testing.[21]

It would be an exaggeration to claim that Greenpeace single-handedly won this unexpected moratorium from President Mitterrand, but the organization's work with Green politicians in the European Parliament and the pressure of its high-profile actions at the test site undoubtedly helped. It is likely that a combination of political and practical factors led to the decision. The key determinant for Mitterrand was the unexpectedly large electoral successes by Les Verts (the French Green Party) in early 1992. The Greens had placed an end to testing high on their list of environmental priorities. Mitterrand may have calculated that the United States, Britain, and China would keep testing—a reasonable bet at the time. Therefore, declaring a moratorium, which could be rescinded after a decent interval, would allow France to take the moral high ground and appear to meet an important pledge of the environmentalists. What was not foreseen was that the French suspension of testing would invigorate U.S. NGOs, resulting in President Bush being maneuvered within the year to sign a moratorium on U.S. testing, an action that made it difficult for France to break its moratorium.

Greenpeace's strength was its international reach (paid campaigners in many countries) and its ability to finance and coordinate large actions quickly and with high-level technical resources, including ships and state-of-the-art communication. Greenpeace clearly understood the importance of timing and media-friendly approaches, combining personal stories and political messages. Selected journalists and photographers (film and still) accompanied every action, ready to project professional-quality footage around the world, thus encouraging the speedy publication of strong images and punchy sound bites. Greenpeace also increased the probability of coverage in key countries by ensuring that its teams of actionists and campaign spokespeople came from a range of target nationalities, which depended on the campaign and the context.

However, the *Rainbow Warrior* effect, which increased the organization's wealth and popularity for several years, diminished in the early 1990s following a series of scandals, misuse of information, and poor leadership. For some years, Greenpeace's disarmament campaigning dropped out of sight. Then, in July 1995, on the tenth anniversary of the bombing of the first *Rainbow Warrior* and one month after President Chirac announced the end of the French moratorium, Greenpeace sent its flagship back to the French test site. A violent boarding of the *Rainbow Warrior* by French naval commandos was dramatically broadcast around the world, as screams interrupted an interview between Greenpeace's on-board campaigner, Stephanie Mills, and the BBC. A few months later, Greenpeace went back to Moruroa, putting more of its boats beside the *Rainbow Warrior*. Again the ships were seized. This time, however, Greenpeace lost the goodwill the previous actions had engendered by treating the seizure as a major defeat and blaming its campaigner in the press.

Whatever disappointment the leadership may have felt, this public and personalized scapegoating of the campaigner, who was in French custody at the time, went down badly with Greenpeace supporters. It was a brutal illustration of the internal problems that had plagued the organization since its inception but had become increasingly destructive in the 1990s. These problems included the persistence of a bar-bonding, heavy-drinking, macho "boys' sailing club" at the top of the informal power structure; a dysfunctional formal structure suffering from overbureaucratized attempts to implement fashionable risk-avoidance "new management" theories; and a growing dependence on large boats and expensive, high-tech machinery, which made Greenpeace look less like David and too much like Goliath. Instead of treating their ships as campaigning tools—like banners or meetings—the effectiveness of which is highly context dependent, Greenpeace's leadership seemed to believe that if they put enough boats around Moruroa they could actually prevent the planned nuclear explosions. When their best boats were impounded by the French navy, as could have been anticipated, they experienced the seizure as a terrible defeat and looked for someone to blame. In fact, as any experienced campaigner would know, the boats were not as important as what they represented. Their power derived from their ability to symbolize the voices of public opinion or to project Greenpeace campaigners romantically as brave Davids willing to risk his body against the wicked tests. Instead, caught up in their own internal rivalries and egos, the leaders of Greenpeace missed a golden opportunity to use the arrests to cast France as an arrogant, bullying, nuclear-addicted Goliath and to call on international public opinion to commit its collective voice of protest in place of the detained ships.

Public Movement Campaigns and Grassroots Activists

Grassroots activists and public movement campaigns played an important part in achieving the CTBT, although they were marginalized in the negotiations on the NPT extension. Disarmament organizations large and small had continued campaigning for a test ban at local and regional levels throughout the wilderness years. One of the most astonishing initiatives arose in Kazakhstan, where the Soviet Union had its principal test site, at Semipalatinsk. In February 1987, soon after Moscow resumed nuclear testing after a nineteen-month moratorium, two explosions released unexpected amounts of radioactive gases into the environment. The pollution galvanized a local Kazakh poet, Olzhas Suleimenov, to use the occasion of a televised awards presentation to call on fellow Kazakhs to shut the Soviet test site down. The popular response was overwhelming. When the first demonstration attracted thousands to the center of Alma-Ata (now Almaty), the Nevada-Semipalatinsk Movement was born.

The name of the Kazakh group made a deliberate link with the American test site. After initiating the movement, Suleimenov recruited local doctors and made contact with IPPNW, Greenpeace, and leaders of the Western Shoshone Nation (whose tribal lands had been taken over for U.S. and British testing in Nevada). During the rest of 1987, the Nevada-Semipalatinsk Movement held meetings and demonstrations in several Kazakh and Russian cities and conducted epidemiological research. They published a series of pamphlets and video documentaries that mixed medical science and harrowing pictures of deformed and brain-damaged children from villages near the test site. Suleimenov's tactics, which combined nationalism with antinuclear environmentalism, are widely credited with forcing the Soviet government to cancel eleven of eighteen scheduled tests in 1989. In May 1990, the Nevada-Semipalatinsk Movement and IPPNW jointly organized the International Citizen's Congress for a Nuclear Test Ban, attracting 600 Soviet and international nongovernmental participants to Semipalatinsk, where rallies were held with thousands of local people. The Kazakh movement against testing grew, incorporating villagers as well as politicians and professionals in the towns. Fearful of the rising appeal of nationalism as its control of the Soviet republics slipped, Moscow canceled more tests and announced that the Semipalatinsk site would be closed by 1993. Meanwhile, the Soviet military began preparing to conduct further underground explosions at its arctic test site on Novaya Zemlya.[22] It is probable that the Nevada-Semipalatinsk Movement would not have been as successful in closing down the test site without the Kazakh nationalist appeal in its antinuclear message. Nevertheless, Suleimenov employed a very effective strategy of local organizing and international outreach, augmenting his group's limited financial resources by linking with larger international NGOs, such as IPPNW and Greenpeace.

Internationally, however, public movement campaigns have proved less successful. At the NPT Review and Extension Conference, some of the NGOs involved in grassroots activism and public movement diplomacy formed an "abolition caucus" that met daily to exchange information and discuss tactics. The caucus included representatives from international bodies such as IPPNW, the International Association of Lawyers Against Nuclear Arms, and the International Peace Bureau.[23] Although participation was international, the abolition caucus meetings were dominated by representatives of U.S. NGOs, including Peace Action, Western States Legal Foundation, and Nuclear Age Peace Foundation, as well as various individuals who were attached to

NGOs or coalitions but did not necessarily represent the views of others in those organizations. Most members of the abolition caucus opposed indefinite extension of the NPT, believing that a short extension would force the nuclear weapon states to agree to pursue real disarmament, rather than face unbridled proliferation.

Other NGOs were wary of holding the NPT hostage to nuclear disarmament. Even before the 1995 conference, there had been clashes between NGOs over this "strange logic of leverage," which relied on threatening the stability and longevity of the nonproliferation regime as a means of exerting leverage on the nuclear powers. The Peace Research Institute, Frankfurt, for example, argued that the actual consequence of a short extension would be increased domestic and military pressure on governments to stay ahead in the nuclear arms race, thereby creating the opposite effect of the one intended. Moreover, it was feared that by persuading some countries to hold out for a short extension, NGOs advocating this position had made it impossible for the Non-Aligned Movement to coalesce around a more credible alternative to indefinite extension.[24] Certainly, the divisions among the nonaligned countries over extension options greatly assisted the Western governments in achieving indefinite extension.

During the early weeks of the conference, the abolition caucus meetings were tense and angry. As the dynamics of big-power politics moved inexorably toward indefinite extension of the treaty, these NGO participants felt themselves and their concerns being sidelined. At one point, it appeared that the caucus would self-combust with acrimony. Instead, shut out from and frustrated by events inside the United Nations, the caucus decided to launch an abolition campaign: on April 28 about sixty NGO representatives issued a joint statement calling for the "definite and unconditional abolition of nuclear weapons," together with eleven steps for eliminating nuclear weapons and creating alternatives to nuclear energy.[25]

Ill prepared and divided over objectives and tactics, the NGOs in the abolition caucus had largely been irrelevant to NPT developments leading up to 1995. By channeling their frustration with the NPT conference into positive campaigning for the abolition of nuclear weapons, however, they managed to rescue themselves and start a network to enable like-minded NGOs to exchange information on nuclear issues and, where possible, cooperate on campaigns.

Their cause was inadvertently helped by the actions of governments. Two days after the NPT review conference closed, and despite
having agreed that "pending the entry into force of a Comprehensive
Test Ban Treaty, the nuclear weapon states should exercise utmost re-
straint,"[26] China exploded another underground nuclear test. Within
a month, President Chirac announced that France would resume nuclear testing in the South Pacific for a final "campaign" of up to eight
explosions before concluding the CTBT. The prospect of France breaking its moratorium, adhered to since 1992, shook the test ban negotiations and caused an international outcry.

The CTBT negotiations seemed to be sinking, not only because of
the Chinese and French tests but also because some states and diplomats were angry and resentful over the way the NPT had been indefinitely extended. The tests appeared to confirm civil society's worst
fears—that the indefinite extension would be treated by the nuclear
weapon states as a carte blanche for nuclear business as usual.[27]

Although Gérard Errera, France's ambassador to the Conference
on Disarmament, spiritedly defended his country against the dismay
expressed by fellow ambassadors, these diplomatic criticisms were not
unexpected or particularly hard-hitting.[28] What did take France by
surprise was the international reaction outside governmental circles,
as demonstrations disrupted French diplomatic residences and companies all over the world. A French consulate in Australia was even set
on fire (although Australian disarmament NGOs were quick to dissoci-
ate themselves and condemn the arson attack). Boycotts against French
goods, especially wine, were started in Japan, Canada, parts of the
United States, and several European and Scandinavian countries. The
boycotts were particularly interesting because they were largely the
spontaneous reaction of the public. Although the International Peace
Bureau and IPPNW and their national affiliates called on members to
boycott French goods and produced stickers to identify French products on supermarket shelves, the sight of restaurateurs pouring
French wine down drains was on television screens almost before the
NGOs had mobilized. Alhough Germany's government said little,
German shoppers boycotted French goods in large numbers. In the
United States, Physicians for Social Responsibility (PSR) convened a
boycott coalition that included diverse groups, including Peace Action, the Women's Action for New Directions, and the Fellowship of

Reconciliation. The coalition asked French-owned companies to make public statements denouncing the tests, promising to exempt them from the boycott if they did so.

Even the implosion of Greenpeace at this time proved to be irrelevant to the wider issue. International public response to the resumption of French testing had already taken off under its own steam. The antinuclear lobby in France had always been rather weak, but it managed to organize two sizable demonstrations. Most importantly, the international boycotts began to bite into commercial and agricultural income, giving rise to interviews with disgruntled farmers and heated discussions in the French media on the costs and benefits of testing. This was worse than Chirac's government had expected. France tried hard to salvage a deteriorating public-relations position. From appearing to be a reluctant participant in the CTBT negotiations, its negotiating posture was transformed to one of constructive and proactive engagement. On July 14, Chirac indicated that France would drop its requirement for a low threshold and then left open the possibility that the test series might be fewer than eight and could finish earlier than May 1996.[29] At the time, hardly anyone noticed, but the concessions France made were significant nonetheless. On August 11, 1995, President Clinton announced a crucial shift in U.S. policy toward the CTBT, dropping the long-standing insistence on permitting very small tests in favor of a total ban. This change, itself the product of civil society mobilization (described later), pushed France into accepting a zero-yield ban. France went ahead with its tests, but it conducted only six and stopped at the end of January 1996, months before the cutoff date given in the original announcement. The flexibility may have been built into the French strategy, but in making such concessions, France was perceived as responding to public and diplomatic pressure.

Abolition 2000: A Global Network to Eliminate Nuclear Weapons was formally established in November 1995 at a meeting in the Hague, the Netherlands. It was not set up as a membership organization, but was open to all who endorsed the April 1995 abolition statement. Communicating principally by e-mail through the Internet and a dedicated server, Abolition 2000 was intended to be a network of regional and working groups encompassing many cultures, languages, and political systems, with an annual international meeting and regional gatherings as desired. In January 1997, Abolition 2000 held its annual meeting in the South Pacific, hosted by Hiti Tau, the Maohi NGO based in Polynesia. In addition to strategizing for the future, the purpose of the meeting was to support the Maohi people's independent health study of test site workers and their families and to "honor the leadership of Pacific nations in facing and preventing further dangers of the Nuclear Age." The 150 participants adopted the Moorea Declaration, recognizing the "unique sufferings and challenges that face indigenous cultures touched by the nuclear chain."[30] By the end of 1999, Abolition 2000 claimed around 2,000 organizational members worldwide and had participated as an active caucus in the various meetings (PrepComs) established under the NPT's strengthened review process, as well as in other initiatives, such as the Hague Peace Appeal.

Analysts and Pragmatists

Whereas direct action and radical appeals worked at key moments to catalyze public opinion and increase the pressure on politicians and governments, analysts and pragmatists were crucial in translating the demands into policy options for government officials to consider and implement.

A number of Washington-based NGOs had spent many years working for a CTBT. Although some of their leaders were activists, most had professional or academic qualifications. These NGOs tended to rely on detailed analysis and insider access, though some backed this up with public mobilization. Seizing the opportunity afforded by the Russian and French testing moratoria, a group of them, notably the Natural Resources Defense Council, PSR, Union of Concerned Scientists, Plutonium Challenge, Arms Control Association, and Institute for Science and International Security, played a crucial role in working with Congress to achieve the moratorium imposed by the Bush administration in 1992. Convinced that arms control opportunities would become closed off if the NPT was not made permanent, these and other NGOs concerned with broader proliferation issues formed a coalition in late 1993 to work for both a CTBT and the indefinite extension of the NPT. The Campaign for the NPT was initiated by Michael Krepon of the Stimson Center, a former staffer for the U.S. Arms Control and

Disarmament Agency (ACDA), together with the W. Alton Jones Foundation, a major U.S. funder of arms control projects. Joseph Cirincione, who had been a staff member of the House Armed Services Committee, was hired in December 1993 to coordinate the political and media strategies, and eighteen of the most influential Washington-based NGOs were soon on board.[31]

Because of the revolving door in U.S. politics, which allows academics, lawyers, and diplomats to be in key governmental positions one day and back in their universities or nongovernmental institutions the next, some of the senior figures in the Campaign for the NPT had themselves been members of past administrations as ambassadors, officials, and treaty negotiators. In addition to senior figures and organizations concerned with nonproliferation, arms control, and the management of nuclear forces, the Campaign included a few activist-oriented NGOs, such as Peace Action and PSR, that were committed to the abolition of nuclear weapons. They backed the indefinite extension of the NPT principally because, in the wake of revelations about the nuclear programs under construction in Iraq and North Korea, they regarded a permanent treaty as necessary to reinforce the international norm against the acquisition of nuclear weapons. But for most, their endorsement was neither unconditional nor uncritical. On the contrary, they repeatedly raised concerns that the United States and the other weapon powers needed to pledge to do more toward implementing the Article VI obligations on nuclear disarmament. During 1994, the Campaign for the NPT castigated the Clinton administration for not paying sufficient attention to the concerns of non-nuclear parties to the treaty. Kept closely informed of the snail's pace of the CTBT negotiations in Geneva through the Acronym e-mails and reports, members of the Campaign publicly criticized the lack of effective American leadership, as well as positions they regarded as counterproductive, such as the option of easy withdrawal from the treaty after ten years and the wrangling over whether to exempt very small nuclear explosions from the scope of the ban.[32]

Initially, prospects for indefinite extension of the NPT did not look promising, and U.S. officials seemed to lack the necessary attention and strategies. After the deadlocked and messy third preparatory meeting for the 1995 NPT conference, which was held in Geneva in September 1994,[33] the Campaign for the NPT stepped up its pressure on ACDA and the U.S. State Department to take the concerns of key nonaligned states more seriously and also to work toward conclusion of the CTBT by April 1995. The Campaign held breakfast and lunch briefings in Washington, to which it invited representatives from the major embassies, the U.S. government, and political media to hear nongovernmental experts or diplomats discuss the major issues and problems. It conducted a well-resourced, carefully targeted media campaign, feeding information and articles to all the important U.S. newspapers and keeping regional press supplied with opinion pieces and apposite quotes.

Since the Campaign's aim was the indefinite extension of the treaty, which was U.S. policy, other NGOs questioned its independence. Indeed, when two Campaign representatives visited Geneva to discuss the NPT with ambassadors from a number of undecided states, some nonaligned diplomats came close to accusing them of being tools of the U.S. Government.[34] These criticisms missed the point, however, for a large part of the Campaign's work was directed toward the U.S. government, and its real impact was on American perceptions.

During 1994 and early 1995, the Campaign for the NPT purveyed two principal messages to the U.S. government: "Wake up—the NPT extension is in jeopardy" and "Show leadership to bring the CTBT to a rapid conclusion." As more nonaligned countries declared their opposition to indefinite extension in the final months before the conference, the Campaign proposed a five-part agenda that it believed would address the underlying concern that indefinite extension would mainly freeze the privileged position of the nuclear five: substantial progress or agreement on a draft text of the CTBT before April 1995, ratification of START II, a halt to the production of fissile materials for weapons, a moratorium on commercial production and civilian use of separated plutonium and highly enriched uranium, and a declaration against the first use or threatened use of nuclear weapons. The Campaign charged that "the Clinton Administration has failed to exert leadership either internationally or in domestic politics to insure that its position—and that of the nonproliferation treaty—would be strong when the formal review begins in April."[35]

Just before and during the review and extension conference itself, the Campaign focused more on procedures and votes. This brought some simmering internal disagreements to a head, resulting in two groups, Peace Action and the Nuclear Control Institute, pulling out of the Campaign before the conference, expressing their dismay at what they viewed as inadequate emphasis on disarmament objectives. Others, such as PSR and Manhattan Project II, issued individual position statements and participated in some of the abolition caucus activities. Led by Cirincione, the Campaign created momentum toward the extension decision by keeping a tally of countries' voting intentions, which was updated regularly and fed to the press in ways that increased the intensity of expectation. It embraced a breakthrough proposal from South Africa that called for a strengthened review process with a defined set of principles and objectives for nonproliferation and disarmament, almost as soon as it went public. It canvassed opinion on how such an approach might work out and briefed the press as conference decisions developed behind closed doors.

The Campaign, unlike other NGOs, was intended as a short-term, focused effort. With the accomplishment of its principal objective, it disbanded after May 1995 but then re-formed as the Coalition to Reduce Nuclear Dangers (CRND) when it became clear that the CTBT and other key negotiations were in trouble. Cirincione stayed on as director of CRND until April 1997, utilizing the strategy and tactics that had proved effective in the NPT campaign: uniting the major U.S. arms control groups around achievable goals and a coherent and practical program, utilizing flexibility in tactics and well-targeted media relations.

The CTBT needed all the friends it could get. After the NPT was indefinitely extended, the U.S. Joint Chiefs of Staff and some important State Department officials backed a reasserted Pentagon demand for the CTBT not to ban nuclear explosions smaller than 500 tonnes (TNT equivalent). The Washington NGOs and others opposed the Pentagon push by rallying a group of 24 senators and 113 representatives to urge Clinton to support a total zero-yield test ban. Together with the grassroots networks, they collected over 35,000 letters and messages, which were dispatched to the White House. The pressure coincided with publication of a report commissioned by the U.S. Department of Energy from several nuclear weapon specialists known as the JASON Group, which concluded that small tests of up to 500 tonnes would not add much to stockpile safety. Public pressure, intensified by outrage over the resumed French testing, was utilized in a pincer action by Acronym in Geneva and NGOs in the United States, which persuaded congressional representatives to write to Clinton, forcing the president to make a decision. The JASON report gave him the scientific arguments he needed to decide in favor of a total ban, thereby excluding the low-yield tests advocated by the Pentagon.[36] U.S. advocacy of a total ban was the fundamental breakthrough necessary to revive the CTBT negotiations. Under pressure, first France, then Britain, and finally Russia followed.

That left one nuclear power, China, still looking for a loophole. Behind the scenes, the Acronym Institute worked with the delegations of Japan, Germany, Australia, and others to block China's demand for a provision permitting requests to conduct nuclear explosions for "peaceful" purposes, such as large-scale excavations. So-called "peaceful nuclear explosions" were not supported by most other delegations, but many were prepared to include a provision as a face-saver for China, provided permission to conduct such nuclear explosions would require consensus among CTBT parties. In their view, such consensus would have been unlikely. The danger was that the provision would have given the nuclear weapon states an excuse to maintain their testing infrastructure and apparatus unhindered, exactly what the Acronym Institute and others wanted to avoid. Once the scope of the CTBT was settled, the treaty was able to be concluded and signed by the end of 1996. Although NGOs such as the Acronym Institute, VERTIC, PSR, and CRND continued their work with diplomats and officials, the intense negotiations and dramas of the final year were conducted mainly among states, with India, Britain, Russia, the United States, China, and the Netherlands (chairing the negotiations) in the lead parts.

Behind-the-Scenes Facilitators

The role of transnational civil society is not always public. There is a long history of academics and think tanks that assist policy transformation by diagnosing problems, facilitating constructive contacts among government officials and diplomats, and exploring workable solutions. At least two behind-the-scenes organizations stamped their influence indelibly on the outcome of the 1995 NPT Review and Extension Conference: the Programme for Promoting Nuclear Non-Proliferation and the Monterey Institute. PPNN held "track one and a half" meetings (gatherings of both government representatives and nongovernmental specialists[37]) twice a year in the run-up to the review conference, at which diplomats from all sides could meet informally and brainstorm about some of the issues likely to arise. In addition, PPNN and the Monterey Institute provided expert analysis, ideas, and a confidential atmosphere for exchanging information and troubleshooting. Senior policy makers from almost all the key governments attended under Chatham House rules, according to which discussions could be summarized in general terms but without attributing specific contributions to named participants.

Without the coordination, information and behind-the-scenes work of such academically based NGOs, the outcome of the NPT conference may well have been quite different, for it was during successive PPNN meetings, over games of pool, that diplomats from three key countries developed the triple-action concept of indefinite extension with a strengthened review process and the set of principles and objectives on nuclear nonproliferation and disarmament. Proposed by South Africa at the review conference and negotiated under the auspices of conference president Jayantha Dhanapala, the three decisions were adopted as a package on the penultimate day of the conference. They succeeded as a compromise between those who wanted indefinite and unconditional extension of the NPT and those who wanted greater leverage on the nuclear weapon states to implement their disarmament obligations.

Dislodging Boulders

The NPT was indefinitely extended, but for the first few years, the review process did not function well and the political environment for nonproliferation, nuclear arms control, and disarmament worsened. The success of the sixth review conference in May 2000, however, has vindicated much of what civil society sought to achieve in 1995. NGOs were more organized and cooperative, and they played an important role in briefing countries before and during the conference, providing expert information, and developing strategies and tactics that were taken up by several governments. A few countries even featured NGOs from PPNN, the Monterey Institute, and some abolition caucus organizations on their delegations. Of most importance for the outcome of the 2000 conference, a group of medium non-nuclear powers known as the New Agenda Coalition ran with a strategy originally outlined in an Acronym paper in 1998. In unofficial partnership with the Acronym Institute and a few European NGOs working with their parliaments, the New Agenda countries managed to persuade the nuclear powers to consent to an unequivocal undertaking to eliminate their nuclear arsenals and to agree on a number of practical, interim steps for nuclear disarmament.

The CTBT has been signed by more than 155 states but may never become legally binding, in large part because Russia, Britain, and China forced through an unusually stringent entry-into-force provision that required the signature and ratification of 44 named nuclear-capable countries. Despite NGO efforts during 1995–96, particularly from the Acronym Institute, VERTIC, and the CRND, it proved impossible to prevent the adoption of this rigid provision, with predictable consequences. India was angered to find itself on the entry-into-force list after declaring that the CTBT was inadequate because it was not tied explicitly to progress on nuclear disarmament. Within two years of opposing the CTBT's adoption by the United Nations General Assembly, India conducted a series of nuclear explosions in May 1998. Pakistan followed within the month. The explosions threatened the international norm against testing, which the CTBT was intended to embed, but they did not violate the treaty itself, since neither India nor Pakistan had signed. Although there were international protests against these tests, they were much weaker than earlier demonstrations against the French. Moreover, the tests were very popular with the general public in both countries. The few Pakistani scientists and journalists who opposed the tests were reviled and even attacked. Many Indian NGOs that had collaborated for years with Western academic institutions and antinuclear groups, including the abolition caucus, sought to justify their country's nuclear ambitions.

In October 1999, the CTBT was dealt a further blow when Republicans in the U.S. Senate maneuvered successfully to prevent U.S. ratification, the first time the Senate had defeated a major international accord since it threw out the 1919 Versailles Treaty. The rejection had less to do with the merits of the CTBT than with domestic politics and Republican hostility toward President Clinton, and it was carried through on partisan lines, after only a derisory debate. Yet it was a defeat for civil society as well as for government, coming only months after an opinion poll showed that over 82 percent of Americans were in favor of the CTBT.[38] A number of NGOs, particularly CRND, had made valiant efforts since 1996 to promote CTBT ratification and persuade the Clinton administration to mobilize Republican supporters, but it was not enough, and the issue, as in 1963, dropped from public sight.

Disarmament is a tough challenge for transnational civil society. Arms control and disarmament objectives cannot be achieved if states consider their national and regional security to be threatened. Nuclear weapons can be eliminated only when they are perceived to have lost their military and political value. At present, nuclear weapons are still central to the military strategy and political identity of their possessors, in ways that other weapons, like land mines, are not. Changing that will require a paradigm shift that may not be within civil society's power to bring about without a cataclysmic event, such as a major accident, near miss, or nuclear exchange.

The track record shows that civil society was most successful when it worked at both the elite and public movement levels, as it did in achieving the moratoria in 1991–93 and the CTBT zero-yield decision in 1995. The very different strategies of prominent public activism and quiet, behind-the-scenes partnerships with policy makers can reinforce each other. Similarly, different types of organization and initiative can accomplish different parts of the process. In relation to defense and security policies, transnational civil society can work most effectively by sustaining a credible base of research and information, working with all sides while retaining independence from governments or parties, and utilizing pincer approaches involving both partnership and confrontation.

Although disarmament NGOs were more obviously active in the 1980s, they were operating in a barren political context. The Cold War was at its height, and the political and strategic conditions for achieving a CTBT were dismal, although the American and European peace movements played an important part in halting the MX missile program and bringing about the Intermediate Nuclear Forces (INF) Treaty in 1987. Although NGOs can contribute to creating and ripening the political conditions, they cannot succeed in a vacuum, no matter how effective their tactics.

Not everything worked as planned. The start of the Gulf War in January 1991 overshadowed the PTBT amendment conference and the mass demonstrations organized by Greenpeace and others at the Nevada test site, at which more than 750 people were arrested.[39] Demonstrations may be useful in instilling NGO bonding and promoting local attention, motivation, and excitement, but to have an impact on national policy and decision making, they need to be unexpectedly large, inspirational or fortuitously timed (preferably all three).

Adversity is good for membership of NGOs but not for their success. When political conditions are unfavorable, the roles of grassroots and direct actionists are likely to be of greater salience than the work of elite NGOs. Since tools for policy input were weak or unavailable during the 1980s, the major role of NGOs was to keep nuclear weapons and testing alive as an issue. Greenpeace actions at the test sites were ideal for this purpose. The technical and policy experts came to the fore when negotiations became complex and when NGO partnerships with government officials or diplomats from key countries could foster positive outcomes. As the case study showed, effective progress required a synergy among direct action to grab media attention, public movement campaigning to increase political pressure, and arms control elites to whisper in decision makers' ears. And, as the example of PPNN showed, some of the most effective work can be conducted without any publicity whatsoever, provided information is targeted wisely.

In what can look like a good cop–bad cop routine, the grassroots and public movement campaigns target their messages and raise expectations; the resulting demands and pressure make the political decision makers insecure, which encourages them to turn to the incrementalists for "reasonable" solutions and reassurance. The elite NGOs should be there, ready with proposals for practical steps and offers of assistance in solving the governments' problems. As long as the national and international pressure is maintained, and provided the incrementalists have not pitched their proposals too low, collective progress toward shared objectives can be made.

Civilians, especially women, are disproportionately harmed by weapons and wars but have little representation where military policies are decided, even in democracies. The hardware, threat assessments, and negotiating postures associated with defense decisions are less open to question and scrutiny than any other area of political decision making. By highlighting dangers, reminding governments of the wider and international implications of their actions, and giving voice to the interests of those who could not expect to be provided with safe bunkers in the event of nuclear policies gone wrong, transnational civil society fulfills a legitimate function of responsible citizenship. The objective is not to replace governments or usurp their decision-making authority but to inform and persuade governments and businesses to adopt or abandon certain policies or positions.

Moral authority derives not only from the objectives but also from the means adopted. Advocates of disarmament customarily abide by nonviolent principles, whereby individuals are required to shoulder responsibility for their own actions and not to harm others. In this philosophy, ignoring a problem is tantamount to choosing in favor of the status quo or ongoing abuse. By contrast, the nuclear weapon scientists and former military or political officials who become advocates of nuclear abolition do not necessarily subscribe to a moral philosophy of disarmament, but they can claim the authority of insider knowledge and the moral ground of having "seen the light" with regard to particular weapons or practices.

The case study shows the importance of the timely use, exchange, and targeting of information. Within transnational civil society, the role of knowledge providers has become an increasingly important source of legitimacy. During the CTBT negotiations, the Acronym Institute came to be regarded by many delegations as the "NGO negotiator" on the treaty. PPNN and the Monterey Institute gained legitimacy through their briefings and expertise on the NPT. The Campaign for the NPT was regarded by the U.S. government as an ally in securing indefinite extension, though this may have reduced its legitimacy in the eyes of others. Inevitably, some civil society actors, especially those with private (and therefore less accountable) sources of funding, pursue agendas and claim to speak for others while representing no one but themselves. Additionally, as civil society is fluid, there is frequently a time lag between political relevance and formal, organizational status on influential bodies. Associated with the United Nations in New York, Vienna, and Geneva, for example, are formally important committees burdened with well-meaning but ineffectual people representing defunct organizations or outdated politics. This is a problem of particular relevance to the disarmament field, which has a long history, diverse groupings, and remnants of Cold War structures and organizational traditions.

The bitter chasm between arms controllers and abolitionists is slowly being bridged, though there are still problems of distrust. Although polarized around the extension of the NPT, the core difficulties were less about political objectives than about ways of working. There is a danger in case studies such as this of oversimplifying the differences: for example, although most were arms controllers, some members of the Campaign for the NPT were grassroots disarmament organizations, and some members of the abolition caucus were professionals or academics with no public movement connections of their own. Moreover, since 1995, more of the NGOs designated "arms controllers" have been addressing how to prohibit and eliminate nuclear weapons altogether.[40] Similarly, growing numbers of abolition advocates now accept that incremental steps do not necessarily entail abandoning radical objectives. The peace movement is proud of its long history, but as the case study shows, this comes with competitive ideological baggage, which may hinder the development of alternative strategies, cross-group coalition building, and creative new approaches, the importance of which was demonstrated by the successful land-mines campaign.

By the prevailing paradigm, nuclear weapons are perceived as necessary and desirable by powerful cliques in a few dominant states. Whereas some campaigns are like a tug-of-war with a length of rope, achieving nuclear disarmament is more like dislodging a massive boulder. It is not a linear process. Eliminating one weapon system or practice is not necessarily the first step toward closing down the next. Deep-rooted ideologies, backed by powerful interest groups within the military, defense industries, and political class, have to be weakened and dismantled. To be successful, therefore, civil society must engage at multiple points: political, legal, environmental, moral, and ideological. Although transnational civil society cannot claim unqualified successes with either the NPT or the CTBT, and the approaches of some NGOs and civil society actors can be criticized as misguided or ineffective, the conclusion of this case study is that the participation of civil society in the disarmament field and in creating and reinforcing nonproliferation, nontesting, and antiwar norms is important and desirable.

Notes

1. Statement by U.S. President Bill Clinton to the United Nations General Assembly, September 24, 1996.
2. The Acronym Consortium of NGOs was formed in January 1994 and dissolved in September 1995. I then formed Disarmament Intelligence Review, which later became the Acronym Institute.
3. Interview with Daniel Ellsberg, reported in R. Johnson, "Visions and Divisions," *NPT Update* 10 (April 28, 1995).
4. *Today*, November 15, 1990.
5. "Mass Break-in at the Palace—The Queen in Residence as Protest Women Scale the Walls," *Evening Standard*, July 6, 1993.
6. I am indebted to Daryl Kimball of the Coalition to Reduce Nuclear Dangers for sharing his research on U.S. NGOs and their work on the test ban.
7. As noted by the Soviet ambassador to the United Nations, Valerian Zorin, quoted in J. Goldblat and D. Cox, *Nuclear Weapon Tests: Prohibition or Limitation?* (Stockholm: Stockholm International Peace Research Institute; Oxford: Oxford University Press, 1988), p. 97.
8. In June 1996, the Conference on Disarmament admitted twenty-three new members. In August 1999, five more countries were admitted, bringing the membership to sixty-six, although since the breakup of Yugoslavia, that seat has remained unoccupied.
9. General-Secretary Gorbachev first announced the Soviet moratorium in October 1990, which Russian President Yeltsin extended in 1991, after the breakup of the Soviet Union.
10. "Blueprint for a Nuclear Weapon–Free World," Campaign for Nuclear Disarmament, London, 1995.
11. See George Bunn and Charles N. Van Doren, "Options for Extension of the NPT: The Intention of the Drafters of Article X.2" in the PPNN pamphlet *Options and Opportunities: The NPT Extension Conference of 1995*, PPNN Study 2, 1991. George Bunn—a former U.S. ambassador, part of the 1960s team of international lawyers who negotiated the NPT, and associated with the PPNN, the Monterey Institute, and the Lawyers Alliance for World Security—developed the concept of a twenty-five-year rolling extension and methods of sustaining leverage on the nuclear weapon states.
12. China advocated a "smooth extension," which was understood to mean indefinite or long term, such as the twenty-five-year rolling extension advocated by Bunn and taken up by several nonaligned delegations during the NPT conference.
13. Michael Szabo, *Making Waves: The Greenpeace New Zealand Story* (Auckland, New Zealand: Reed Books, 1991).
14. The origin of this description, frequently heard among Greenpeace's female (and some male) employees in the 1980s, is not known.
15. For an analysis of the NPT review conference in 1990, see John Simpson, "The 1990 Review Conference of the Nuclear Non-Proliferation Treaty," *Round Table* (April 1991).

16. From August 1988 to 1992, I worked for Greenpeace International, coordinating first the International Test Ban Campaign and then the International Plutonium Campaign.

17. This research ended up as the basis for a successful exposure of Chinese testing by VERTIC in October 1993, long after Greenpeace had lost interest. See "Britain Scores First on Rumbling Test," *Guardian*, October 6, 1993; "China Explodes Nuclear Device Despite US Plea," *Financial Times*, October 6, 1993; and "Waiting for the Earth to Move," *Independent*, October 11, 1993.

18. "Protest Dive off Tower Bridge," *Daily Express*, November 13, 1990; "Nuke Ban Daredevils Jump off Deep End," *Daily Star*, November 13, 1990; "Svenskan som protesterade högt i London," *Aftonbladet*, November 19, 1990.

19. "Greenham Girl Halts Nuclear Blast 7 Minutes from Death," *Today*, November 15, 1990; "N-bomb Halted by Women," *Daily Mirror*, November 15, 1990; "Nevada Blast Is Delayed," *Times*, November 15, 1990; "Nuclear Test Delayed After Three Women Infiltrate Site," *Daily Telegraph*, November 15, 1990.

20. Testimony of witnesses of French nuclear testing in the South Pacific, Greenpeace International, August 1990; "Memorandum: Preliminary Proposals for Research on Nuclear Test Sites in French Polynesia" (Moruroa and Fangataufa), Greenpeace International, October 1990.

21. "France Calls Off Nuclear Testing," *Times*, April 9, 1992; Tim Wichter, "France to Suspend N-tests in Pacific," *Daily Telegraph*, April 9, 1992, p. 15.

22. "Testing Decision on Semipalatinsk by Kazakhstan," *Soviet Weekly*, January 10, 1991. Much of this section is derived from contemporaneous notes of meetings I had with members of the Nevada-Semipalatinsk Movement in 1990, 1995, and 1999. I also participated in the 1990 Citizen's Congress.

23. These three NGOs spearheaded the World Court Project, which succeeded in 1996 in obtaining an influential advisory opinion on the use and threat of use of nuclear weapons from the International Court of Justice.

24. See the section on NGO participation in R. Johnson, "Extending the Non-Proliferation Treaty: The Endgame," *ACRONYM Report* 5 (February 1995): 11.

25. The abolition statement can be found in various publications, including "Creating a Nuclear Weapons Free World," Waging Peace Series Booklet No. 38, Nuclear Age Peace Foundation, Santa Barbara, Calif., August 1997, pp. 16–17.

26. Decision 2 on Principles and Objectives for Nuclear Non-Proliferation and Disarmament, 1995 Review and Extension Conference of the Parties to the Treaty on the Non-Proliferation of Nuclear Weapons, Final Document, Part I (NPT/Conf. 1995/32).

27. See R. Johnson, "Indefinite Extension of the Non-Proliferation Treaty: Risks and Reckonings," *ACRONYM Report* 7 (September 1995): 70, n. 22, quoting British and French officials.

28. See R. Johnson, "Geneva Update No. 20," *Nuclear Proliferation News* 28 (June 30, 1995).

29. The French tests ended in January 1996 after six rather than eight explosions. The conclusion was timed to give a boost to the CTBT negotiations at the start of the Conference on Disarmament's 1996 session.

30. The 1997 Moorea Declaration is in "Creating a Nuclear Weapons Free World," p. 18. The Maohi are the Polynesian people of the South Pacific. They were related many centuries ago to the Maori of New Zealand.

31. Members of the Campaign for the NPT were the Arms Control Association, British-American Security Information Council, Center for Defense Information, Committee for National Security, Council for a Livable World, Institute for Science and International Security, Lawyers Alliance for World Security, Manhattan Project II, Natural Resources Defense Council, Nuclear Control Institute, Peace Action, Physicians for Social Responsibility, Plutonium Challenge, Public Education Center, Henry L. Stimson Center, Union of Concerned Scientists, Washington Council on Non-Proliferation, and Women's Action for New Directions.

32. Since the U.S. Department of Energy was prepared to provide only a ten-year assurance of the reliability of U.S. arsenals, the United States initially proposed a ten-year opt-out or "easy exit" clause that would allow any state to withdraw temporarily from the treaty to test its nuclear weapons for "safety and reliability." There was overwhelming opposition to such a provision, which was perceived as discriminatory and as undermining the indefinite and universal character of the treaty. See *Nuclear Proliferation News* 10 (September 2, 1994) and *Nuclear Proliferation News* 18 (February 17, 1995). On scope, see R. Johnson, "The CTBT Endgame: The Major Obstacles," in *Verification 1996*, ed. John Poole and Richard Guthrie (Boulder, Colo.: VERTIC, Westview, 1996).

33. See R. Johnson, "Strengthening the Non-Proliferation Treaty: Decisions Made, Decisions Deferred," *ACRONYM Report* 4 (September 1994).

34. A newspaper article actually described the Campaign for the NPT as having "close ties to ACDA" (Josh Friedman, "Nuclear Pact at Turning Point," *Newsday*, January 24, 1995).

35. Barbara Crossette, "Atom Pact Runs into a Snag," *New York Times*, January 26, 1995.

36. Kimball, unpublished research.

37. In diplomatic parlance, discussions involving only governments are track one, and meetings among nongovernmental experts from several countries are denoted track two. Hence, meetings between governmental representatives and nongovernmental specialists are referred to as track one and a half.

38. "Eight in Ten Americans Support Test Ban Treaty: More Want Senate Approval of Pact in Year Since South Asian Blasts," news release, Coalition to Reduce Nuclear Dangers, July 20, 1999.

39. "Britons Held," *Times*, January 7, 1991; "250 Nevada Test Site Arrests," *Morning Star*, January 7, 1991; "Nuclear Conference to Debate Total Test Ban," *Independent*, January 8, 1991; "UN Conferees Press for Test Ban," *International Herald Tribune*, January 8, 1991; "Testing Time for Treaty," *Independent*, January 14, 1991.

40. See, for example, the Henry L. Stimson Center Project on Eliminating Weapons of Mass Destruction.

4

Toward Democratic Governance for Sustainable Development: Transnational Civil Society Organizing Around Big Dams

Sanjeev Khagram

AROUND THE WORLD, perhaps the most dramatic conflicts over how to pursue sustainable development with democratic governance have occurred in the contestation over big dams.[1] The massive scale of these projects, and their seeming ability to bring powerful and capricious natural forces under human control, historically gave them a unique hold on the social imagination.

For proponents, dams symbolize temples of progress and modernity, from a life controlled by nature and tradition to one in which the environment is ruled by technology, and tradition by science. But a growing number of opponents see the same projects as destructive of nature and indigenous cultures, imposing unacceptable costs while rarely delivering on their ostensible benefits.

This chapter tells the story of the conflicts between a powerful set of interests (government agencies, international organizations, multinational corporations, and domestic industrial and agricultural lobbies) that favor dam construction and the affected peoples groups and civil society coalitions that oppose them. It explores what could prove to be an important model for global governance that incorporates all these stakeholders: the World Commission on Dams.

Today, big dams contribute 20 percent of global electricity generation.

In sixty-five countries, hydropower produces more than 50 percent of electricity; in twenty-four more than 90 percent.[2] Worldwide, agricultural crops currently get more than 30 percent of their water from irrigation, a lion's share of which comes from big dams. Future increases in agricultural production to meet the needs of a growing global population will require greater numbers of irrigation dams.[3] Moreover, nearly 1 billion people still do not have adequate supplies of drinking water, 2 billion people do not have access to electricity, and the need for better flood management seems undeniable (witness the massive and destructive floods that have engulfed various regions of the world over the past several years).

Given the seemingly tremendous need for the benefits generated by big dams, and the powerful groups and organizations promoting them, the dramatic decline in the construction of these projects globally over the past twenty-five years is puzzling. The number of big dams built annually grew from virtually zero in 1900 to nearly 250 by midcentury. The rate exploded thereafter and peaked at around 1,000 big dams being finished annually from the mid-1950s to the mid-1970s. But the number fell precipitously to less than 200 by the 1990s—a 75 percent drop in just over a decade.

There are technical, financial, and economic factors behind this trend, but they do not tell the whole story. The technical argument highlights the decreasing availability of sites for big dams. However, as of 1986, 95 percent of big dams were concentrated in 25 countries that had built more than 100, while less than 2 percent were spread over the more than 150 other countries where sites were still available, even plentiful.[4] In other words, sites remain plentiful in many countries.

Financial and economic factors, such as funding shortages and the increasing viability of "conventional" alternatives, are two other possible explanations.[5] The worldwide recession during the 1980s, the growth in indebtedness by many Third World states, donor fatigue among foreign lenders, and a strategy shift toward privatization all contributed to the decreasing availability of public and international financing. The decreasing costs of conventional alternatives, particularly natural gas power plants for electricity generation, made big dams relatively more expensive, especially as dam projects encountered increasing time and cost overruns.

But many of the largest financial and economic blows have come from political opposition of domestic civil society organizations in dozens of countries—opposition that has become transnationally linked. Mounting public protests against these projects have caused time overruns in their implementation, which in turn have produced cost overruns. Costs have escalated further because big dam builders and authorities have been compelled by civil society critics to first investigate and then prevent or mitigate the negative environmental and social impacts of these projects. These impacts are often enormous. For example, it is estimated that 40 million people, many indigenous or tribal, were displaced by big dams in the twentieth century. Rarely did these oustees receive just compensation, let alone real development benefits. As social and environmental costs are more fully internalized, economic benefit-cost or financial rate of return criteria justifying the building of these projects have become more difficult to achieve.[6]

The technical factor of site depletion generated political opposition to big dams, in addition to directly contributing to the decline in big dam building. Particularly in North America and Western Europe, the continual loss of free-flowing rivers from the damming of more and more sites sparked much of the initial criticism of domestic conservation groups. The success of these early campaigns against big dams played a critical role in the growth of national environmental movements in the West from the 1950s to the 1970s.[7]

Over the last two and a half decades, coalescing from a multitude of struggles and campaigns waged all around the world, domestic and transnational civil society organizations have dramatically altered the dynamics of big dam projects. Environmental nongovernmental organizations (NGOs) from the First World and at the international level, along with those working on human rights and the protection of indigenous peoples, increasingly focused on slowing or halting the global spread of big dams. Often independently and before this, directly affected local peoples, social movements, and domestic NGOs in other parts of the world began mobilizing to reform or block the completion of these projects in their own countries. Over time, coalitions were formed between these like-minded domestic and foreign groups. Thus, transnational civil society coalitions were formed from the domestic successes and subsequent internationalization of environmental and human and indigenous rights organizations in the West and the linkages and coalitions forged with people's groups and social movements struggling worldwide against big dam building.

The Rise of Domestic Opposition

Transnational civil society advocacy efforts are often criticized as being more Western than transnational, thus supposedly representing a narrow range of elite values and interests. This may be true for some issues, but it is not true of the historical dynamics around big dams. Domestic opposition has been independently organized in numerous countries outside the West, such as in India, Thailand, Indonesia, Brazil, Chile, Hungary, the former Soviet Union, and South Africa, to name just a few. Space does not allow a comprehensive review of them all, but some typical cases can be highlighted.[8]

In India, for example, domestic opposition began as far back as the 1940s, when authorities initiated one of the most prolific dam-building programs in history. The Hirakud dam, one of independent India's first multipurpose projects, provides a clear demonstration of this opposition. An anti-Hirakud campaign involving the full range of lobbying and pressure tactics was waged immediately after independence. The campaigners were so strident that they disobeyed orders prohibiting further public opposition against the project; 30,000 villagers and townspeople even protested in front of the state governor. Such purely domestic campaigns were generally unsuccessful through the 1960s.

Nevertheless, domestic civil society opposition to big dam building in India mounted during the 1970s and 1980s. The campaign against the Silent Valley hydroelectric project in Kerala, one of the first to eventually draw support from international NGOs, was a harbinger of trends to come. Grassroots mobilization against the project emerged in 1976 when a group of local teachers began assisting villagers who feared the loss of their livelihoods from the destruction of forest resources. At the same time, the World Wildlife Fund for Nature began to highlight internationally the project's negative environmental consequences on the pristine Silent Valley Forests and the endangered lion-tailed monkey.[9]

The Silent Valley campaign grew in size and strength over the subsequent decade. Domestic and foreign critics and opponents wrote letters, staged protests, lobbied officials, and filed court cases to halt the project. During the same time, environmental issues increased in prominence domestically in India and internationally in the aftermath of the United Nations Conference on the Human Environment held in Stockholm in 1972. As a result of the sustained opposition, the Silent Valley project was halted in 1984.

Cancellation of the Silent Valley project inspired big dam opponents throughout India and all over the world (see the next section). Within India, opposition mounted against such projects as the Tehri, Bodhghat, Subarnarekha, and, most visibly, Sardar Sarovar-Narmada River Valley. By the end of the 1980s, a meeting of over eighty prominent social movement leaders, activists, scholars, and critics representing millions of Indians called for a moratorium on big dam building in an "assertion of collective will against big dams" until domestic decision-making processes became more participatory and the results of projects more socially just and environmentally sustainable. At the same time, critiques of big dams became more widespread in popular and scholarly Indian publications.[10] Several of these pieces found their way into international journals and publications, contributing to transnational linkages.

The two most well-known campaigns in India, the first to reform and the second to halt completely the World Bank–funded Sardar Sarovar-Narmada project, were spearheaded not by foreign or international NGOs, but by local and domestic groups that eventually developed into the powerful social movement known as the Narmada Bachao Andolan (Save the Narmada Movement). Indeed, mobilization against the Sardar Sarovar in the form of rallies, mass protests, letter-writing campaigns, political lobbying, and scientific critiques began as early as the late 1970s, half a decade prior to the active involvement of transnationally linked allies. The degree of opposition, symbolized by the willingness of local people to drown rather than be displaced by the Sardar Sarovar project, was not motivated by outsiders but actually strengthened the organizing efforts of nondomestic supporters (discussed later).

India was not unusual. The campaign of cordilleran peoples in the Philippines against the Chico River project in the mid-1970s became known worldwide for the confrontations between opposition and government. As a result of the sustained and (atypical for antidam movements) violent grassroots opposition, the World Bank eventually withdrew its funding from the project. Similarly, from the 1970s on in Brazil, a nationwide movement of dam-affected peoples grew in size and strength. Combining civil society campaigns against projects in various regions of the country, the movement contributed not only to domestic social and environmental policy reform but also to the broader democratization process in Brazil.

This widespread domestic opposition did not flow from a Western-inspired or -funded agenda. These were primarily indigenous initiatives, and often successful ones, especially in democracies. Indeed, where domestic mobilization and organization were strongest is where the formation of transnational civil society was most likely.

The case of the Lesotho Highlands Water Project (LHWP) demonstrates the limits on what transnational civil society can accomplish when domestic members are weak. Initiated in the 1980s by the apartheid regime of South Africa, the project involved the export of water to the thirsty regions of South Africa in exchange for monetary compensation for Lesotho. But the project would also displace indigenous highlands people and inundate scarce agricultural lands in Lesotho. Not until the late 1980s did civil society organizations internationally begin aggressively criticizing the project. Around the same time, both South Africa and Lesotho initiated transitions to democracy, and domestic civil society opposition emerged. This empowered the transnational campaign and resulted in substantial reforms in terms of compensation, resettlement, and environmental protection. But the relative weakness of domestic civil society organizations and the unevenness of domestic democratization meant that the decision to replace the LHWP with a potentially more cost-effective and sustainable demand-side management program in South Africa was not made.

The more successful domestic antidam campaigns in the United States and Western Europe certainly contributed to the subsequent formation of transnational civil society coalitions. During the 1950s, 1960s, and 1970s, civil society groups critical of big dam building emerged in many European countries.[11] New laws requiring public disclosure of information and mandating environmental impact assessments on large projects both resulted from and added to the success of these efforts.[12] These successful campaigns contributed to the broader decline of big dam building in most European countries by the 1970s.

As in Western Europe, the earliest domestic campaigns to reform or halt big dam building in the United States were led primarily by nature conservationists. These early environmentalists, fighting to protect the natural beauty of the American West, achieved major victories by stopping construction of the Echo Park Dam in 1956 and two other big dams proposed for the Grand Canyon in 1967. The struggles against the Grand Canyon dams that began in the mid-1950s heralded the end of the expansion years of big dam building and played a central role in fostering the growth of a national environmental movement in the United States.[13]

During the 1970s, civil society critics of big dams became progressively better organized, losing some battles, but eventually winning the war. In 1972, the Environmental Policy Center (EPC; later the Environmental Policy Institute [EPI]) was established to lobby the federal government against large-scale water projects. One year later, the American Rivers Conservation Council (ARCC) was set up with an office in Washington, D.C. These two organizations arranged and sponsored the first national Dam Fighters Conference in 1976, which became an annual meeting. Between 1972 and 1983, EPC/EPI, the ARCC, and other civil society reformers and critics helped stop hundreds of big dam projects. When the U.S. Army Corps of Engineers completed the Lower Granite Dam on the Snake River in Washington State in 1975, it was to be one of the last massive river projects to be built in the United States.

As Robert Devine noted in a recent review, "The very success of the dam-building crusade accounts in part for its decline; by 1980 nearly all the nation's good sites—and many dubious sites—had been dammed. But two other factors accounted for most of the decline: public resistance to the enormous cost and pork-barrel smell of many dams, and a developing public understanding of the profound environmental degradation that building dams can cause."[14] A further blow occurred in 1987 when the U.S. Congress decided to limit the huge taxpayer subsidy for large water projects by requiring that local beneficiaries pay 25 percent of the cost. By 1994, the commissioner of the U.S. Bureau of Reclamation acknowledged that "we have recognized our traditional approach for solving problems—the construction of dams and associated facilities—is no longer publicly acceptable.... Our future lies with improving water resource management and environmental restoration activities, not water project construction."[15]

The Building of Transnational Linkages

By the 1970s, as civil society groups in the West succeeded in reforming and halting big dams domestically, they realized that similar projects were being formulated and implemented elsewhere. Not surprisingly, big dam proponents moved their activities to countries where demand for these projects was still high, international funding available, criticism of big dam building less organized, and democratic and environmental norms less institutionalized. In fact, more than two-thirds of new big dam starts occurred in the Third World during the 1980s.

In response, European NGOs such as the Ecologist, Survival International, Berne Declaration, Urgewald, and European Rivers Network were formed or shifted their focus to big dam projects in Southern Europe, Eastern Europe, the Soviet Union and its successor states, and the Third World. These indigenous peoples, human rights, environmental, and even sustainable development NGOs consciously built coalitions with allies all over the world.

U.S. groups followed the same path. During the late 1970s, Philip B. Williams, a hydrologist living in San Francisco who had long supported environmentalists campaigning against large water projects in California, began conducting research on the social and environmental effects of big dams worldwide. Williams found:

> As we were becoming successful in stopping dams in the U.S., we saw the same obsolete big dam technology being exported to the third world, disregarding the devastating ecologic damage and huge economic costs that the U.S. had incurred in its dam building boom in the 50's and 60's. Yet at the same time we saw successful examples of citizens groups' resistance in the early 1980s, most notably the cancellation of dams on the Franklin River in Tasmania, the Silent Valley in India, and the Nam Chaom Dam in Thailand. Around the world big dams were being promoted to gullible and corrupt politicians as a quick road to economic development by an international syndicate of self serving interests: international consultants, construction firms, and development bureaucrats.... We believed that by cooperating with and coordinating

with nongovernmental organizations fighting dams in international policy arenas we could counter the influence of these international interests.[16]

In 1982, he urged U.S. dam-fighter Brent Blackwelder of EPI to organize a session on big dam building globally to be held in conjunction with the annual national dam fighters' conference in Washington, D.C.

The transnational coalition received a boost with the initiation of a new campaign that opposed many of the practices of multilateral development banks, including their support for dams. The connection began when Bruce Rich, an attorney with the Natural Resources Defense Council who had been investigating the negative impacts of mega projects funded by the World Bank and other international development organizations, attended the dam fighters' meeting.[17] As the next section describes, the antibank campaign quickly gathered momentum.

Overlapping the initiation of the anti–multilateral development bank campaign was the publication of the first volume of Edward Goldsmith and Nicholas Hildyard's *The Social and Environmental Effects of Large Dams*, which further strengthened emergent transnational connections.[18] The study was the first to systematically integrate the main arguments against big dams and to insist that the problems caused were largely inherent to the technology.

The growing local, national, and transnational civil society organizing around specific dams, the anti–multilateral bank campaign, and the publication of the first Goldsmith and Hildyard volume all contributed to the establishment of the transnational NGO eventually known as the International Rivers Network (IRN). Encouraged by these developments, Philip Williams motivated a group of volunteer environmentalists in California to start a bimonthly *International Dams Newsletter* in late 1985. The newsletter was intended "to help citizen's organizations that are working to change policies on large dam construction throughout the world" and to serve "as one channel of communication for activists in all parts of the world, so that lessons learned in one place can be put to use in another."[19] The first issues included critiques of Chile's Bio, China's Three Gorges, Malaysia's Bakun, India's Sardar Sarovar, and other projects that were considered hot spots, often written by or in conjunction with representatives of civil society organizations in those countries. Within one year, 1,500 copies of the newsletter were being distributed to individuals and organizations in fifty-six countries.

Feedback from readers and activists and a series of internal discussions resulted in the creation of a more formalized organizational structure to increase the potential impact of the *International Dams Newsletter* volunteer group. In mid-1987, the group formally became the IRN, and the newsletter was renamed *World Rivers Review*.[20] The IRN organized a conference on the social and environmental effects of big dams in San Francisco in 1988, at which sixty-three civil society activists and scholars from twenty-three countries met. The participants drew up the San Francisco Declaration, demanding an independent assessment of big dam projects and a moratorium on all projects not having the participation of affected persons, free access to project information, environmental impact assessments, comprehensive resettlement plans, and full cost-benefit analyses. They also endorsed a watershed management declaration recommending numerous alternatives to big dams.[21]

The San Francisco Declaration, and the subsequent Manibeli and Curitiba Declarations discussed later in this chapter, articulated an evolving sets of norms on indigenous peoples, human rights, the environment, and democratic governance for sustainable development that were being promoted by civil society organizations working specifically in those areas. The declarations applied the new standards directly to the issues of big dam projects, river basin management, and the provision of water and power services. Groups from very different societies found common ground by developing these norms. They also used these norms strategically, first as guidelines for appropriate policy prescriptions and subsequently as a means of holding authorities accountable when these norms became institutionalized into the procedures and structures of governmental agencies and intergovernmental organizations.

By 1989, according to Williams:

> IRN had evolved into a structured organization and our vision had expanded and changed. While our analysis of the problem remained the same, we now understood that the destruction of rivers was as much a social and human rights issue as environ-

mental. We started to see the importance of dams as center-pieces of an inappropriate development ideology and realized we could use dam fights as important weapons in a larger war against institutions like the World Bank or against dictatorial governments.

Our vision of how IRN could operate most effectively in these bigger arenas also changed. As we learned more about the internal dynamics of the international environmental movement we realized the impracticability of coordinating a formal international structure for IRN, and instead recast ourselves as a U.S. based organization that derived our legitimacy from the respect of the individual groups we worked with all over the world. We saw ourselves as one part of a larger citizen-based movement working on these issues.[22]

The IRN quickly became a lead NGO in the growing transnational civil society network around big dams and sustainable development, as well as in the continuing anti–multilateral bank campaign. The IRN began publishing another newsletter, *Bankcheck Quarterly*, a precursor to the Fifty Years Is Enough campaign against the World Bank; established an office in Brazil; and significantly expanded its linkages with NGOs and social movements all over the world.

This transnational civil society network grew and became increasingly better connected and more sophisticated, especially from the mid-1980s on. Diverse civil society organizations such as Probe International in Canada; the European Rivers Network (ERN) in France; the Association for International Water and Forest Studies (FIVAS) in Norway; Friends of the Earth in Japan; Both Ends in the Netherlands; the Berne Declaration in Switzerland; Urgewald in Germany; Aid-Watch in Australia; Christian Aid, Oxfam, and Survival International in the United Kingdom; the IRN, Environmental Defense Fund (EDF), Cultural Survival, and Lawyers Committee for Human Rights in the United States; the Narmada Bachao Andolan in India; the Movimento dos Antigidos por Barragens in Brazil; Help the Volga River in Russia; the Project for Ecological Recovery in Thailand; and the Lesotho Highlands Church Action Group became members of the network. The third volume of *The Social and Environmental Effects of Large*

Dams, published in 1992, attempted to review the enormous expansion of critical materials that had emerged as the transnational civil society network became increasingly institutionalized. Although Goldsmith and Hildyard were again the editors, volume three was the collaborative product of an international set of reviewers, demonstrating and contributing to the growing transnational antidam network.[23]

By the 1990s, virtually any big dam being built or proposed in the world became a potential target, a fact that big dam proponents bemoaned. In 1992, the president of the International Commission on Large Dams—the professional association of big dam engineers—warned that the big dam industry faced "a serious general countermovement that has already succeeded in reducing the prestige of dam engineering in the public eye, and it is starting to make work difficult for our profession."[24]

Taking on the World Bank

The World Bank has been the central international organization promoting big dam building around the world since its founding. The Bank's initial loan to fifteen Third World countries was for big dam projects, starting with loans in 1949 and continuing through Lesotho's first loan in 1986. The World Bank's largest borrower through 1993, India, had received $8.38 billion for the construction of 104 big dams, far more than any other country. World Bank technical support is often critical to the initiation and management of big dam projects, and Bank-arranged cofinancing generally increases the funds available for big dam projects between 50 and 70 percent. The Bank has also contributed to the creation of numerous dam-building bureaucratic agencies in the Third World, such as Thailand's Electricity Generating Authority and Colombia's Interconexión Eléctrica SA.[25]

But the Bank's long experience with big dam building did not produce any significant policy or practical changes with respect to social and environmental issues through the 1970s. A few individuals within the Bank, notably Michael Cernea and Robert Goodland, began to recognize the problems in these areas but were unable to independently bring about visible reform within the organization. Thayer Scudder, a development anthropologist and World Bank consultant who has investigated the effects of dams for more than forty years, confirmed that "during the 1950s and 1960s, engineers, academics, and development practitioners had no clue of the tremendous negative social and environmental effects of large river basin projects. While incremental learning began to produce some change at the World Bank by the late 1970s, without environmental and human rights activists and movements, the broader reforms would never have happened."[26]

The growing transnational efforts to halt big dam building overlapped with the emergent campaign against the World Bank and other multilateral development banks in the early 1980s. Transnational antidam coalitions linking groups in the West with those elsewhere were critical in broadening and strengthening what was initially conceived as primarily a Western-based conservationists' campaign against multilateral banks. As Paul Nelson suggests, "The agenda of the campaign was initially concerned with protecting river basins, preserving tropical forests and biodiversity, and promoting demand reduction and efficiency in energy lending. However, three related issues have come to equal, and sometimes eclipse, these conservationist themes: involuntary resettlement of communities from dam projects, protection of indigenous peoples' lands, and accountability and transparency at the World Bank."[27] These were among the highest-priority issues for domestic groups from the South fighting big dams.

As part of the broader anti–multilateral development bank campaign, antidam opponents compelled the Bank not only to reduce its involvement in big dam projects but also to adopt new policies and mechanisms for resettlement, environmental management, indigenous peoples, information disclosure, monitoring, and appeals. The cumulative effect of transnationally allied civil society lobbying against World Bank support for dams over the last twenty-five years is most clearly demonstrated by the more than 60 percent decline in Bank funding for these projects—from approximately $11 billion between 1978 and 1982 to an estimated $4 billion between 1993 and 1997. Under sustained pressure, the Bank finally conducted its first comprehensive review of the big dams in which it had been involved after being in the business for forty years. Civil society critiques of the Bank's review, in turn, sparked the creation of an independent World Commission on Dams.

The World Bank adopted general environmental norms, at least formally, as early as 1970. Scholar Robert Wade states in his authoritative review of the Bank's changing environmental policy from 1970 on: "As the recognized lead agency in the work on development issues, the Bank could not remain oblivious to this rising tide of concern, particularly because many in the environmental movement were saying that economic growth should be stopped, an idea fundamentally opposed to the Bank's mission. In addition, the Bank had to consider what position it would take at the United Nations Conference on the Human Environment scheduled for 1972 in Stockholm."[28] The World Bank's then president, Robert McNamara, who had been convinced of the importance of environmental issues by prominent conservationists, responded by establishing the post of environmental adviser. The Bank's first environmental adviser, James Lee; senior Bank official Mahbub ul Haq, who convinced developing countries worried about their sovereignty that they should participate; and McNamara, who delivered the keynote address, played a central role at Stockholm.[29] The World Bank thus gave itself a reputation at the time as one of the leading agencies addressing international environmental issues.

But newly adopted environmental norms played a marginal role in World Bank activities throughout much of the 1970s and early 1980s. The Bank's Office of Environmental Affairs, created after Stockholm, remained small during this period; by 1983, the office had only three regular specialists out of a total World Bank professional staff of nearly 2,800. In addition, most Bank staff ignored environmental factors and continued working as if no new requirements existed. When environmental issues were emphasized, the focus was generally on disease prevention, occupational health and safety, and the reduction of air and water pollution, which largely neglected the types of human ecology, natural resource, and ecosystem issues that were the cornerstone of the anti–multilateral development bank campaign of the 1980s and 1990s.[30]

As pressures from the transnational antidam campaign mounted, World Bank policies and practices began to change. For example, opposition to the World Bank–funded Chico Dam project in the Philippines in 1974 focused attention on the detrimental effects of large-scale Bank-funded projects on indigenous and tribal populations. It compelled McNamara to state that "no funding of projects would take place in the face of continued opposition from the people"[31] and led the Bank to adopt a new policy on "Social Issues Associated with Involuntary Resettlement in Bank-financed Projects,"[32] which set novel standards for appropriate practices with respect to the resettlement of people displaced by World Bank projects.

The Bank's subsequent involvement in Brazil's Polonoreste project, an infrastructure-based colonization program that severely threatened some indigenous peoples in the Amazon, catalyzed the establishment of standards "to follow in situations where projects funded threatened to infringe the rights of residual ethnic minorities." These new standards were influenced by NGOs and experts concerned with the rights of indigenous peoples, such as the Boston-based NGO Cultural Survival and the U.S. section of Survival International, which consulted with members of the Bank's in-house sociology group.[33]

One mechanism by which reforms occurred involved the empowerment of like-minded Bank staff by the increasing effectiveness of pressure being leveled by NGOs from the outside.[34] As Lee later acknowledged, "There were a number of outside groups who were quite vociferous ... groups like Amnesty International, the Harvard group Cultural Survival ... and others. They were quick to chastise us and rightly so. ... And so ... my office moved out in front on this."[35] Civil society helped shape World Bank environmental adviser Robert Goodland's report, "Economic Development and Tribal Peoples: Human Ecologic Considerations," and subsequently a policy document, Operational Manual Statement (OMS) 2.34, "Tribal People in Bank-Financed Projects," in 1981 and 1982, respectively. As with the earlier policy on resettlement, the policy on tribal peoples was full of problems and inconsistencies, but it established norms and procedures that transnationally allied civil society organizations exploited from the early 1980s on.

The level of external pressure escalated in 1983 with the initiation by the Washington D.C.-based National Resources Defense Council, National Wildlife Federation, and Environmental Policy Institute of the aforementioned anti–multilateral development campaign. The basic strategy was to publicize a small number of destructive large-scale projects and use them as levers on donor governments to pressure the World Bank to institute reforms. Over the next four years, more than twenty hearings on the performance of multilateral banks were held before six subcommittees of the U.S. Congress, and similar events subsequently took place across Europe and in Japan.[36] In addition, civil society organizations held regular public demonstrations in front of World Bank headquarters in Washington, D.C., and regional offices in other countries.

These tactics quickly produced change; in 1984, the World Bank introduced OMS 2.36, "Environmental Aspects of Bank Work," which stated that the Bank would "endeavor to ensure that . . . each project affecting renewable natural resources does not exceed the regenerative capacities of the environment" and that the "Bank would not finance any projects that . . . would severely harm or create irreversible environmental deterioration" nor "displace people or seriously disadvantage certain vulnerable groups without undertaking mitigatory measures."[37] The network then used the Bank's new guidelines and public statements on the environment, human rights, and indigenous peoples to hold staffers accountable.

The campaign achieved its first major victory when the World Bank suspended its loan disbursements for Brazil's Polonoreste project in 1985, on the basis of a transnational campaign that identified the project's destructive consequences for the environment and indigenous peoples. The campaign scored another victory in 1986 when the U.S. executive director voted against the World Bank's proposed Brazil power-sector loan, which was to help finance the construction of 136 dams—the first time any of the Bank's member governments had voted against a loan on social and environmental grounds. Moreover, transnational lobbying in which two Kayapo tribal leaders and ethnobotanist Darrell Posey traveled to the United States to protest specific dams to be built by Brazil with the power-sector loan led to a suspension of the second $500 million tranche.

Responding to the mounting pressure for reform, then World Bank president Barbar Conable announced on May 5, 1987, that the Bank was "creating a top-level Environment Department to help set the direction of Bank policy, planning and research work. It will take the lead in developing strategies to integrate environmental considerations into our overall lending and policy activities."[38] One month later, the Bank released a five-year review of the 1982 OMS 2.34, "Tribal People in Bank-Financed Projects," conducted by its Office of Environmental and Scientific Affairs. It stated that although the Bank's identification of indigenous peoples issues had slightly improved, "there was a general tendency among Bank staff to underestimate the unique social, cultural, and environmental problems that both tribal and indigenous or semi-tribal populations face in the process of development."[39] Senior Bank management renewed the pledge to prioritize issues of environment, resettlement, and tribal and indigenous peoples in project lending, but critics were not satisfied.

By nearly unanimous agreement, the transnationally allied opposition to India's Sardar Sarovar-Narmada River Valley projects—led by the powerful domestic Save the Narmada movement—produced the most visible change. The World Bank's Operations Evaluation Department (OED) acknowledged this fact in 1995: "The Narmada Projects have had far-reaching influence on the Bank's understanding of the difficulties of achieving lasting development, on its approaches to portfolio management, and on its openness to dialogue on policies and projects. Several of the implications of the Narmada experience resonated with recommendations made by the Bank's Portfolio Management Task Force . . . and have been incorporated into the 'Next Steps' action plan that the Bank is now implementing to improve the management of its portfolio."[40] The Bank's subsequent reforms included initiatives in a range of areas, from resettlement and environment to procedural mechanisms that would increase the transparency and accountability of Bank activities.

Criticism of the high social costs related to the displacement caused by Bank-funded projects, especially big dams, had prompted a 1985 portfolio review of resettlement practices in hydro and agriculture projects over the previous six-year period. The portfolio review's conclusion that there had been only marginal improvement in Bank compliance with the 1980 OMS on resettlement prompted a significant policy revision in 1986. However, as political scientist Jonathan Fox states, "the 1986 policy revisions led to few improvements (in practice) until after 1992 when awareness of the issue increased due to the Narmada debacle."[41] In fact, resettlement had been a central issue in the first transnational campaign to reform the Sardar Sarovar-Narmada River Valley projects from 1983–84 on.

The second transnational campaign, which was organized to halt the Sardar Sarovar Dam altogether rather than merely reform the project, led the World Bank to establish the first independent review of a Bank-supported project under implementation.[42] The independent commission, known as the Morse Commission, issued a report that concluded that the Bank had not complied with its own resettlement and environment policies and that it should take a step back from the project. The conclusions surprised Bank management, which immediately responded by sanctioning a comprehensive review of resettlement problems throughout its portfolio. According to staffer Michael Cernea, who proposed the idea, the Bank's managing director, Ernst Stern, "agreed to a new review because it was part of the formal report to the Board and the public answer to the Morse Commission," and the Bank was eager to find out if there were "other Narmadas hidden in the portfolio."[43] The resettlement review, which was published in 1994, acknowledged that progress in the Bank's resettlement efforts was often "a consequence of public opinion demands, of resistance to displacement by affected people, and of strong advocacy by many NGOs."[44]

The Narmada campaigns also influenced environmental practices at the World Bank. The network emphasized the Bank's failure to comply with its own 1984 policy guidelines (OMS 2.36) on environmental issues and its willingness to fund the Sardar Sarovar Project even though it had not been sanctioned by India's Environment Department. Linkages among the Environmental Defense Fund, Survival International, and the emergent Narmada Bachao Andolan, established in 1986, helped the network spur the Bank's internal reform process, initiated in 1987. The upshot was both organizational change, such as the hiring of regional environmental directors in 1987, and policy reform, most notably Operational Directive 4.00 on environmental policy for dam and reservoir projects in 1989.[45]

That operational directive mandated that for any World Bank–supported dam with a height greater than ten meters, a panel of independent and internationally recognized specialists was to be established to advise on the environmental aspects of the project. But NGOs, which were not consulted during its drafting, quickly compelled a reformulation of the document through continued lobbying efforts and protests. A substantially revised policy, Operational Directive 4.01, was completed by October 1991. It stated that "the purpose of EA (environmental assessment) is to ensure that the development options under consideration are environmentally sound and sustainable"; it also strictly mandated information disclosure to and consultation with civil society actors and required borrowing countries to release environmental assessments to the executive directors of the Bank. Moreover, as Robert Wade writes,

> around 1992 and 1993 the more comprehensive ideas of the "environmental management" paradigm began to take hold at senior management and operational levels. The conversion came partly from love and partly from fear. Narmada was the fear factor. By the early 1990s staff throughout the Bank were aware of the NGOs' anti-Bank campaign. As a division chief in the Africa region put it, Narmada had become a "four letter word" . . . managers in other parts of the Bank reinforced their signals to staff that environment and resettlement should not be ignored or fudged.

The Bank seized the opportunity to turn around the negative image imposed by the anti-Narmada and anti–multilateral bank campaigns and demonstrate its leadership by unveiling a new environmental management paradigm at the 1992 United Nations Conference on Environment and Development.[46]

The World Bank also created in 1993 an inspection panel to assess violations of policies with respect to large-scale development programs.[47] Again, these reforms flowed directly from the institution's humiliating experience with Sardar Sarovar-Narmada River Valley projects and had immediate effects. The inspection panel's first decision was to mandate the withdrawal of Bank support for Nepal's proposed Arun hydroelectric project. The following year, the Bank established its Public Information Center to ensure greater availability of Bank documents based on its information disclosure policy. The International Narmada Action Committee and other NGOs, utilizing similar tactics of pressuring their governments to withhold funds to the Bank until reforms were instituted, were once again critical motivators of these changes.

These reforms did not satisfy the campaigners, who expected that practice would lag behind rhetoric. In 1994, the antidam campaign issued the Manibeli Declaration, which built on the previous San Francisco Declaration. As activist Patrick McCully wrote, this document, drawn up by IRN in coordination with colleagues in India and elsewhere, was submitted to then World Bank President Lewis Preston in September 1994 during the Bank's 50th anniversary celebrations. It calls for a moratorium on World Bank funding of large dams until a number of conditions are met including the establishment of a fund to provide reparations to people forcibly evicted without adequate compensation, improved practices on information disclosure and project appraisal, and an independent review of the performance of all dams built with World Bank support. The Manibeli Declaration was endorsed by 326 groups and coalitions in 44 countries.

If the member organizations of coalitions are counted separately, the number of individual endorsements for the Manibeli Declaration rises to more than 2,000 from all regions of the world.[48] That same year, Bruce Rich of the Environmental Defense Fund published his book *Mortgaging the Earth: The World Bank, Environmental Impoverishment, and the Crisis of Development*, which leveled a scathing critique of the Bank's assistance for large-scale development projects, especially big dams.

World Bank management responded to the ever-mounting pressure by prompting its OED to initiate the first systematic review of big dam projects supported by the Bank. The OED draft report was completed on August 15, 1996. The report acknowledged the role that external pressure, particularly the transnational campaign against the Sardar Sarovar-Narmada River Valley projects, played in catalyzing reforms at the Bank and motivating the study itself:

Large dams used to be synonymous with modernization and development. But in the 1970s and 1980s, their adverse indirect and secondary impacts became the target of public criticism. As a result, starting in the World Bank, new policies and standards emerged to help avoid or mitigate the adverse environmental and social consequences of large dams in developing countries....

The advent of these new directives did not still public controversy, partly because of serious implementation problems in a few visible cases and also because, by then, the debate had turned bitter and polarized....

The large dams controversy reached a new peak and focused more directly on the Bank in the 1990s, mainly as a consequence of the Bank-financed Narmada (Sardar Sarovar) projects in India. ... The Bank's role in financing this project and its inadequate management of the resettlement and environmental aspects before India's cancellation of the Bank loan in 1993, disturbed and alienated many environmentalists, and intensified their opposition to large dams....

The controversy surrounding large dams has made potential borrowers reluctant to approach the World Bank and other development agencies for assistance even for justified projects. Yet, many developing countries are unable to finance on their own the scale of investments required to tap fully the economic and social development potential of their river basins and meet the ever more pressing demands for additional water, power and flood control. To draw appropriate lessons and clarify the issues involved in deciding on such projects in the future, this report initiates a review of the Bank experience with large dams.[49]

The OED analysis, based on a desk assessment of fifty World Bank–assisted projects, determined that big dams continued to be effective and thus desirable development initiatives. The report argued that although only about one-third of the projects had fulfilled Bank guidelines, "mitigation of the adverse social and environmental consequences of large dams would have been both feasible and economically justified in 74 percent of the cases." It thus concluded, "These results go a long way to help answer the basic question: 'Should the World Bank continue supporting the development of big dams?' Based on the sample reviewed, the answer is a conditional yes, the conditions being that: (i) the projects comply strictly with the new Bank guidelines; and (ii) the design, construction and operation of new projects take into account the lessons of experience."[50]

The Genesis of the World Commission on Dams

Not surprisingly, the transnational civil society network around big dams criticized the OED report as methodologically flawed and biased. But OED knew that limitations in this preliminary analysis were inevitable and thus proposed convening a representative group of stakeholders to review the report and formulate plans for a second phase. At a workshop in Gland, Switzerland, in April 1997, the World Bank and the World Conservation Union brought together thirty-nine representatives of governments, international development agencies, the private sector, and transnational civil society. Representatives of governments and international development agencies participated because they were interested in finding means of achieving the various benefits generated by big dams while avoiding the tremendous social and environmental costs associated with building them.[51] Participants from the private sector attended because of the reputational and financial risks they face from the continuous campaigns. "With a multi-million dollar dam the costs of long political delays are enormous," said Jan Strombland of ABB, the dam-building multinational that had received a beating from pressure groups for its involvement in such projects as Malaysia's Bakun Dam.[52]

Representatives of transnational civil society seized the opportunity afforded by the Gland workshop to push for an independent and comprehensive review of big dams, a demand that they had been pursuing for several years and had recently articulated in the Curitiba Declaration. That declaration had been drafted and approved at the historic first International Conference of People Affected by Dams held in Curitiba, Brazil, between March 11 and 14, 1997, and attended by more than 100 dam-affected people and dam critics from seventeen countries.[53] The 1997 Declaration of Curitiba, which affirmed the right to life and livelihood of people affected by dams, built on the norms and goals espoused in the San Francisco Declaration of 1988 and the Manibeli Declaration of 1994.[54] The primary principle espoused was opposition to the construction of any dam that had not been approved by the negatively affected people, especially those to be displaced, through an informed and participatory decision-making process. The declaration demanded the establishment of an independent commission to conduct a comprehensive review of all large dams supported by international agencies, subject to the involvement of representatives of transnational civil society, and similar reviews for each national and regional agency that had supported the building of big dams.

At the Gland workshop, the thirty-nine participants unanimously agreed to this demand, and the World Commission on Dams (WCD) was established shortly thereafter. The WCD is an independent international body composed of twelve commissioners known for their leadership roles in social movements, NGOs, academia, the private sector, and governments directly involved with dam building from all over the world. The unprecedented mandate of the WCD is to (1) conduct a global review of the development effectiveness of dams and assess alternatives for sustainable water resources and energy management, and (2) develop internationally accepted criteria and guidelines for decision making in the planning, design, appraisal, construction, monitoring, operation, and decommissioning of dams.[55] Arguably, the WCD is the most innovative international institutional experiment in the area of democratic governance for sustainable development today, and if it is successful, the WCD could pave the way for a wave of novel multistakeholder global public policy processes in the twenty-first century.

The WCD initially faced tremendous opposition from dam proponents—including many governments. They argued that the inclusion of four civil society representatives among the twelve commissioners, including Medha Patkar—the famous leader of the Save the Narmada Movement—meant that the WCD was biased and antidam. The WCD responded by repeatedly demonstrating the balance of perspectives among the commissioners; by raising its funds from across a spectrum of public, private, and nonprofit entities; and by conducting an independent and comprehensive work program that touched all regions of the world, in addition to other tactics. Momentum behind the commission has grown, but as it enters its last phase of formulating conclusions and recommendations, it remains to be seen whether it will be able to successfully fulfill its mandate. The lessons learned from the WCD process, no matter what happens, should certainly contribute to better practice in multistakeholder engagement on significant global public policy issues—lessons that international institutions like the

World Trade Organization and International Monetary Fund might find valuable.

Toward Democratic Governance for Sustainable Development

Power

A profound change in the global dynamics of development has occurred since the 1970s as a result of two interacting trends: the emergence and growing strength of transnationally allied civil society organizations, and the global spread and international adoption of norms on the environment, human rights, and indigenous peoples. The declining construction rate of big dams worldwide, reforms and funding shifts at the World Bank with respect to these projects, and the establishment of an independent, multistakeholder WCD clearly demonstrate the powerful effects of these two trends.

But that power depends on the vibrancy and strength of domestic civil societies and democratic institutions. When buttressed by strong social mobilization in democracies, transnational civil society has contributed to the reform or halting of big dam projects all over the world. This interactive effect is most visible in the case of India. China, as evidenced by the hundreds of big dams it continues to build and symbolized by the mammoth Three Gorges project, vividly depicts a case in which the absence of these critical domestic factors has posed a formidable barrier to the impact of transnational civil society and international norms.

Just as civil society needs democracy, democratization often needs civil society. Civil society organizing around big dam building has contributed to democratization in many countries, because demands for free access to information, adherence to civil rights and political liberties, and greater citizen participation in decision-making processes are central to most antidam campaigns. This was certainly true in the case of Indonesia, where a wide array of civil society actors focused on the Kedung Ombo project to protest not only the abuses but also the very existence of the domestic authoritarian regime. In Brazil, civil society dam critics fought for democratization precisely because democracy offered greater political opportunities to alter dam-building practices.

But the installation of a democracy does not in and of itself ensure the halting or dramatic reform of dam-building practices, as the LHWP shows. Despite the relatively recent and uneven transitions to democracy in Lesotho and South Africa, the lack of organized mobilization by project-affected people and supporting NGOs resulted in completion of the first and continued construction of the second of the five big dams that constitute that project, albeit with significant reforms in resettlement planning in the latter. The continued weakness of democratic institutions and civil society organizing in Lesotho, however, has been balanced by the gradual deepening of democratic institutions and mounting strength of civil society in South Africa since the successful regime transition in 1994. As a result, the future of the remaining big dams proposed for the LHWP remains in doubt.

Sustainability

Despite its power, several factors constrain the sustainability of the transnationally allied civil society network around big dam building. Building sustainable transnational coalitions across wide geographical, cultural, and linguistic boundaries is extremely difficult. To then have these transnational coalitions buttressed by the institutionalization of supportive international norms in countries with persistent democratic institutions and linked to strong domestic social mobilization raises the threshold for success even higher.

And big dam proponents may put up more of a fight in the future. Initially caught off guard by the opposition, they are now organizing to defend their interests. The international secretariats and national chapters of organizations such as the International Commission on Large Dams, International Hydropower Association, and International Commission on Irrigation and Drainage, not to mention domestic and multinational corporations and consulting companies, are now mounting stronger campaigns to improve the public perception of big dam projects.[56] The WCD offered them an arena to more effectively assert their interests.

The transnational interactions linked with the processes of privatization and economic liberalization that are shaping sustainable development and democratic governance more broadly may also pose a counterbalance to transnationally allied organizing around big dams. This marketization of development not only potentially increases the financing available for big dam projects, it also threatens the victories on improved social, environmental, and decision-making procedures that have been won since the 1970s. For example, Peter Bosshard of the Swiss civil society organization, the Berne Declaration, notes:

> The guidelines on the environmental analysis of IFC [International Financial Corporation] and MIGA [Multilateral Investment Guarantee Agency] projects are less strict and comprehensive than the World Bank's respective Operational Directive. The assessments can be done later in the project cycle, when critical decisions about the project have been taken and the analysis of alternative options does not make sense.[57]

Professor Thayer Scudder of the California Institute of Technology adds that the 1998 IFC draft guidelines on involuntary resettlement "not only perpetuate the flaws of the 1980 World Bank policy document and its 1990 revision (in this area), but further weaken those guidelines."[58] And private-sectors arms of development agencies like the IFC and MIGA, not to mention private-sector firms, are generally much less transparent and accountable to the public than are states (especially those with democratic regimes) or even the World Bank. These potential setbacks from the privatization and liberalization of the financing and building of big dam projects are thus a central issue on the agenda of the WCD.

For the time being, the transnational civil society network described in this chapter continues to grow in strength. This is exemplified by the growing number of groups participating in the International Day of Action against Dams and for Rivers, Water, and Life held on March 14 in 1998, 1999, and 2000, and in the network's active involvement in the World Commission on Dams. Indeed, a transnational civil society movement for sustainable development might be in formation.[59] As L. David Brown and Jonathan A. Fox suggest, "in the long run, such transnational coalitions may generate the social capital—reflected in the proliferation of bridging organizations and individuals capable of building relationships and trust among diverse actors—required to construct effective transnational movements."[60]

Moreover, the progressive consolidation of transnational civil society networks (on indigenous peoples, human rights, the environment, big dams, and others) and the increasing transnational solidarity among domestic civil society groups on promoting democratic governance for sustainable development may make strong domestic social mobilization less necessary in the future. The emergence of cross-national social mobilization and the potential deepening of transnational linkages among grassroots groups of peoples affected by dams may empower and thus increase the effectiveness of previously weak and disorganized domestic groups.[61]

The continuing institutionalization of supportive norms at various levels of authority, from local implementing agencies to international organizations, is also likely to contribute to this trend. Domestic conditions may become more hospitable if democratic regimes are consolidated in the scores of countries that have undergone transitions from authoritarian rule over the last three decades and as others (such as Indonesia and Nigeria) move slowly but surely down the path of political liberalization and democratization. The importance of internationally institutionalized norms and democracy domestically suggests that transnationally allied civil society actors promoting sustainable development should concentrate on promoting these principles and structures in their campaigns.

Desirability

Although the transnationally allied civil society activities around big dams are generally organized internally in a democratic and nonhierarchical manner, the degree of representation of and accountability within transnational civil society organizations, coalitions, and networks in this area remains a challenge. Although much of the moral authority of transnationally allied civil society dam activity is based on the leadership of civil society organizations constituted by historically marginalized and oppressed big dam–affected peoples, positions and tactics are often articulated in international arenas by NGOs and activists that are not directly linked or clearly accountable to big dam–affected peoples. NGOs from the North with more resources, such as the IRN, tend to be much more active in shaping campaign strategies and gaining access to decision makers. This asymmetry is further exacerbated because mechanisms for resolving differences among network groups remain underdeveloped.[62]

Moreover, while transnational organizing has been extremely successful in reforming and halting big dam building, it has been much less successful in promoting alternatives to these projects. Although big dam critics have argued for such alternatives as improvements in the functioning of existing big dams, demand-side management, traditional water harvesting practices, and solar and wind power projects, the comparative time and resources spent on this agenda have been far less. There are serious long-term costs to the decline in big dam building in the absence of clear and viable alternatives: critical shortages of drinking water, irrigation for food production, and electricity remain, and these shortages affect mostly the poor and the marginalized. The transnational coalition can also be questioned for not fully taking into account the negative social and environmental effects from the more conventional alternatives to big dam projects, such as the global warming effects of coal-fired thermal plants that are likely to occur if other alternatives to big dams are not more readily available.[63]

Although the transnational coalition has a pressing agenda on its hands, it also has much cause for pride. The individuals and groups involved in the network, the norms they promote, and the campaigns they execute have certainly had a dramatic and overall positive effect on democratizing governance toward transparency, participation and accountability, as well as promoting sustainable development that is more socially just and environmentally sound.

Notes

1. Big dams are those taller than fifteen meters—the height of a four-story building. In this chapter, "big dams" and "dams" are used interchangeably.
2. International Hydropower Association, *Hydropower for Sustainable Development: A Vision for the 21st Century* (London: IHA, 1998).

3. Sandra Postel, *Pillar of Sand: Can the Irrigation Miracle Last?* (New York: W. W. Norton, 1999).

4. International Commission on Large Dams, *World Register of Dams* (Paris: ICOLD, 1998), p. 1. Only slightly more than 10 percent of the world's technically available hydropower potential has been developed. See Jose Roberto Moreira and Alan Douglas Poole, "Hydropower and Its Constraints," in *Renewable Energy: Sources for Fuels and Electricity*, ed. Thomas B. Johansson et al. (Washington, D.C.: Earth Island Press, 1993).

5. This does not include nonconventional and renewable sources of energy production such as wind or solar power.

6. The World Bank estimates that a one-year delay in completion reduces the benefit-cost ratio by one-third and a two-year delay by over one-half, and that costs associated with resettlement can increase project costs up to 30 percent (World Bank, *The Bankwide Review of Projects Involving Involuntary Resettlement* [Washington, D.C.: World Bank, April 8, 1996]).

7. For the United States, see Tim Palmer, *Endangered Rivers and the Conservation Movement* (Berkeley: University of California Press, 1986), and R. Gottlieb, *Forcing the Spring: The Transformation of the American Environmental Movement* (Washington, D.C.: Earth Island Press, 1993).

8. See Sanjeev Khagram, "Dams, Democracy and Development: Transnational Struggles for Power and Water," unpublished manuscript, Kennedy School of Government, Harvard University.

9. See Darryl D'Monte, *Temples or Tombs? Industry Versus Environment: Three Controversies* (New Delhi: Centre for Science and Environment, 1985).

10. These began with *Major Dams: A Second Look*, a 1981 book edited by L. T. Sharma and Ravi Sharma of the Gandhi Peace Foundation, a domestic human rights NGO, and several high-profile newspaper articles such as Darryl D'Monte, "A Question of Survival," *Illustrated Weekly of India*, May 1984; it peaked with the publication of B. D. Dhawan's edited volume of the views of proponents and opponents, *Big Dams: Claims, Counterclaims* in 1990.

11. In Europe, most big dams were built during the first half of the twentieth century, particularly in countries such as Austria and Switzerland in the Alps. In France, most dams were built after World War II, spurred by the Marshall Plan. Dams were built primarily for hydroelectric purposes in countries that had few other energy sources and were often located in the mountains, where they displaced few people. This section is heavily indebted to Roberto A. Epple, "Popular Control/ Democratic Management of River Basins," paper presented to the first International Conference of Peoples Affected by Dams, Curitiba, Brazil, March 10, 1997.

12. See Patrick McCully, *Silenced Rivers: The Ecology and Politics of Large Dams* (London: Zed Books, 1996), p. 282, and A. D. Usher, *Dams as Aid: A Political Economy of Nordic Development Thinking* (London: Routledge, 1997).

13. See Robert S. Devine, "The Trouble with Dams," *Atlantic Monthly*, August 1993, pp. 64–71; Palmer, *Endangered Rivers and the Conservation Movement*; Marc Reisner, *Cadillac Desert: The American West and Its Disappearing Water* (London: Secker and Warbary); Gottlieb, *Forcing the Spring*; "The Big One," *Economist*, March 29, 1997, pp. 27–28; and "Dammed if You Do," *Economist*, March 29, 1997, pp. 28, 33.

14. Devine, "Trouble with Dams," p. 65.
15. Daniel P. Beard, speech to the International Commission on Irrigation and Drainage, Varna, Bulgaria, May 18, 1994, p. 4.
16. Philip B. Williams, "The Experience of the International Rivers Network 1985–1997," paper presented to the first International Conference of Peoples Affected by Dams, Curitiba, Brazil, March 10, 1997.
17. See Bruce Rich, *Mortgaging the Earth: The World Bank, Environmental Impoverishment, and the Crisis of Development* (Boston: Beacon Press, 1994), pp. 111–47. See also David Wirth, "Partnership Advocacy in World Bank Environmental Reform," in *The Struggle for Accountability: The World Bank, NGOs, and Grassroots Movements*, ed. Jonathan Fox and David Brown (Cambridge, Mass.: MIT Press, 1998).
18. Edward Goldsmith and Nicholas Hildyard, *The Social and Environmental Effects of Large Dams*, vol. 1, *Overview* (Cornwall, England: Wadebridge Ecological Centre, 1984).
19. *International Dams Newsletter* 1, no. 1 (winter 1985–86): 1–2.
20. See *World Rivers Review* 2, no. 6 (November–December 1987).
21. See Owen Lammers, "IRN's Programmatic Evolution," unpublished manuscript, 1998. See also International Rivers Network, "San Francisco Declaration" and "Watershed Management Declaration," September 1988, at www.irn.org.
22. Philip B. Williams, "A Historic Overview of IRN's Mission," unpublished manuscript, 1998.
23. Edward Goldsmith and Nicholas Hildyard, eds., *The Social and Environmental Effects of Large Dams*, vol. 3, *A Review of the Literature* (Cornwall, England: Wadebridge Ecological Centre, 1992). Interestingly, there seems to have been no explicit connection between Goldsmith and Hildyard's volumes and the emergence of transnational linkages in Europe that eventually led to the formation of the European Rivers Network.
24. Wolfgang Pircher, "36,000 Large Dams and Still More Needed," paper presented at the Seventh Biennial Conference of the British Dam Society, University of Stirling, June 25, 1992.
25. See Leonard Sklar and Patrick McCully, "Damming the Rivers: The World Bank's Lending for Large Dams," IRN Working Paper No. 5, November 1994.
26. Telephone interview with Thayer Scudder, April 29, 1997. The United Nations did convene a panel of experts to prepare a report on integrated river basin development that was published in 1958 and revised in 1970, but it did not highlight the severity of problems related to the environment and resettlement. See Department of Economic and Social Affairs, *Integrated River Basin Development: Report of a Panel of Experts* (New York: United Nations, 1958; rev. ed., 1970).
27. Paul Nelson, "Internationalising Economic and Environmental Policy: Transnational NGO Networks and the World Bank's Expanding Influence," *Millennium: Journal of International Studies* 25, no. 3 (1996): 609–10.
28. Robert Wade, "Greening the Bank: The Struggle over the Environment, 1970–1995," in *The World Bank: Its First Half Century*, vol. 2, ed. Davesh Kapur, John P. Lewis, and Richard Webb (Washington, D.C.: Brookings Institution, 1997), pp. 619–20. Much of this section's analysis of environmental reform at the World Bank builds on Wade's essay.

29. See Robert McNamara, "Address to the UN Conference on the Human Environment, Stockholm, Sweden, June 8, 1972" (New York: United Nations, 1972).

30. Wade, "Greening the Bank," pp. 628–29.

31. Quoted in Andrew Gray, "Development Policy–Development Protest: The World Bank, Indigenous Peoples and NGOs," in Fox and Brown, *Struggle for Accountability*, p. 7.

32. Operational Manual Statements were the policy guidelines of the World Bank at the time; see "Social Issues Associated with Involuntary Resettlement in Bank-financed Projects," Operational Manual Statement 2.33, 1980. See also Michael Cernea, "Social Science Research and the Crafting of Policy on Population Resettlement," *Knowledge and Power* 6, nos. 3–4 (1993), and "Social Integration and Population Displacement: The Contribution of Social Science," *International Social Science Journal* 143, no. 1 (1995).

33. Gray, "Development Policy," pp. 9–10.

34. See Fox and Brown, *Struggle for Accountability*, chap. 1.

35. Quoted in Wade, "Greening the Bank," p. 630.

36. Wade, "Greening the Bank," p. 656.

37. Quoted in Wade, "Greening the Bank," p. 634.

38. Quoted in Wade, "Greening the Bank," p. 673.

39. World Bank Office of Environmental and Scientific Affairs, "Tribal Peoples and Economic Development: A Five Year Implementation Review of OMS 2.34 (1982–1986)," and "Tribal Peoples' Action Plan," 1987, p. 13.

40. World Bank Operations Evaluation Department, "Learning from Narmada," OED précis, May 1995, p. 7.

41. Jonathan Fox, "When Does Reform Policy Influence Practice? Lessons from the Bankwide Resettlement Review," in Fox and Brown, *Struggle for Accountability*, p. 309. The World Bank extended its involuntary resettlement guidelines to all projects in 1990; see "Involuntary Resettlement," Operational Directive 4.30.

42. See Bradford Morse and Thomas Berger, *Sardar Sarovar: The Report of the Independent Review* (Ottawa: Resources Futures International, 1992).

43. Quoted in Fox, "When Does Reform Policy Influence Practice?" p. 311.

44. Social Policy and Resettlement Division, "Resettlement and Development: The Bankwide Review of Projects Involving Involuntary Resettlement, 1986–1993," Environment Department Paper No. 032 (Washington, D.C.: World Bank, 1996), p. 99.

45. Operational Directives succeeded Operational Manual Statements at the World Bank.

46. Wade, "Greening the Bank," pp. 685–87, 709–10.

47. World Bank, "Bank Procedures, Disclosure of Operational Information," BP 17.50 (Washington, D.C.: World Bank, September 1993), and "The World Bank Inspection Panel," Resolution 93-10 (Washington, D.C.: World Bank, September 1993). For an analysis, see Ibrahim F. I. Shiata, *The World Bank Inspection Panel* (Oxford: Oxford University Press, 1994), especially pp. 9–13, and Lori Udall, "The World Bank and Public Accountability: Has Anything Changed?" in Fox and Brown, *Struggle for Accountability*.

48. See McCully, *Silenced Rivers*, p. 308.

49. Operations Evaluation Department, *The World Bank's Experience with Large Dams —A Preliminary Review of Impacts* (Washington, D.C.: World Bank, August 15, 1996), pp. 3, 12, 15.

50. Operations Evaluation Department, *World Bank's Experience with Large Dams*.
51. See in Stephanie Flanders, "Truce Called in Battle of the Dams," *Financial Times*, April 14, 1997.
52. Quoted in Flanders, "Truce Called."
53. See the various documents presented and generated at the conference published in *Proceedings: First International Meeting of People Affected by Dams* (Berkeley, Calif.: International Rivers Network, June 1997).
54. The following is based on "Declaration of Curitiba," in *Proceedings: First International Meeting of People Affected by Dams*, pp. 11–13, and personal observation of the declaration drafting process.
55. See International Union for the Conservation of Nature, "Large Dams: Learning from the Past, Looking at the Future," "Workshop Proceedings," and "WCD Mandate" (Cambridge: IUCN, August 1997 and February 1998).
56. See, for example, the publications of the International Commission on Large Dams, the International Hydropower Association, and the International Commission on Irrigation and Drainage from the early 1990s, in which the importance of big dams is much more clearly articulated. Interestingly, many of these more recent arguments in favor of big dams defend them on the basis of novel norms such as basic needs and environmental sustainability.
57. Quoted in Nicholas Hildyard, "Public Risk, Private Profit: The World Bank and the Private Sector," *Ecologist* 26, no. 4 (July–August 1996).
58. Thayer Scudder, "Critique of the 1998 IFC Draft Involuntary Resettlement Guidelines (OP 4.12)," e-mail document, February 19, 1998.
59. See Sanjeev Khagram, Kathryn Sikkink, and James V. Riker, introduction to *Restructuring World Politics: The Power of Transnational Agency and Norms* (Minneapolis: University of Minnesota Press, forthcoming).
60. L. David Brown and Jonathan A. Fox, "Accountability Within Transnational Coalitions," in Fox and Brown, *Struggle for Accountability*, p. 476.
61. For the skeptical view on transnational movements, see Sidney Tarrow, "Fishnets, Internets and Catnets: Globalization and Transnational Collective Action," in *Challenging Authority: The Historical Study of Contentious Politics*, ed. Michael Hanagan et al. (Minneapolis: University of Minnesota Press, 1998).
62. See Kathryn Sikkink, Sanjeev Khagram, and James Riker, "Conclusions," in *Restructuring World Politics*; Brown and Fox, "Accountability within Transnational Coalitions."
63. See Robert Goodland, "The Big Dam Controversy: Killing Hydro Projects Promotes Coal and Nukes," paper presented at the GTE-Technology and Ethics Series, Michigan Technological University, Houghton, 1995.

5

Transnational Networks and
Campaigns for Democracy

Chetan Kumar

OVER THE PAST DECADE, armed insurgencies have abounded around the world. Most are lucky to garner an occasional headline abroad. However, a visit to the Zapatistas in Cyberspace web site[1] suggests that the uprising by the Zapatistas in Mexico is no ordinary one. The web site provides access to an impressive collection of worldwide resources on the Ejercito Zapatista de Liberacion Nacional (EZLN), with links to pro-Zapatista groups in Austin, Texas; Melbourne, Australia; Torino, Italy; Quebec, Canada; Amsterdam, the Netherlands; and Dublin, Ireland. The domestic politics of Mexico, it seems, has become the focus of an extensive transnational network.

The Chiapas case is unusual but hardly unique. A growing number of domestic struggles for democracy are attracting the attention of civil society groups abroad. While other transnational campaigns target substantive areas of international policy making such as human rights or the environment, these campaigns have targeted the very nature of specific *governments*. Some of the resulting transnational networks aim to democratize an existing government, as seems to be the case for many of the groups focusing on China. In other cases, a transnational network may aim for the overthrow of a nondemocratic regime, as was the case in Haiti (discussed later).

These pro-democracy transnational campaigns matter. They influence political developments within countries directly and by mobilizing foreign governments and corporations. Their effects can be as dramatic as that of the antiapartheid campaign against South Africa or as simple as the success of the Free China Movement in persuading Adidas to abandon the manufacture of soccer balls in China due to allegations of forced labor.[2]

This chapter examines two transnational campaigns to promote democratic governance—in Mexico and in Haiti. Although both campaigns have been about democracy, they have differed on their specific objectives. The Haiti campaign targeted a pariah regime, while the Mexico campaign targeted an internationally recognized and well-established government. The Mexico campaign started with the limited objective of preventing a violent repression of the Zapatista uprising by the Mexican government. Subsequently, its objectives, which constitute a long-term and evolving agenda, have expanded to include the rights of native peoples in Mexico, the broad parameters of democratization in that country, and the reversal of the perceived adverse impact of global market forces on marginalized populations in developing countries. The Haiti campaign had far more specific objectives: the restoration of ousted President Aristide, and changes in the U.S. policy of repatriating without asylum hearings those Haitian refugees who were fleeing the repression of the military. After the restoration of Aristide in 1994, remnants of the campaign continued a low-key activism on issues ranging from the rights of Haitian immigrants in the United States to the impact of structural adjustment on Haiti. However, in the absence of massive popular engagement within both Haiti and the United States, this activism no longer constitutes a focused campaign.

This chapter compares the origins, evolutions, and results of these campaigns to shed light on three questions:

1. What are the actual impacts of these networks?

2. What factors can allow such networks to achieve their goals, even in a limited fashion? And how sustainable are these factors?

3. To what extent are actions of transnational civil society in promoting or focusing changes in governance legitimate in the

specific countries as well as in the broader international community?

The Chiapas Campaign

This is the story of a local uprising that turned into a worldwide campaign for democracy and against neoliberalism in Mexico.[3] The 1990s were a decade of considerable change in Mexico. Mexico entered into a free-trade agreement with the United States and Canada and, as a part of the process of becoming a credible partner for its two northern neighbors, also began to liberalize its economy and its one-party polity. Hence, it came as a surprise to many when a violent uprising broke out in the impoverished province of Chiapas in 1994. A little-known guerrilla group called EZLN, which had been founded in 1982 but had previously laid low, captured four towns. Equally rapidly, the Mexican government sent in armed forces to quell the rebellion. This inspired an overwhelming reaction from civic groups throughout the United States, which feared a repeat of the military barbarism that had occurred throughout Central America during the 1980s. Perhaps not wanting to be seen as an inadequate partner for the United States and Canada, Mexico put its forces into a holding pattern, and a cease-fire was agreed on. Shortly thereafter, the Zapatistas and the transnational network that was rapidly coalescing around them moved to a broader set of objectives. Claiming, with justification, that the indigenous populations of Mexico had been left out of the country's economic and political life, the Zapatistas and their transnational allies sought an explicit recognition of the problems of these populations within the country's democratization process.

Who were these transnational allies? A quick survey of the memberships of two coalitions of organizations engaged with Chiapas—the seventy-five-member Mexico Solidarity Network, founded in 1998,[4] and the fifty-member International Service for Peace (SIPAZ),[5] founded shortly after the start of the Chiapas uprising—reveals four types of organizations. The first category includes organizations affiliated with the Catholic Church and the more progressive Protestant denominations (Methodists, Lutherans, Episcopalians) that had protested Cold War–era U.S. military support for authoritarian governments in Central America during the 1980s. The second category consists of campus student and faculty organizations, particularly from universities in Texas and California (the two states with the greatest interest in America's southern neighbors), that had existed since the 1980s to oppose U.S. policies in Central America or were started explicitly to publicize or support the Zapatistas. A third category includes U.S. and European think tanks and nongovernmental organizations (NGOs) that conduct research, advocacy, networking, and fund-raising activities for civil society initiatives in the developing world in the areas of democratization, conflict resolution, and social reform. These include the Washington Office on Latin America, Peace Brigades International, Global Exchange, Witness for Peace, Grassroots International, and International Fellowship of Reconciliation (the Netherlands). The fourth category comprises local organizations, often started and linked via the Internet, formed by supporters of the Zapatista cause (including from among the Hispanic American diaspora). Examples include the Chiapas Coalition (Denver), Gainesville Committee for Democracy in Mexico (Florida), NY Zapatistas (New York), and North Americans for Democracy in Mexico (Sacramento, California).

Although many of these organizations had previously been active on other Central American issues, their actions on Mexico differed from earlier campaigns in several ways. First, the coincidence of the launch of the North American Free Trade Agreement (NAFTA), which was seen as a major defeat for antiglobalization activists from the Left in the United States, and the start of the Chiapas uprising brought together the traditional supporters of peace in Central America and those acting on behalf of peasants and indigenous populations allegedly adversely affected by NAFTA. Second, the availability of the Internet, particularly on campuses, allowed the dissemination of information and consequent mobilization to proceed more rapidly than in the 1980s.[6] The ideology of the EZLN could be made available to a global audience immediately. Third, the relative accessibility of Mexico as compared with El Salvador and Guatemala in the 1980s allowed organizations such as Peace Brigades International and Global Exchange to conduct highly successful monitoring and observation programs that made information about the indigenous populations of Chiapas and their political and economic aspirations available outside Mexico. More significantly, these programs may have dissuaded the Mexican government from pursuing harsher policies toward the Zapatistas and their sympathizers.[7]

A Chronology of the Uprising

On January 12, 1994, barely two weeks after the start of the uprising, the entry into force of NAFTA, and a large demonstration for peace in Mexico City, the government declared a cease-fire and agreed to negotiate. Possibly in a move to strengthen its position before peace talks, it issued arrest warrants for several EZLN leaders and moved aggressively into Zapatista-held areas. The leaders withdrew into the hills and asked for civil society assistance. They also asserted that the existence of oil in Chiapas had caused the government's actions, and they made an issue of the damage caused to local communities by the oil industry. Environmental degradation was thus added to poverty and human rights among the basket of issues on the Zapatista agenda.

In August 1994, the Zapatistas convened a national civil society convention in Aguascalientes. Representatives of numerous Mexican pro-democracy organizations participated. Delegates put the EZLN and its goals not just in the context of indigenous rights but more broadly in the context of the empowerment of communities and of civil society after a long history of authoritarianism in Mexico. When, in November 1994, Ernesto Zedillo Ponce de Leon became president after what were perhaps the freest elections in Mexico up to that point, the Zapatistas and many others claimed fraud by the ruling party in the provinces, particularly in the remote areas, and added this issue to their growing list of causes.

Subsequently, the rebels and the government signed the Joint Declaration of San Miguel on April 9, 1995, in which they agreed to resolve all issues through dialogue.[8] They also agreed to negotiate at San Andres with the assistance of Bishop Samuel Ruiz of the CONAI, a commission formed specifically for the purpose of mediating between the two sides. The talks ran into trouble right at the start. The government objected to the presence of large numbers of civilian EZLN supporters in

San Andres, and the EZLN, in turn, claimed that the Chiapas communities supporting them had rejected the government's initial proposals. With CONAI's assistance, however, the talks continued.

In June 1995, the Zapatistas called for another consultation with national and transnational civic actors. Held in mid-1995, the consultation allowed the Zapatistas to establish a *national* civil society agenda instead of one that was limited to Chiapas. More significantly, the Zapatistas and their transnational partners issued a call for a series of Declarations for Humanity and Against Neoliberalism, the first of which was issued from La Realidad in January 1996. These actions made allies out of those organizations both within and outside Mexico that had been protesting the perceived adverse effects of rapid economic liberalization on Mexico. The core of the Zapatista argument was that sustainable economic growth and development were not possible unless decisions regarding the use of economic resources, trade in various products, and the raising of capital for market activities were made at the community level. The role of national governments in this paradigm was to serve as forums for participatory debate whereby common strategies would be developed that were implemented at the community level. Although this paradigm did not provide specifics regarding policy or implementation that matched, for instance, the very detailed provisions of NAFTA, it provided a rallying point for those opposed to economic liberalism, or neoliberalism. With these declarations, the Zapatistas became an important focus for organizations and individuals around the world who opposed the advent of the global economy.

Despite the worldwide image of the Zapatistas as resisting the onslaught of globalization, it is not clear whether they adopted this stance to gain more allies in their struggle against the Mexican government or whether the stance against neoliberalism represented an indigenous evolution of Zapatista thinking. The movement's leader, a former professor at the Metropolitan Autonomous University of Mexico by the name of Rafael Sebastian Guillen Vincente (known to his followers as Marcos), certainly seemed to have the intellectual wherewithal, with his bourgeois family background and his education as a philosophy student, to play with various threads of global leftist thought. Conversely, remote and poor Chiapas suffered more from the problems of old-fashioned Latin American authoritarianism than the ravages of the high-tech global economy. Probably, the Zapatista allegiance to the global anti-neoliberal cause as a backdrop for more down-to-earth struggles on behalf of the rights of Mexico's indigenous population was a mix of genuine intellectual conviction and pragmatic strategy on the part of its leadership.

In January 1996, the San Andres accords were agreed on between the government and the Zapatistas, and they were signed on February 17.[9] The accords acknowledged that indigenous forms of government were valid at the municipality level, stipulated a number of constitutional and legal reforms in order to institutionalize this acknowledgment, and established a congressional commission (COCOPA) to assist with further negotiations and develop the provisions of the stipulated reforms.[10] Also in January, the Zapatistas convened a National Indigenous Forum in San Cristobal and made the decision to launch a political wing of the EZLN known as the FZLN. They issued a call for transnational conferences on globalization, to be called "encounters" for humanity and against neoliberalism. In July, the first such encounter was held in Chiapas. Three thousand individuals from forty-three countries participated.

After the signing of the San Andres accords, discussions between the Zapatistas and the government followed a rocky path. In summer 1996, the Zapatistas broke off talks with the government on the implementation of the accords, claiming racism on the part of the government delegation and accusing the government of engaging in a covert military buildup in the province. In January 1997, the government rejected an implementation proposal prepared by the COCOPA. The government claimed that several of the proposals were at variance with the Mexican Constitution and federal and local laws.[11]

Throughout 1997, evidence mounted of increased military activity in Chiapas. Most alarming were reports of paramilitary violence reminiscent of death squad activity elsewhere in Central America during the 1980s. Apparently, most of this activity was targeted not at the EZLN cadre but at the numerous community organizations and cooperatives that had flourished in the space provided by the EZLN.[12] To the extent that most of the members of these organizations were women, they appeared to challenge the local power structures in terms of both economics and gender. Certainly, paramilitary violence appeared to bear out the claims of the Mexico network that since the

Zapatista phenomenon challenged neoliberal orthodoxy, it would face increasing repression.

The second of the encounters for humanity and against neoliberalism initiated by the Zapatistas was held in Spain in July 1997. The gathering drew about 3,000 participants from roughly fifty countries. The substantive message of the gathering was a mélange of ideas under the general theme of emphasizing production for the survival of communities instead of profit. A more significant outcome of the gathering was the creation of relatively sophisticated plans for alternative communications networks, largely Internet-based, that could allow this global coalition to press its agenda more effectively.[13]

Following the encounter, the Zapatistas held the founding congress of the FZLN, their political wing, in Mexico City. The government initially refused to let EZLN members travel to Mexico City, only to relent and let 1,000 of them attend the founding congress in September. This congress marked the formal arrival of the Zapatistas on the national political scene. The goals established by the FZLN at the congress were significant. In the short term, the FZLN was to campaign for the revival of the implementation of the San Andres accords. In the longer term, the FZLN's agenda included a reversal of the amendments to Article 27 of the Constitution, which, according to the Zapatistas, had ended land reform in Mexico; attention to environmental degradation; a campaign to call for a new Constitution; and "ongoing work toward the establishment of true grassroots democracy in Mexico."[14] These goals fit the Zapatista strategy of positioning themselves not just as an uprising but as a movement for a better democracy in Mexico.

The delays in the implementation of the San Andres accords prompted a march by 10,000 residents from throughout Chiapas in Cristobal de las Casas on November 29. The size of this demonstration pointed to the growing reach of the Zapatistas. But paramilitary violence continued to mount. Bishop Ruiz, the widely respected mediator of the government-Zapatista dialogue, was the subject of an assassination attempt in November. The climax of this violence, however, was the massacre of forty-five civilians at Acteal on December 22, 1997.[15] Following the massacre, the governor of Chiapas and the Mexican interior minister resigned, and the Mexican Human Rights Commission implicated a former governor in the massacre.[16] Violence continued, as police and military units began attacking and dismantling the various indigenous municipalities that the Zapatistas had incorporated. In January 1998, the two Mexican peace commissions, the COCOPA and the CONAI, issued a joint declaration in which they urged both the government and the Zapatistas to create the conditions for relaunching the dialogue and criticized the government for placing troops in Zapatista communities.[17]

The government's increasingly hard-line attitude led to Bishop Ruiz's resignation from CONAI in June 1998. Shortly thereafter, CONAI was dissolved. In response to the government's hostility, the Zapatistas boycotted the elections in the state of Chiapas in October. Subsequently, though, they called for a national consultation on ways of reviving the talks and offered to meet with COCOPA in Chiapas. Three thousand individuals from Mexican civil society attended a consultation in Chiapas in November 1998. They agreed to hold a bigger national consultation in March 1999 and to organize a poll to gauge the level of public support for the proposals developed by COCOPA for the implementation of the San Andres accords.[18]

The EZLN and its civil society allies conducted this unofficial poll in 1999. The participation of 2.8 million Mexican citizens in this poll pointed to the Zapatistas' success in putting their agenda on the national stage. Some 96 percent of the participants reportedly supported the COCOPA proposals (even though COCOPA disassociated itself from EZLN efforts in order to maintain its overall neutrality).[19] The goal of the EZLN effort was to persuade Mexican legislators to introduce the proposals as a part of the legislative agenda. For its part, the government continued to maintain its objections to the COCOPA proposals on legal and constitutional grounds and even launched a series of unilateral political and economic initiatives in Chiapas in mid-1999 designed to provide relief to the province's population.

Meanwhile, the government's human rights policies came under increasing international and transnational criticism. In August 1998, the Subcommittee for Prevention of Discrimination and the Protection of Minorities of the United Nations (UN) Human Rights Commission called on the Mexican government to take steps to protect the human rights of indigenous peoples and relaunch the peace process in Chiapas. Amnesty International, Human Rights Watch, and the Inter-American Human Rights Commission of the Organization of American States (OAS) all released reports criticizing the government for human rights violations in Chiapas and other provinces. On a visit to Chiapas, the British vice-minister for foreign relations, Tony Lloyd, met with several NGOs. Subsequently, he commented that "the Mexican government is aware that the framework of the commercial treaty between Mexico and the European Union requires respect for human rights within the participating nations."[20]

To summarize, in 1999, the short-term goals of the Zapatistas and the transnational network supporting them remained the revival of talks to implement the San Andres accords and the prevention of government violence against the Zapatista communities. Longer-term goals included building the Zapatista position within the national debates on democratization and the rights of indigenous peoples, as well as within the transnational debate on the impact of globalization on marginalized populations in developing countries.[21]

Transnational Civil Society and Human Rights Observation

There exists a formal, legal precedent for human rights monitoring at the international level. Human rights monitoring missions can be mandated by the UN General Assembly, as occurred recently in Guatemala and Haiti. An Organization for Security and Cooperation in Europe (OSCE) mission was fielded in Kosovo in 1998. However, such missions can occur only in the context of prolonged internal conflict when an international organization is assisting with mediation or peacekeeping. This context did not exist in Mexico. The Mexican government was also very unlikely to invite an international mission to its territory. This prompted Bishop Ruiz and the Coordination of Nongovernmental Organizations for Peace (CONPAZ) to request international civil society observation in 1995. The presumption was that it was not enough to put the cause of the Chiapas Indians on the Internet and global media in order to stay oppression. The presence of live observers, equipped with cameras and accompanying the most vulnerable groups and individuals, would act as a deterrent both to acts of violence by all sides and to human rights violations.

Several prominent NGOs responded to Ruiz's request. These included the Washington Office on Latin America, Christian Peacemakers Teams, Peace Brigades International, Global Exchange, and

Pax Christi USA. As indicated earlier, many of these organizations, and others that subsequently joined them, had grouped themselves into the SIPAZ in 1995, which sent the first volunteer observers into Chiapas later that year.

Global Exchange, in a 1998 report titled *Foreigners of Conscience*,[22] made the legal case for such observation. Articles 1 and 2 of the Mexican Constitution of 1917 guarantee for foreigners in Mexico the same fundamental rights as Mexican citizens. However, Articles 33, 34, and 39 of the Constitution, taken together, limit political activity within Mexico to Mexican nationals only. Simultaneously, Article 33 reaffirms the right of foreigners living in Mexico to freely express themselves and their opinions on the same basis as Mexican citizens. Additionally, Articles 5 and 32 guarantee the right of foreigners to work in various professions in Mexico. Taken together, Articles 5, 32, and 33 imply that although foreigners cannot participate in political activity, they can certainly observe and express their opinions on various political actions while living and working in Mexico. This implication has been used by members of the SIPAZ network to justify their monitoring activities, whereas the government has used Articles 33, 34, and 39 to justify the expulsion of foreigners engaged in such activities.

Foreign monitors were able to conduct their activities without too many obstacles during 1996 while the negotiations between the government and the Zapatistas appeared to be making progress, but the subsequent deadlock in the talks coincided with a hardening of the Mexican government's stance toward both the Zapatistas and foreign observers.[23] Mexican criticism of foreign observers mounted through 1997 and culminated in the first expulsions in February 1998. Prominent among those expelled was French priest Miguel Chanteau, who had been a pastor in Chiapas for three decades and had laid responsibility for the Acteal massacre on the government's shoulders. Another fourteen observers were expelled in April. The biggest expulsion was of 120 Italian observers, who were collecting statements on human rights violations, in May. Expulsions on a smaller scale continued through the rest of 1998–99. It should be noted that the view that foreign observers violated Mexico's sovereignty was not held by the Mexican government alone. The National Commission on Human Rights, which had otherwise been critical of the government's Chiapas policy, was critical of the July 1999 visit of the UN special rapporteur for extrajudicial executions, Asma Jahangir, to Mexico.

Evaluation

When evaluating the activities of the Zapatistas and their transnational supporters, one has to keep in mind the highly favorable regional environment at the time of the uprising. The Clinton administration had to first persuade a reluctant Congress to ratify NAFTA and then make the case for an expensive bailout of the Mexican economy in 1995. The Mexican government thus had the burden of proving itself to be a responsible and mature state, worthy of American partnership and assistance, rather than another failing totalitarian state. Hence, the government was constrained in the amount of force it could openly use to repress the Zapatistas. Also, in 1991, all Latin American states had signed the Santiago Declaration, under which any violent regime change could become the target of regional sanctions. Although the declaration was aimed against the illegal overthrow of governments, the broader regional norms for democracy also increasingly frowned on violent government repression of genuinely democratic movements. To the extent that the Zapatistas were able to establish themselves as a credible force campaigning for a better Mexican democracy, they were no longer in the same league as the Peruvian guerrillas, for instance, who had absolutely no legitimacy regionally.

The most significant element in the Zapatistas' overall impact has been the worldwide network that mobilized to support them. Here, three factors have been critical: the role of the Internet; the ability of the Zapatistas to build a programmatic agenda that does not stop with the indigenous population of Chiapas but includes indigenous rights at the national level, the nature of Mexican democracy itself, and the global debate on the merits of economic neoliberalism; and the ability of the Zapatistas to form a firm alliance with Mexico's emergent civil society. In a background paper prepared for a congressional hearing on Chiapas on July 29, 1998, the Washington Office on Latin America pointed out "that despite their limited military capacity, the Zapatistas have developed strong political support in Chiapas, throughout Mexico, and internationally." Of course, the Zapatistas have also benefited from the space that has opened up for civil society under Mexico's democratization program and throughout Latin America generally. With the end of the Cold War, both Latin American and major Western governments take a far more benign view of civic activism, particularly Left-oriented activism.

To what extent has the Zapatista movement depended on this transnational network? Certainly, the pressure exerted on the Mexican government would not have been possible without the assistance of the network. Also, the network helped build alliances with civil society for the Zapatistas not just globally but also within Mexico, particularly in the initial stages of the uprising, when the EZLN was confined to the hills of Chiapas. However, the Mexican government's ambiguous response to the Zapatista phenomenon has also benefited the EZLN. In a time of transition, different sectors of the state have responded differently to the uprising, and different agendas and policies appear to have been simultaneously pursued. This lack of policy coordination has allowed the Zapatistas to obtain the positive interest of certain sectors of the state. It has hurt them, however, when other sectors of the state have responded with violence.

While the reach of the Zapatistas has not been in question, the legitimacy of transnational activity to support them has been. Certainly, the transnational network has assisted in building an agenda that goes well beyond the limited concerns of a small peasant uprising, and it has given the Zapatistas credibility and a presence on the Mexican national stage that they would not otherwise have had. However, the formulation of this agenda in antiliberal terms, and the tendency of some members of the transnational network to view the actions of the Mexican government and the international community in conspiratorial terms, has meant a lack of substantive engagement with policy makers in the United States, which is the most critical foreign government as far as Mexico is concerned. Additionally, many in Mexico's ruling establishment, who would otherwise be sympathetic to the cause of democracy, may have been alienated by the constant excursions of members of the transnational network in Mexico, which are seen as violations of Mexican sovereignty.

On balance, however, transnational civil society *has* made a difference. Although developing regional norms for democracy have clearly made it impossible for any government to practice the kind of mass repression found in earlier decades, a series of regional preoccupations in the 1990s—such as the crisis in Haiti, rapid economic integration, and the market shocks of 1997—might have meant a quick eclipsing of the Zapatista cause and a greater degree of repression against its sympathizers had it not been for the transnational network.

The Haiti Campaign

In the fall of 1990, Haiti, under considerable international pressure, conducted the first free and fair elections in its history. Marc Bazin, a liberal technocrat, was widely expected to win, but the actual winner, by an overwhelming majority, was a popular priest named Jean-Bertrand Aristide. Few outside Haiti had ever heard of him. However, in the months leading up to the elections, he had become a lightning rod for a phenomenon that had been developing throughout Haiti for the past decade. Many Haitians had finally decided to challenge two centuries of neglect and repression by a small urban political class and formed numerous "popular organizations" that sought to advocate the interests of grassroots Haitian communities at the national level. Among the political class, only Aristide seemed to sense what this popular awakening represented. As a liberation theology priest, he had helped to bring it about. He termed this phenomenon Lavalas, or "flood," and subsequently gave his political platform the same name. He had not intended to run for president. However, the left-wing coalition opposing Bazin feared losing to the latter's well-funded campaign and invited Aristide to run. At the last moment, Aristide accepted. Seeing an opportunity to finally have representation at the national level, the popular organizations ensured that Haitians turned out in overwhelming numbers to vote.

After being inaugurated as president, Aristide began to implement the Lavalas agenda. The Lavalas coalition included not just popular organizations but also many members of the progressive middle class who wanted to remove the structural constraints on Haiti's development. They crafted an economic agenda that focused on issues such as fair tax collection, the removal of monopolies in trade and business, and the provision of appropriate kinds of credit and market assistance to Haiti's informal sector and peasantry. The economic plan won accolades from international financial institutions, but it earned the ire of Haiti's traditional elite, which was the biggest beneficiary of nonpayment of taxes and trade monopolies. Aristide's plans also ran into trouble with the Haitian parliament, which was still dominated by traditional politicians beholden to the elite. When Aristide asked his supporters to demonstrate in the streets in support of his plan, the elite claimed that he was trying to subvert democracy by threatening violence. On September 30, 1991, he was overthrown in a coup. Concluding that the military was out to kill him, he fled first to Venezuela and then to the United States. Under the terms of the Santiago Declaration of 1991, both the United States and OAS members refused recognition to the coup leaders and called for a return to democracy in Haiti. The OAS called for a voluntary trade embargo against Haiti.[24]

However, no one in the international community was prepared for the extent and brutality of the military repression that ensued. The military and its elite allies saw the Lavalas phenomenon as a threat to the traditional order in Haiti. They decided to physically eliminate Lavalas. For the next three years, the appearance of dozens of horribly mutilated bodies in Haiti's streets became an almost daily occurrence. Figures vary as to how many were killed, from a low of 3,000 to as many as 10,000. These are large numbers for a country with a population of only 6 million. Another 300,000 Lavalas supporters became internal refugees as they fled for their lives into the interior.

Many others began to leave Haiti in rickety boats headed for the shores of Florida. The Bush administration declared them economic refugees, and those who were picked up were deported back to Haiti, where they were targeted again by the military. The claim that economic considerations were responsible for the refugee outflow was refuted by the fact that in the first six months of military rule, 38,000 people took to the sea; in comparison, only a few individuals had left Haiti during the six months of the Aristide presidency before he was overthrown. Also, despite having recognized Aristide as the legitimate president of Haiti, the United States did not immediately try to restore him. There had been reservations in the U.S. policy establishment about his populist rhetoric, some of which had been targeted at the United States.

The response of many civil society groups was starkly different. A key role in mobilizing a transnational network in support of better treatment of Haitian refugees and a return to democratic government in Haiti was played by the New York–based National Coalition for

Haitian Refugees (NCHR), an organization whose members included representatives from the National Association for the Advancement of Colored People (NAACP), Human Rights Watch, AFL-CIO, Lawyers' Committee for Human Rights, Hebrew Immigrant Aid Society, and United States Catholic Conference. Members also included organizations of the Haitian diaspora in the United States, such as the Haitian Refugee Center, Coalition for Haitian Concerns, and Haitian-Americans United for Progress. The Washington Office on Haiti, which espoused concerns closely related to the Lavalas program, was also a member.

The NCHR and its allies protested the Bush administration's refugee policy and its apparent indifference to reviving Haitian democracy, and they quickly developed guidelines for an alternative U.S. policy. Key elements of these guidelines included the appointment of a special envoy to conduct negotiations among the military, Aristide, and the international community; achievement of a "comprehensive settlement" for the restoration of democracy in Haiti, including assistance for Haiti's fragile democratic institutions and a heavy international presence to guarantee against further repression; the creation of a development package for Haiti by international donors; and a nuanced refugee policy under which interdicted refugees would first be taken to a neutral territory in the Caribbean, where their asylum claims would be processed by the UN High Commissioner for Refugees, and then they would be sent to the United States or to other Caribbean countries, according to a predetermined formula. The suggestions made by the NCHR and its allies displayed sensitivity toward the United States' difficulty in opening its doors to thousands of refugees; they were also specific and constructive.

The fact that many organizations representing minority communities opposed Bush's Haiti policy prompted Bill Clinton, who was courting the minority vote, to promise a different Haiti policy upon his election. On December 1, 1992, the NCHR and its civil society allies wrote a letter to President-elect Clinton detailing their specific proposals for reforming the Haiti policy of the United States. On assuming office, Clinton appointed Lawrence Pezullo as his special Haiti envoy.

By June 1993, the combined efforts of Pezullo and UN envoy Dante Caputo had produced a binding resolution of the UN Security Council, imposing an embargo on oil and weapon sales to Haiti and freezing the overseas financial assets of the coup leaders. The military responded by agreeing to negotiate with Aristide, and negotiations were held on Governors Island in New York in July 1993, under the sponsorship of the United States and the UN. Largely because of the considerable international pressure to do so, both parties signed what many members of the Haiti campaign considered a flawed accord. The accord provided for the immediate lifting of sanctions on Haiti and the resignation of the coup leader, General Cedras, and the return of President Aristide by October 30. Aristide agreed to pardon Cedras and also agreed to let his return be preceded by a small UN Mission in Haiti, which would attempt to retrain the police and the army.

The accord had been critiqued by members of the Haiti campaign on the grounds that it lifted sanctions on the military regime well before the actual departure of Cedras. These fears were also shared by the Aristide camp.[25] Members of the Haiti campaign were proved right shortly thereafter when the military launched a new paramilitary death squad called FRAPH, which assassinated Antoine Izmery, a businessman friend of Aristide's, and Guy Malary, justice minister under Robert Malval, who had been appointed prime minister by Aristide following the Governors Island accord. In October 1993, when the advance team of the UN Mission tried to land in Port-au-Prince, it was met by a demonstration of right-wing thugs. Since this happened only a week after eighteen American soldiers had been killed in Somalia, a jittery Pentagon withdrew the mission. Subsequently, the embargo was reimposed on Haiti.

Two points are of note regarding the actions of the Haiti network during this period. First, both President Aristide and his allies in the Haiti network refrained from calling for violent resistance by Lavalas activists in Haiti. Instead, they called for and supported the UN's actions aimed at sanctioning the military regime. By taking this route, they retained the moral high ground. Second, the Haiti network collected and disseminated detailed information in the United States and around the world on the systematic way in which the military regime was attempting to eliminate the network of cooperatives and community organizations that had flowered in the short time the Lavalas movement had occupied the national stage. This information, obtained through the strong links that many in the Haitian diaspora retained in their homeland, was disseminated widely through e-mail and the Internet and by the NCHR through its various publications and reports.

Following the coup leaders' failure to implement the accord, the United States issued an ultimatum to the Haitian junta that if it did not depart by January, it would face additional sanctions. However, many U.S. officials also had reservations about Aristide. A report leaked by U.S. intelligence sources suggested that he was mentally unstable. Although subsequently proved false, the report crystallized many of the fears that U.S. officials had always had about Aristide's rhetoric. According to a study by the Institute for National Strategic Studies, "the US government wavered, uncertain about Aristide's ability to govern or his commitment to reconciliation. Policy focused on building support for a broad moderate coalition in Haiti." This policy, coupled with the complete lack of any progress on the refugee issue, infuriated members of the Haiti network. On January 14–16, 1994, Aristide convened a broad-based conference in Miami to renew the confidence and solidarity of his supporters.[26] Among the participants were twenty-seven Haitian parliamentarians, members of the Congressional Black Caucus, diplomats from all the key actors involved with Haiti, and members of numerous civic organizations. The conference produced heavy criticism of the Clinton administration's Haiti policy with regard to both refugees and the lack of stronger action against the military. The joint participation by both governmental and nongovernmental actors at the conference was a strong indicator of the increasing role of civil society in international affairs.

The Miami conference resulted in increased activism. Members of the Haiti network began to circulate almost daily reports of the brutalities being committed in Haiti. Most poignant were stories of asylum seekers being repatriated back to Haiti, only to be horribly murdered by the military.[27] A joint report of the NCHR and Human Rights Watch/Americas "severely criticize[d] the Clinton administration for its diplomacy in Haiti, the lip service it has paid to the Governors Island agreement, and its indifference to the actions of the Haitian army."[28] On March 23, 1994, an open letter to President Clinton was published in the New York Times in which several personalities including members of the Congressional Black Caucus, representatives from the NAACP and the American Jewish Congress, the Reverend Jesse Jackson, and producer-director Jonathan Demme criticized the Clinton administration's policy of repatriating Haitian refugees without asylum hearings. The Congressional Black Caucus subsequently called for a complete trade embargo on Haiti and the deployment of a multilateral border patrol on Haiti's border with the Dominican Republic to prevent a violation of the embargo. Shortly thereafter, legislation was introduced in both the Senate and the House of Representatives to enact the suggestions of the caucus.

On April 12, Randall Robinson, executive director of TransAfrica, began a hunger strike for the Haitian refugees and threatened to continue the strike until the administration changed its policy on refugees. On April 20, ten human rights organizations sent a letter to President Clinton asking for a stronger condemnation and denunciation of the human rights violations of the military regime than had hitherto been offered, and asking for a change in refugee policy. These organizations included the National Coalition for Haitian Refugees, Amnesty International, Lawyers Committee for Human Rights Watch, and Physicians for Human Rights.

On April 25, the Haitian army massacred as many as fifty people in the Raboteau section of the town of Gonaives. In some instances, the soldiers chased people into the sea as they ran for their lives and shot them there. The Haiti network quickly carried the details of the massacre around the world; the resulting international outcry added to the overall momentum building toward stronger action against the illegal regime. On May 16, Senator John Kerry published an article in the *New York Times* arguing that the United States should be ready to use military force to oust the dictatorship if aggressive negotiations and a total embargo failed.

Meanwhile, faced with increasing criticism of its Haitian policy, the Clinton administration finally changed course. On April 22, the United States announced that it would seek a total international economic embargo on Haiti and introduced a resolution to this effect in the UN Security Council on April 28. On April 26, Pezullo, who had been widely criticized for treating the Haitian military with kid gloves, resigned as special adviser. Clive Gray, head of the Congressional Black Caucus, was appointed Clinton's new envoy for Haiti. On May 6, the UN Security Council approved a complete embargo on Haiti, including a ban on any travel by Haitian military officers and their families. On May 8, bowing to the pressures from civil society and the Congressional Black Caucus, Clinton announced that the United States would no longer automatically repatriate Haitian refugees picked up by sea but would instead hold asylum hearings on U.S. ships or in other countries. On the same day, Robinson ended his hunger strike.

Following the imposition of the embargo, the Haitian military ordered all UN observers in Haiti to leave the country and increased its repression even further. As the number of refugees skyrocketed, the United States became convinced that the only lasting solution to the refugee problem was to oust the junta. Also, the international community realized that the total embargo imposed on Haiti could not be sustained indefinitely without completely destroying the Haitian economy. Hence, on July 31, 1994, the UN Security Council authorized the use of "all necessary means" to restore democracy. Seven weeks later, the first U.S. troops landed in Haiti.

Several factors accounted for the success of the Haiti campaign. The Haitian diaspora's commitment to democracy in Haiti was crucial. The diaspora remained heavily invested in its homeland on a day-to-day basis. Diaspora organizations demonstrated in New York and Miami against the coup and the U.S. refugee policy; they constantly lobbied their representatives in Congress; and through their families still in Haiti, they ensured that the details of the military's repression were made known to the world.

Equally critical was the fact that many influential international and U.S. NGOs with significant policy access were involved in the campaign from start to finish. Here, the untiring networking and alliance-building activities of individuals such as Jocelyn McCalla, executive director of the NCHR, were essential. Also essential was their ability to keep the issue in the forefront of public attention through detailed coverage of the horrors going on in Haiti and the consequences of U.S. policy toward refugees.

In some ways, the campaign was helped by circumstances. To the extent that it was targeting an illegal tyranny, the agenda was straightforward and appealing. Also, the campaign was largely based and carried out in the United States, where technology and civil liberties combined to provide the most favorable terrain for civic organization. On the other side of the equation, the campaign faced a U.S. government that, while officially recognizing Aristide as president, was reluctant to deal comprehensively with Haiti until the last few months of the crisis.

The members of the campaign were able to present their criticisms of U.S. policy not as ideology or rhetoric but as suggestions for better policy implementation that would contribute toward realizing long-term U.S. foreign policy goals of promoting stability and democracy in the hemisphere. In doing so, they were helped by the active interest and involvement of the Congressional Black Caucus and by key senators such as John Kerry and Christopher Dodd.

From the two cases presented here, one can certainly conclude that transnational civic activism is here to stay, not just in specific areas of government policy, such as the environment or development, but *with regard to the nature of governments themselves.* But what will be the long-term impact of such activism?

There is no doubt that the Haiti campaign helped obtain the best possible outcome at the time—an end to a brutal and illegal dictatorship. It is quite likely that without the campaign to change U.S. policy, American troops would never have restored Aristide. Yet circumstances helped. The campaign relied greatly on the skills, professionalism, and dedication of the Haitian diaspora. Members of the diaspora felt great pride in their homeland as well as in their new country; from their perspective, the resources of the latter were best put to use in the service of the former. Also, the Clinton administration could not afford to let the refugee crisis continue for long. It was losing popularity points at home, particularly in Florida, which was run by Democrats up for election. One could therefore argue that Aristide's restoration resulted from a fortuitous combination of an active and skilled diaspora, the interest of a number of influential American and international NGOs, and the interests of a superpower. It should also be remembered that when U.S. troops finally went to Haiti, they did so as part of a multinational force that had been authorized by the UN Security Council. Hence, legitimacy was conserved.

Will it be possible to create the same serendipitous set of circumstance elsewhere in the world? The first two components—an enthusiastic diaspora and influential NGOs—might be easier to come by than the third—the interests of a superpower. But sometimes, even superpowers have to be reminded of where their interests lie. For instance, if the Congolese diaspora in the United States or France were to carry out a concerted campaign for either of those governments to back a series of concrete actions designed to bring better government to Congo (Kinshasa), and if in so doing they repeatedly emphasized the consequences if Central Africa were not stable, one might see results. A clear articulation of Congo's great mineral wealth and potential economic strength, along with a delineation of how a superpower's response could be made congruent with the interests of the Congolese people, might even create enough of an interest in the limited use of force to obtain a desirable outcome. But this is speculation. All that can be said for sure is that, given the right circumstances—an international interest in getting rid of a widely hated regime and a more specific interest on the part of a major power capable of using force—civil society might be able to play a role in getting rid of nasty dictatorships.

Chiapas presents more of a dilemma. Quite likely, in its absence, the Mexican government would have used greater force against the Zapatistas. Also, the Zapatistas have taken the right steps to consolidate themselves. They have created a political presence, thus helping to institutionalize the voices of the indigenous peoples of Mexico on the national political stage. As a Mexican organization, the Zapatistas have the right to demand that they be heard on issues such as indigenous rights and democratization. Given the fact that Mexico is still in the process of building democratic institutions after decades of authoritarianism, one could even argue that they have the right to an insurrection to make themselves heard, if that is what it takes.

The uncertainty comes with the transnational network. Do foreign activists have the right to influence the internal political developments of another country? Can civil society boldly tread where governments still fear to go? Apparently so. International law does not forbid private citizens of one country to travel to another and express their opinions during their travels within the limits of the laws of the host country. In this context, it would be interesting to see what would happen if Mexico asked the United States to extradite a member of the peace observation team on the grounds that he or she had violated Mexican law by undertaking political actions that resulted in tension or violence. Very likely, this scenario will not arise, since Mexico has constantly sought the best relations with its North American partners. In addition, there are regional norms that require Mexico to be a good regional citizen. Both the democracy norms of the OAS and participation in NAFTA require that Mexico be a free-market democracy that allows as much freedom as possible to its citizens. Hence, a key element here is the existence of regional norms. Although these norms do not justify external interference, they clearly indicate that a country's sovereignty is abridged the moment it violates its social contract with its citizens.

The experiences of Haiti and Mexico also show that networks campaigning for specific short- to medium-term objectives are likely to be successful. The Zapatistas' participation, accompanied by an attempt to play a leadership role, in the global anti-neoliberal agenda may have won them a few more friends in far-off places such as Australia but perhaps lost them more powerful allies closer to home. For many, the challenge of globalization is not figuring out how to revive the rhetoric of the Cold War era but discovering creative and credible ways to protect indigenous populations and other minorities from adverse impacts and enable them to play a profitable role in the world economy. The discovery of such ways will be an enterprise supported by many; it is a concrete and identifiable goal, as opposed to a never-ending class struggle.

Can transnational networks be formed to help other oppressed groups elsewhere gain more recognition and representation? If one goes by regional norms, this can happen only in Latin America and Western Europe—the only two regions of the world that have explicit norms regarding democracy. What should perhaps happen first is the formation of transnational networks to campaign for regional norms of good governance in other regions of the world.

The case of China shows just how difficult it can be to form effective transnational campaigns for democracy in other regions. There are many groups outside China pushing for democracy within the country. Most are based in the United States, often supported by private American foundations, and many include prominent Chinese exiles. Yet their influence on U.S. policy toward China has been limited, and their influence on China itself even less. This is perhaps not surprising—China is, and behaves like, a major power, and one that has recently achieved a most impressive increase in the standard of living for most people.

The moral dilemma presented by the current transnational China democracy campaign is whether, by heightening the Chinese government's perceptions of being under attack by a foreign-funded conspiracy, the campaign is not shutting off whatever natural impulses the government might have for gradual reform.[29] Even the limited foreign support for the democracy movement has probably bolstered Chinese government perceptions that a small but powerful foreign constituency is attempting to undermine the Chinese state. If this is the case, the campaign might be doing more harm than good. In the case of Haiti, this dilemma did not exist, because the country's real government was in exile, and what was being targeted was an illegal regime. In the absence of the transnational campaign, the only natural impulse of the illegal regime would have been to further destroy its own country. In the case of Mexico, the dilemma does not exist in the same form as in China. The issue is not whether, in the absence of the Chiapas campaign, the government will carry out political reform but one of the pace and extent of the political reform process on which the government has already embarked. Is the Chiapas transnational network conducting an immoral act by supporting an armed insurgency against the government of Mexico? The networks would probably say that they are supporting the forceful demand for their rights by Mexico's indigenous population, who have been repressed and neglected for too long. Here, they are on firmer moral ground. A growing trend in regional and international norms holds states accountable for their behavior toward their citizens. Membership in organizations such as the North Atlantic Treaty Organization, the European Union, the OAS, and the various subregional Latin American trade arrangements all require adherence to certain minimum codes of conduct by member governments. Presumably, citizens of these member nations also have the right to exercise vigilance over the citizens and governments of other countries that are participating in the same regional arrangements.

What is the future of transnational networking of the kind described in this chapter? One interesting aspect that is common to both campaigns, and to the China network as well, is the extent of the participation by the diaspora, particularly in North America. This involvement was extensive in Haiti, substantial in China, and more limited in Chiapas. This may point to a wave of the future. The Kosovar diaspora, for instance, united behind the Kosovo Liberation Army (KLA) demands for an independent Kosovo. Of course, one could also argue that the same diaspora effort that helped focus the international community's attention on Kosovo also made it difficult for the international negotiators at Rambouillet, France, to impose a solution on the KLA, thus precipitating the bombing of Yugoslavia. The KLA, buoyed by support and arms from around the world, refused to accept any compromise. A similar argument could be made for the LTTE in Sri Lanka. Supported by sections of the Tamil diaspora, it has refused to negotiate constructively with the Sri Lankan government and has been placed on many international lists of terrorist organizations for its attacks on civilians. In fact, resolutions adopted by the UN Security Council and the General Assembly toward the end of 1999 aimed at curbing international terrorism were widely perceived as having hindered the LTTE's international network of support. Diaspora engagement with political issues in their homelands is obviously a mixed blessing.

An important concern involving global civil society networks remains the extent to which networks focused on governance may use their cause as a means for pushing other agendas or as permanent life lines for various institutions and organizations. Certainly, perennial proponents of the idea of a vast corporate, right-wing conspiracy to destroy the peoples of the world at the altar of corporate greed have received a new boost to their sagging fortunes from being involved with the Chiapas uprising. And allying with the global opponents of globalization and corporate power might have given the Zapatistas greater worldwide visibility. But is continually being in the limelight more significant than moving quickly toward a constructive resolution of the issue by building alliances with well-meaning people in the center of the Mexican political spectrum?

It is difficult to address the issue of what kinds of inputs are needed to make transnational networks better tools for reforming governments or dealing with illegal regimes. Specifics will vary from case to case. However, certain broad points apply generally:

- First, regional norms are an important factor. Citizens are empowered to a greater extent if their countries are participating in regional arrangements that emphasize state accountability and good governance. Citizens can then hold their governments, and their neighbors' governments, to these norms. In East Asia, with individual exceptions such as Japan, South Korea, the Philippines, and Taiwan, current regional norms empower governments, with their emphasis on stability and economic growth. However, there is no reason why there cannot be a civil society discourse on regimes and their transformation that spans regional boundaries within East Asia.

- Second, organized and well-led diasporas play a critical role. Western donors that support democracy-related activities, as well as students of foreign policy, ought to look at this issue more closely.

- Third, information technology remains one of the most critical ingredients of networking activity. The organizations involved in the campaigns described in this chapter have all overcome the shortcomings of limited resources and staff by making heavy use of computers for purposes that vary from mass mailings to joint planning. The key is to identify organizations that have the ability to move flexibly and rapidly with information technology. Organizations with great institutional weight and inertia apparently do not make good networkers.

- Fourth, campaigns against specific governments occur in the context of the broader discourse on the nature of the social contract between states and their citizens in an increasingly globalized society and economy. Once again, international donors to transnational networking activities should encourage participants in these networks to engage in discussions of their rights and duties vis-à-vis states and to develop a discourse that enables everyone involved—states, activists, and donors—to develop a more concrete sense of the possibility of economic or political transformation.

Notes

1. http://www.eco.utexas.edu/faculty/Cleaver/zapsincyber.html.
2. See *Free China Movement Update* 1, no. 5 (July 25, 1998), at http://www.freechina.net/fcmupdate/v1n5.html.

3. The narrative of events in Chiapas presented here is drawn largely from the chronology of Chiapas-related events provided on the "Towards a History of Events in Chiapas" page, available at http://flag.blackened.net/revolt/mexico/ralertdx.html, and from the detailed and updated chronology of events in Chiapas provided by the International Service for Peace (SIPAZ) at its web site (http://www.sipaz.org).
4. http://www.mexicosolidarity.org/.
5. See http://www.sipaz.org/frme.htm.
6. For a comprehensive study of the role of the Internet in the Zapatista story, see Harry Cleaver, "The Zapatistas and the Electronic Fabric of Struggle," available at http://www.eco.utexas.edu:80/Homepages/Faculty/Cleaver/zaps.html.
7. See "Foreigners of Conscience: The Mexican Government's Campaign Against International Human Rights Observers in Chiapas," a report by Global Exchange available at http://www.globalexchange.org/.
8. The text of the Joint Declaration of San Miguel is available at http://www.global exchange.org/.
9. The detailed text of the accords is available at http://www.presidencia.gob.mx/welcome/chiapas/document/sanadres/.
10. See Eric Olson, "WOLA Background Paper for Congressional Hearing on Chiapas," July 28, 1998.
11. A detailed explanation of the government's objections can be found at http://www.presidencia.gob.mx/welcome/chiapas/document/cocopa.htm. Details of the EZLN's critique of COCOPA's revised proposals can be found at http://flag.blackened.net/revolt/mexico/reports/cocopa_ezln_mar97.html.
12. See "A Background to the Current Violence in Chiapas" page, at http://www.flag.blackened.net/revolt/mexico/womindex.html.
13. See http://www.geocities.com/CapitolHill/3849/gatherdx.html.
14. See http://flag.blackened.net/revolt/mexico/reports/fzln_outcome_sep97.html.
15. An account of the massacre and its aftermath can be found at http://thedagger.com/appel.html. The author is Kerry Appel, director of the Human Bean Company.
16. http://www.sipaz.org/frme.htm.
17. Andrea Becerril, "COCOPA and CONAI Identify 10 Points for Renewing Dialogue," *La Jornada*, January 23, 1998, available at http://www.sipaz.org/ch1998e.htm#1998.
18. *SIPAZ Report* 4, no. 1 (February 1999), available at http://www.nonviolence.org/sipaz/v04no1/sume.htm and at www.sipaz.org.
19. See "Chiapas Report Summary," *SIPAZ Report* 4, no. 2 (May 1999), available at http://www.sipaz.org/frme.htm.
20. "Update—Chiapas: One Step Forward; One Step Back," *SIPAZ Report* 4, no. 1 (February 1999), available at http://www.sipaz.org/frme.htm.
21. The Canada-based Chiapas Alert Network, which has thirty members, succinctly states these goals in its own mission statement.
22. Available at www.sipaz.org.
23. This and subsequent details on human rights observation were obtained from the chronology of Chiapas-related events available from SIPAZ's Web site.
24. David Malone's authoritative and detailed work, *Decision-Making in the UN Security Council: The Case of Haiti, 1990–1997* (Oxford: Clarendon Press, 1998), pro-

vides the best account of the complexities of international decision making on Haiti in the aftermath of the overthrow of President Aristide in 1991.

25. See James Ridgeway, ed., *The Haiti Files: Decoding the Crisis* (Washington, D.C.: Essential Books/Azul Editions, 1994), p. 224.

26. Howard W. French, "Aristide Seeking to Rally Support," *New York Times*, January 18, 1994.

27. See Toni L. Kamins, "Death and Life in Haiti," *Haiti Insight* 5, no. 3 (May 1994).

28. Ahpaly Coradin, "Joint Efforts for Refugees," *Haiti Insight* 5, no. 3 (May 1994).

29. In a significant development, China invited the Carter Center to observe township elections in Chongqing municipality on January 7–15, 1999. According to the Carter Center's report, "The delegation was impressed by the large turnout of voters at the elections of deputies to the TPC and by the eagerness of the elected deputies in critiquing the governance of the township government. It did not see any coercion or manipulation in the three elections that it had observed. . . . However, the delegation were mostly concerned with the incompatibility of the electoral laws governing township elections and the Organic Law of Villager Committees, *which imposes a much stricter electoral procedure* [emphasis added]. . . . Recommendations to improve the quality of these elections were made to the officials of the NPC at a series of meetings. . . . Chinese officials responded positively to these suggestions." According to the Carter Center, "This Mission was very significant for several reasons. First of all, no foreign agencies or representatives had ever been invited to observe township elections. Secondly, unlike villager committees which are, as defined by Chinese Constitution, autonomous units of self-government, self-service, and self-education, townships are the building block level of the formal, national Chinese government structure. These elections lead upwards through a series of indirect elections to the National People's Congress." These excerpts from the Carter Center's report (available at http://www.cartercenter.org/CHINA/dox/reports/199.html) suggest that even though the Chinese government has continued to crack down on the more overt challenges to its authority, such as in the case of the Chinese Democratic Party or the Falun Gong sect, it has continued to build a popular role in ensuring an honest and accountable officialdom, first at the village level, and then more tentatively at the township level. Clearly, Chinese authorities are aware of the necessity of having capable officials to run a rapidly globalizing economy.

6

Building Partnerships toward a Common Goal: Experiences of the International Campaign to Ban Landmines

Motoko Mekata

IN DECEMBER 1997, the International Campaign to Ban Landmines (ICBL) and its coordinator Jody Williams jointly received the Nobel Peace Prize for helping to establish an international convention that bans antipersonnel land mines. Half the prize money went directly to Williams, but the other half had to wait nearly a year to reach the ICBL. Why? Because the ICBL did not legally exist. It was an amorphous network of nongovernmental organizations (NGOs), not registered as an entity anywhere in the world. Yet this network achieved what critics had derided as a "utopian" objective, and it did so less than five years after its inception. This chapter tells the story of the ICBL.

The Problem with Antipersonnel Land Mines

Few would contest the claim that antipersonnel land mines pose a significant threat to human well-being. The International Committee of the Red Cross (ICRC) estimated that such land mines victimize 2,000 people every month in some sixty countries around the world and that they have inflicted "more death and injury than nuclear and chemical weapons combined" over the past fifty years.[1] A prosthesis costs about $1,000 (all amounts are in U.S. dollars) and needs to be replaced every few years, often thirty times in a lifetime. While it costs from $3 to $20 to make an antipersonnel land mine, the average cost of removing a mine is $300 to $1,000. Mine clearance is very labor intensive and risky, with mines being lifted from the ground one at a time.

General international humanitarian law prohibits the use of indiscriminate weapons, as well as the use of weapons that cause unnecessary suffering.[2] These rules are part of international customary law, so they apply to all states irrespective of their treaty obligations. However, enforceable compliance mechanisms do not exist.

Before the ICBL was born, only one international treaty directly addressed land mines. The United Nations (UN) Convention on Prohibitions or Restrictions on the Use of Certain Conventional Weapons Which May Be Deemed to Be Excessively Injurious or to Have Indiscriminate Effects (the CCW Convention), adopted in October 1980, came into force in December 1983. Protocol II of this convention, the Protocol on Prohibitions or Restrictions on the Use of Mines, Booby-Traps and Other Devices, prohibited the indiscriminate use of antipersonnel mines. However, this treaty failed to address the most egregious problem of antipersonnel mines. Unlike other conventional weapons, mines long outlive the conflicts that generate them; they remain in the soil unless someone removes them—or steps on them.

Protocol II had other serious loopholes as well. For example, it was not applicable to internal armed conflicts (which accounted for most mines used in the 1980s); it did not prohibit the use of nondetectable mines; it did not assign clear responsibility for mine clearance; and it lacked implementation, monitoring, and compliance mechanisms. Furthermore, only forty states had signed the convention by the end of 1993, ten years after its entry into force. Major producer and exporting countries such as Britain, Israel, Italy, and the United States remained outside the convention, as did mine-infested countries such as Afghanistan, Angola, Bosnia, Cambodia, and Mozambique.

When the campaign to ban land mines began in the early 1990s, over 100 companies and government agencies in fifty-two countries were manufacturing more than 340 types of antipersonnel mines. An average of 5 million to 10 million antipersonnel mines had probably been produced annually over the past twenty-five years, about ten times the volume identified in past published reports.[3] The U.S. State Department estimated that the world was infested with some 80 million to 110 million mines and that each year only 80,000 mines were being cleared, while some 2.5 million new mines were being planted.[4]

In short, despite the 1980 treaty, the problem was getting worse. Antipersonnel mines were being laid much faster than they were being cleared, and the end of the Cold War revealed uncontrolled use of antipersonnel mines in internal conflicts. A growing number of relief and humanitarian organizations reached the conclusion that unless antipersonnel mines were eradicated totally, the scourge would not end.

Emergence of the International Campaign to Ban Landmines

The ICBL began with a fax. Bobby Muller of the Vietnam Veterans of America Foundation (VVAF) sent a fax to Thomas Gebauer of medico international (medico) in Frankfurt on April 9, 1991, asking for Gebauer's cooperation on mine victim assistance projects.[5] The VVAF and medico had jointly been organizing support for a prosthesis program for war and mine victims in El Salvador since 1989. Muller had founded the VVAF in 1980 to help Vietnam War victims. He himself had been wounded in Vietnam in 1969 when a bullet severed his spinal cord. He visited Cambodia in 1987 and was struck by the devastating legacy mines leave long after a war is over. Gebauer had been working as a psychologist on projects helping war victims in Central America. Insurgency groups often scattered mines during civil conflicts, and he witnessed the effects on a large group of amputees. Muller visited Gebauer in Frankfurt in the first week of May 1991 to discuss further cooperation on projects, including possible political or legal means of getting rid of land mines. They agreed that "the most effective assistance one is able to give to people surrounded by mines is the ban."[6] Subsequently, Gebauer visited Washington several times. The two agreed to call jointly for an international campaign against antipersonnel mines and decided first to hire coordinators to set up the campaigns in their own countries. Muller hired Jody Williams, then the director of children's projects for Medical Aid for El Salvador, and Gebauer hired Angelika Beer, a former member of parliament in Germany.

Six organizations—Handicap International (HI), Human Rights Watch (HRW), medico, Mines Advisory Group (MAG), Physicians for Human Rights (PHR), and the VVAF—gathered in New York on October 2, 1992 to formally launch the ICBL. None of the founding members were from the traditional disarmament community. Instead, they were mostly humanitarian organizations working directly in mine-affected countries. HI had been providing prostheses to mine victims among Cambodian refugees on the Thai-Cambodian border since 1979 and had been working with MAG on mine awareness education in several mine-infested countries. Rae McGrath, the founder of MAG, had served in the British army for eighteen years. He began working in mine-infested areas in Afghanistan in 1988 and established MAG in 1991 to help affected communities cope with the threat posed by uncleared mines. Since then, MAG had been clearing mines in Cambodia, Kurdistan, Mozambique, Laos, Nicaragua, and Angola. Asia Watch of HRW and PHR had jointly published a book, *The Coward's War: Landmines in Cambodia*, in September 1991, portraying the reality of random land-mine use once a conflict is over.

In New York, the six organizations agreed on the following goals:

- An international ban on the use, production, stockpiling, and sale, transfer, or export of antipersonnel mines.

- The establishment of an international fund, administered by the UN, to promote and finance mine victim assistance programs and land-mine awareness, clearance, and eradication programs worldwide.

- Mandatory contributions to the international fund by countries responsible for the production and dissemination of antipersonnel mines.[7]

The banning of specific weapons was not unprecedented. Conventions had previously banned chemical and biological weapons because they, like land mines, were deemed to be indiscriminate and inhumane. However, unlike with chemical and biological weapons, neither governments nor the public in the major Western countries knew much about the long-lasting, indiscriminate, and inhumane effects of antipersonnel mines. Most Western countries had not used land mines since World War II, except for the United States, which had used them heavily during the Korean and Vietnam Wars. Land mines had largely been regarded as a weapon of defense, and there was no general perception that the weapon was "bad." So the ICBL set out to create that perception.

The London Conference

The first challenge for the ICBL was to raise international public awareness of land-mine issues and to expand its network to other countries. The ICBL convened its first international NGO conference in London on May 24, 1993. The six founding organizations were appointed as the steering committee, and Jody Williams was officially appointed coordinator of the ICBL. More than fifty organizations from different fields came together at this gathering.

Working groups on national and international lobbying efforts, grassroots organizing, and media and public education discussed detailed, concrete steps and strategies for adoption by each national campaign.[8] The working-group reports reflect the wide range of strategies and policies the ICBL adopted in subsequent years. The heavy emphasis on using the power of the media is particularly noteworthy. The ICBL decided then that "press and TV coverage had been minimal, both in Europe and in North America," so campaign efforts to create public information and awareness were emphasized. The content of this information had to be "immediately emotive, easy to understand, and non-ideological, without the political baggage of other disarmament issues." It was also recognized that antipersonnel mines were "remote from the lives of most Europeans and Americans" and that "the proposed solutions are sometimes complex." The ICBL concluded that "it was desirable to have a simple message 'ban mines' and to stigmatize mines."[9]

The ICBL consciously sought to add moral authority to the campaign. Use of figures such as surgeons, de-miners, mine victims, and military figures who were against the use of mines was crucial to relating directly to the public. The ICBL also concluded that involving national Red Cross Societies would add weight to the campaign in respective countries and that calls for consumer boycotts of mine manufacturers and attention-grabbing media events should form part of the strategy.

Participants had mixed feelings about lobbying for ratification of the 1980 CCW Convention and Protocol II. Since Protocol II was not even close to a ban on mines, members felt that it made little sense to spend energy pushing for ratification. Yet it was recognized that "a country cannot get to the ultimate goal all at once." Thus, working for early ratification or an export moratorium was considered a reasonable short-term objective. "Any movement in the right direction was considered positive."[10]

Participants acknowledged and welcomed the loose associational character of the ICBL network to maximize and respect the autonomy of national actions, but they also believed that participating organizations must at least endorse the ultimate goal of a total ban. Organizations under the ICBL were thus united in having achievement of a total ban as their ultimate goal, but short-term goals were left to the discretion of each national campaign.

The Work of Domestic Civil Societies

In the early days of the campaign, although the cause was global, the focus of the work was mostly domestic. NGOs and national campaigns shared information and strategies, but the imperatives of each national situation necessitated flexibility. The United States was the first country to report good news to the ICBL. Congress passed legislation imposing a one-year moratorium on the sale, export, or transfer abroad of antipersonnel land mines, and President George Bush signed the bill into law on October 23, 1992.

An amendment to the Moratorium Act declared that the United States "should actively seek verifiable international agreements or a modification of the landmine protocol to prohibit the sale, transfer, or export." However, the United States was in the "embarrassing position of not having ratified the protocol."[11] Senator Patrick Leahy, who had a long-standing interest in helping land-mine victims, wrote a letter to HI, encouraging it to call on the French government to convene a review conference.[12] Any state party could call for a review session ten years after the protocol entered into force, and that time was coming up at the end of 1993. France had ratified the protocol in 1988, and HI was already actively pressing its government for a review. To that end, in 1992, HI translated *The Coward's War* into French and distributed it to all French legislators and all members of the European Parliament. HI convened conferences in Paris on mines in 1992 and 1993 to bring together government authorities, journalists, and the general public, while it also called for petitions endorsing a ban on land mines. Visual materials portraying the devastating physical damage of land mines had a significant impact on the public. French authorities were said to have "discovered for the first time the magnitude of the global landmine problem and pressed the NGO community for more evidence and documentation."[13] And HI presented Senator Leahy's letter to officials at the Ministry of Foreign Affairs.

Thanks in part to such pressure from HI and its civil society associates in France, on February 11, 1993, President Francois Mitterrand announced the French government's intention to request a CCW review conference during an official visit to Cambodia. In December 1993, the forty-eighth session of the UN General Assembly adopted a resolution calling for a review conference of the 1980 convention.[14]

The Belgian Campaign

On March 2, 1995, Belgium became the first country in the world to ban the production, storage, and export of antipersonnel mines.

Early in the summer of 1993, Senator Martine Dardenne received a letter from HI Belgium,[15] along with a book, *Hidden Death—Antipersonnel Mines in Iraqi Kurdistan*. At HI Belgium's request, Dardenne helped distribute the book to everyone in the Senate and Chamber and wrote an accompanying letter in which she relayed her intent to take action on the issue. She received an unexpected number of encouraging responses from colleagues. HI Belgium also contacted other organizations for their support. At the time, the Belgian campaign had not yet been formally launched, and the initiative comprised just a few loosely connected organizations. HI Belgium was the only Belgian organization working directly on projects linked to antipersonnel mines, so it seemed natural for it to perform most of the daily work once the Belgian campaign was officially launched in March 1994.

Apparently "unaware of the gravity of the matter before receiving the book from HI Belgium,"[16] Senator Roger Lellemand of the Socialist Party became interested in the issue and suggested drafting legislation jointly with Dardenne. Lellemand's involvement was instrumental in building consensus within Parliament as he is a prominent figure on the Belgian political scene. In the buildup to passage of the legislation, his policy assistant Verschvelen maintained close daily contact with HI Belgium to exchange information and strategize on winning support.[17] This communication was vital, because the government opposed Belgium taking any initiative on the land-mine issue when other European countries were not undertaking similar measures. The Ministry of Defense protested strongly, demanding continued use of land mines for North Atlantic Treaty Organization (NATO) joint exercises where other member states would be using them. The government had also suggested selling stockpiled mines instead of destroying them. But Parliament overruled these arguments and unanimously passed legislation banning antipersonnel mines on March 8, 1995, less than a year after the formal launch of the Belgian campaign.

There are mixed views about the degree to which Belgian civil society influenced the passage of the legislation. Lellemand believed that "it was a parliamentary initiative rather than a popular movement which was the driving force"[18] and that the legislation did not generate any opposition because it was fairly simple. Also, Belgium had not used land mines since 1951 and had ceased production in 1991. Building consensus within Parliament was thus not particularly difficult for Lellemand. Dardenne, however, saw the role of the Belgian campaign somewhat differently, saying that "civil society played a crucial lobbying role with Parliament."[19] At a minimum, the Belgian campaign was crucial to making parliamentarians aware of the gravity of the issue and convincing them of the importance of taking urgent action, despite strong government opposition.

In a notable demonstration of the importance of domestic nodes in the outcome, the Belgian campaign hardly ever used the ICBL or the transnational network to elicit either legitimacy or credibility. As a member of the Belgian campaign noted, "the methods for campaigning must be adapted according to the political culture of the country."[20] Rather than relying on inputs from the ICBL, the Belgian campaign sought its own strategies by utilizing HI's accumulated information and expertise from its fieldwork. This authoritative knowledge and firsthand information were key in convincing parliamentarians and government authorities.

Campaign Strategies

The crucial role of authoritative knowledge was also clear from the experiences of the Dutch campaign. Pieter van Rossem of Pax Christi, who led the campaign in the Netherlands, was an expert on small-arms trade and developing economies. He had coordinated a Dutch campaign against arms exports in the early 1980s, so he was experienced in managing networks and lobbying government authorities. Van Rossem carefully selected just a few organizations to be involved in the Dutch campaign to facilitate decision making and avoid bureaucratization. Again, information was key for the domestic network. "What's needed in a campaign is an ongoing flow of new information to keep the subject alive in newspaper and politics."[21] The campaign reported any mine incidents daily to the spokespersons of every political party that discussed the subject in parliamentary hearings.

Through the Pax Christi network, Van Rossem also assisted in launching the campaign in Ireland. Tony D'Costa of Ireland had previously been engaged mainly in nuclear disarmament issues until the official launching of the anti–land mine campaign in Ireland. D'Costa made maximum use of his connections to focus heavily on media campaigns and to create public events for advocacy work. He visited schools, universities, and youth groups to discuss the land-mine problem; he organized a letter-writing campaign for children; and he invited ICBL members with firsthand knowledge to talk to the public and to government officials. Bringing a range of "witnesses" from the field was crucial, because "one can sell the story to the media by having different faces and different dimensions." Initially, D'Costa did much of this work alone; many organizations declined to be involved, as "they had to protect their interests and [it] could be detrimental to be involved in political issues" such as the land-mine campaign.[22]

While ICBL affiliates in the United States, the Netherlands, and, to a certain extent, France utilized personal skill, connections, and expertise as leverage, other networks mobilized the masses to effect a policy shift. Mine Action Canada (MAC) began its campaign with a very simple step: letter writing to ministries and parliamentarians. After attending an NGO meeting in Geneva in May 1994, MAC coordinator Celina Tuttle began a letter-writing campaign. She kept it up until one official asked MAC to stop sending letters because they were taking up too much space in the prime minister's office and the Departments of Foreign Affairs and National Defense.[23]

Public education was key to the campaigns in all the countries. Rae McGrath, the founder of MAG, the British mine-clearing organization, gave talks in schools. "The basis of all effective campaigning is education . . . because a campaign is essentially an intellectual battle and in order to emerge victorious you must transfer the relevant knowledge which underpins your campaigning logic to the public."[24]

Some ICBL member organizations engaged in research work targeting mine producers. For example, HRW compiled a report that was "the basis for a 'stigmatization' campaign by the USCBL [U.S. Campaign to Ban Landmines] to press all companies that have been involved in antipersonnel mine production in the past to renounce any future activities related to antipersonnel mine production."[25] Many components of land mines are also used in consumer appliances, such as personal computers, refrigerators, and beepers. HRW thus called on companies to "make every effort to insure that their products are not used in antipersonnel mines, so that the same chips that power children's computers in the United States do not end up in landmines that might one day blow up children in another country." Of the forty-seven companies named on the HRW producer list, seventeen resolved that they would "renounce any future involvement in antipersonnel mine production."[26]

Most of the national campaigns in the early days involved loose networks. In some cases, there was more of a structure, with perhaps a steering committee drawn from member organizations, with each paying dues to hire a full-time coordinator. Yet this was rare, at least in the early years.

Mobilizing International Public Opinion

Once the French campaign convinced its government to call for a review session of Protocol II of the CCW, the ICBL concentrated its energy on informing international public opinion. The ICBL convened an expanded steering committee meeting in Rome in March 1995 to discuss in detail a wide range of issues relating to the CCW conference to be held in September in Vienna. After the Rome meeting, the ICBL consciously tried to expand the campaign to countries in which there were no ICBL affiliates, especially those countries that were regarded as problematic in terms of mine production or export record. This was done mainly through personal ties and organizational connections. The ICBL had learned that a campaign could be successful only if a local NGO was willing to become actively involved. Indeed, the initiative and readiness to start projects had to come from the national civil society.

International and Regional Organizations

The accumulated work of national networks under the ICBL began to resonate in international organizations as well, largely because these international institutions were active in field operations in mine-infested countries. In September 1994, UN secretary-general Boutros Boutros Ghali submitted his report on "decontamination," a supporting document for the creation of a fund for mine-clearing activities. He noted that "the best and most effective way to solve the global landmine problem is a complete ban on the use, production, and transfer of all landmines."[27]

The UN Department of Humanitarian Affairs sponsored the first International Meeting on Mine Clearance in Geneva to raise funds for its Voluntary Demining Trust Fund in July 1995. More than 1,000 delegates from nearly every country attended and agreed to coordinate and exchange information on de-mining initiatives. Boutros Ghali cited the Chemical Weapons Convention and called on countries to be inspired by its spirit. Sadako Ogata of the UN High Commissioner for Refugees called for a total ban, announced that the UNHCR would not knowingly purchase products from companies that sold or manufactured antipersonnel land mines or their components, and suggested that they should be considered "criminals against humanity."[28]

At a press conference prior to the expert meeting of the CCW review session, President Sommaruga of the ICRC strongly supported a worldwide ban and stressed that it would be the only truly effective solution, a position the ICRC had been advocating from a humanitarian law perspective. The ICRC then engaged in an unprecedented level of campaigning. It had already organized a conference in Montreaux in May 1993 that brought together military experts, humanitarian organizations, and war surgeons, the first comprehensive meeting on the land-mine issue. The ICRC also issued a report challenging the military utility of land mines.

Regional organizations also became vocal on the issue. In May 1995, the Council of the European Union (EU) announced a partial moratorium on the export of antipersonnel land mines, support for the promotion of the convention's universality and the reinforcement of Protocol II, and an EU contribution to international de-mining initiatives. In June 1995, the Organization of African Unity's Council of Ministers adopted a resolution calling on member states to support a common African position in favor of a total ban. Pope John Paul II also launched an appeal in May 1995 for a definitive end to the manufacture and use of antipersonnel mines.

Meanwhile, national campaign efforts in many countries gradually bore fruit. In 1994 alone, Argentina, Britain, the Czech Republic, Greece, Italy, the Netherlands, South Africa, Spain, Sweden, and Switzerland, for example, initiated some measures toward controlling land mines. These steps ranged from total bans to one-year or permanent export moratoria and the destruction of stockpiles, and the means varied from simple declarations to the passing of legislation. International momentum was being generated.

The CCW Conference

By the time of the CCW conference in Vienna in September 1995, the total number of NGOS within the ICBL reached 350 from thirty-two countries, and over sixty NGOs gathered in Vienna to follow the diplomatic negotiations. Affiliated organizations under the ICBL included grassroots and international NGOs working in the field of mine clearance, victim assistance, relief, human rights, environment, development, and refugees. The involvement of religious organizations also expanded the scope of the network. By mobilizing the resource bases and networks of all the NGOs, the ICBL was able to make maximum use of local and international media. It held regular media briefings and issued *CCW News*, which included information on developments at the conference, testimonies and stories from the field, and a list of "good" and "bad" countries. Land-mine victims from Afghanistan, Cambodia, Mozambique, and the United States gathered to share their experiences.

On the eve of the conference, the ICBL organized a series of simultaneous mine awareness actions in countries such as Belgium, Canada, Great Britain, France, Germany, Ireland, and South Africa. HI and the French Red Cross created a shoe pyramid in front of the Eiffel Tower to symbolize those who had lost limbs by land mines. The Belgian campaign held a de-mining demonstration for the media. The VVAF in the United States released *After the Guns Fall Silent: the Enduring Legacy of Landmines*, a report on the socioeconomic impact of land mines. For the first time, the ICBL as a coalition lobbied governments attending the review session. The ICBL was allowed to address the plenary session, and more than twenty speakers representing mine victims and humanitarian, relief, human rights, and religious organizations demanded an immediate ban on antipersonnel mines.

Three weeks of diplomatic negotiations in Vienna revealed a wide difference of opinion among states. Austria, Denmark, Ireland, Norway, and a few others supported a total ban, with Australia, Britain, and India objecting. The British delegation emphasized that "landmines were a legal defensive weapon," while India objected to compliance mechanisms. The biggest stumbling block proved to be agreement on the definition of antipersonnel mines. Land mines include a wide range of types within the definition; indeed, no other weapon has such diversity in design.[29] Britain and the United States pushed hard for continued use of smart mines, mines with self-destructive or self-neutralizing devices so that they lose effect after a set period, and the prohibition of old-fashioned mines, which remain active until they are cleared or stepped on. But China, India, and Russia, which could not afford to match U.S. defense expenditures, strongly opposed the idea. The most inexpensive land mine can be purchased for $3, while smart mines can cost as much as $300.

The conference adjourned without a treaty, agreeing only to discuss limited technical matters in Geneva in January 1996 and to reconvene in May 1996. The ICBL condemned states for not appreciating the urgency of the problem, noting that "in the three weeks while delegates struggled to protect their own stockpiles of landmines, more than 1,600 people around the world were killed or maimed by landmines."[30]

The First NGO-Government Meeting

Members of the ICBL felt that no meaningful advance could be expected from the Geneva conference in January 1996. Three weeks of negotiations in Vienna had been inconclusive, and a week in Geneva would likely have the same result. There was an urgent need for a breakthrough. On January 15, 1996, van Rossem of the Dutch campaign came up with the idea of bringing together those governments that had officially announced support for a total ban. Since Vienna, the number of states supporting a ban had increased to over twenty. Most ICBL members opposed the idea, fearing that if an attempt to bring pro-ban states together failed, it could weaken the momentum and discourage new state initiatives.[31] But van Rossem decided to proceed, organizing the meeting under the banner of the Dutch campaign.

Van Rossem envisaged something quite casual. His intention was to "talk heart to heart, think together with delegates about the difficulties they are confronting, encourage them, and get them out of the normal disarmament context."[32] Yet it was also important to create "an event" for which governments could prepare. Van Rossem additionally wanted to find out how many states were really committed to taking action immediately—instead of eventually—toward a total ban.

The historic meeting, the first step of what would develop ten months later into the Ottawa Process, took place on January 17 at the UN office building in Geneva. Invitations for the meeting were extended to twenty-two delegations, of which eight (Austria, Belgium, Canada, Denmark, Ireland, Mexico, Norway, and Switzerland) attended. Van Rossem chaired the discussion and asked those gathered for their governments' positions on a total ban. They also exchanged ideas about possible initiatives for the CCW. ICBL members, for example, urged delegates to engage in bilateral or multilateral cooperation to create mine-free zones. They also suggested using good-governance criteria developed by the World Bank or International Monetary Fund for demanding bans from developing countries within development assistance schemes. Country delegates and ICBL members agreed to keep in contact and to explore whether there were other governments that might wish to join the group. One NGO member recalled the atmosphere as "heartwarming" and said that it "felt for the first time that a ban was within reach." An Irish delegate later reported to a parliamentary hearing in Dublin that "the CCW would be highly disappointing, but one good thing is happening: an embryo is developing, the beginning of a sense that pro-ban countries identify and associate with each other and in a most tentative possible way are assuming an identity as a group."[33]

The Canadian Initiative

A delegate from Canada, Bob Lawson, who was present at the meeting felt that Canada could assume leadership on the issue. He wrote a memorandum to newly appointed Foreign Minister Lloyd Axworthy right after he returned to Ottawa and proposed exploring the possibility of Canada taking some initiative. The minister's response was simple—"yes."

However, Canada had not yet endorsed a total ban. In fact, van Rossem had not even invited a Canadian delegation to the first NGO-government meeting.[34] He had sent invitations only to those states on a "good country" list the ICBL had prepared. But Canada shifted its policy to supporting a total ban after the first NGO-government meeting and during the January review session in Geneva.

Canada subsequently decided to open a small conference for pro-ban states in the fall of 1996. This idea was unofficially suggested during the second NGO-government meeting that took place on April 22, 1996, at the Quakers' office in Geneva during the final CCW review session. Fourteen countries participated in this meeting, and most of them were supportive of the Canadian initiative. Canada officially announced its intention to convene a strategic conference on May 3, 1996.

The ICBL had already been informed about the Canadian initiative through the ICBL network in Canada. MAC sent an e-mail in April, informing ICBL members that the Department of Foreign Affairs was considering a "Canadian Action Plan on Landmines" based on the "pro-ban countries' meeting" in Geneva in January. The plan "included hosting a small international strategy workshop with experts, officials, and pertinent NGOs to develop a global and regional action plan on landmines in a post-CCW context." MAC asked for suggestions from ICBL members, for it did not "want this initiative to turn into a flag-waving exercise for [the Canadian] government."[35] In cooperation with the Quakers' UN office in Geneva, the ICBL carefully coordinated the April meeting to make sure that the occasion would not be used for lobbying governments but would instead be an opportunity for building solidarity among governments and mobilizing one another for further steps.[36] The NGOs would be present to bring expertise and perspective.

The final session of the CCW review closed on May 3, 1996 without achieving a total ban. Although Protocol II was revised to extend the sphere of application to internal conflicts and to prohibit the use of old-style mines, it allowed continued use of smart mines. The ICBL criticized the negotiation process, saying that it "show[ed] the continued weight given to military concerns instead of granting meaningful protection to non-combatants" and suggested that "the result of two years of international negotiation is a shameful betrayal of tens of thousands of innocent civilians who live in mine-affected regions and those of future generations who will fall victim to this inhuman weapon. In reality the new document is not a step out of the mine-field."[37] The UN secretary-general lamented that by the next review conference, estimated to take place in 2001, "an additional 50,000 human beings will have been killed, and a further 80,000 injured, by landmines. Furthermore, 10 to 25 million landmines will have been added to the 110 million already uncleared," and "the world cannot wait for the eventual elimination of landmines. They must be eliminated now."[38]

The ICBL could not hide its huge disappointment with the CCW outcome. Members had been realistic and had not held high expectations, having witnessed the slow progress made during the 1994–95 preparatory committee meetings. Yet international momentum had been building, and international organizations had also demonstrated strong support for the cause. The next opportunity for effecting progress would be the conference in Ottawa.

Unconventional Diplomacy: The Ottawa Process

The International Strategy Conference Toward a Global Ban on Antipersonnel Mines took place in Ottawa on October 3–5, 1996. Fifty countries attended as full participants, and twenty-four as observers. The Canadian government had initiated an innovative new method of "self-selecting" participants in the conference. A plan of action was circulated to all governments before the conference convened, and they were invited to participate only if they agreed to the text. Although fifty states had claimed to support the text, at the conference most delegates merely reiterated their support for an "eventual" ban. But the Canadians had something more dramatic planned.

The highlight of the conference came on the last day, when Foreign Minister Axworthy challenged the world by announcing that Canada would host a treaty-signing conference in December 1997. Axworthy stated that "there is momentum, there is political commitment, and most importantly, the peoples of the world support what we are trying to do." Speaking of the ICBL, he added that "the challenge is also to the International Campaign to ensure that governments around the world are prepared to work with us to ensure that a treaty is developed and signed next year. This is not far-fetched. You are largely responsible for our being here today. The same effective arguments you used to get us here must now be put to work to get foreign ministers here to sign the treaty."[39] The Austrian government was assigned the task of preparing a treaty text based on the draft text it had circulated in Ottawa.

Creating a New Forum

Axworthy's challenge was unconventional in several ways. First, it set a clear deadline for signing a comprehensive ban treaty, putting an end to the "eventual" response to solving the problem. Second, Axworthy proposed conducting treaty negotiations outside existing diplomatic fora. Finally, the Canadian government demonstrated a degree of willingness to work with transnational civil society that was unknown in the international community. Why did Canada make such a bold challenge?

Canada decided to host the strategic conference because it had witnessed the failure of the CCW review sessions, despite increased international awareness of the problem. What had impeded the negotiations was the CCW's consensus mechanism. Some states were at least rhetorically ready to commit to banning land mines but met strong opposition from less enthusiastic states, especially the United States, China, and Russia.

Other traditional intergovernmental fora for negotiations were no more promising. A joint action adopted by the EU two days prior to the Ottawa conference had carefully accommodated contradictory stances held by member states. While stating that the EU would commit to totally eliminating land mines and would "work actively towards the achievement at the earliest possible date of an effective international agreement to ban these weapons worldwide,"[40] it also stated that the negotiation would take place at "the most appropriate international forum,"[41] and the question of which forum was left open. France was trying to push the Conference on Disarmament (CD) as the appropriate forum for further discussions. During Canadian-French bilateral meetings prior to the Ottawa conference, France made it clear that any statements about further negotiations had to include a reference to the CD.[42] The United States and Italy also made statements favoring the CD for follow-up negotiations. However, it was clear to Canadian officials that concrete results could not be achieved in such a consensus-based forum because the governments' positions were simply too diverse. Furthermore, the membership of the CD was limited to thirty-eight (before it expanded to sixty-one in June 1996), including such ban opponents as Russia, China, and India, and it had no history of negotiating the disarmament of conventional weapons. A new forum was desperately needed if a total ban were to be achieved any time soon.

Yet there was also a danger of undermining existing international settings. Ambassador Johan Molander, chair of the CCW review session, emphasized the importance of "the universality of the UN, which is its weakness but also its strength." He cautioned that the Ottawa Process could be regarded as "being led by a couple of Western countries who are trying to establish an international norm that is higher than what the rest of the world can achieve."[43] But proponents of the Ottawa Process saw the problem of land mines as a humanitarian emergency that demanded an immediate international response.

It seems unlikely that Axworthy would have made his bold announcement had he not been sure of strong ICBL support. He informed a few ICBL individuals (along with the UN secretary-general and the ICRC president) in advance, although Axworthy did not consult a single government in making his final decision. This was not because he valued the role of transnational civil society and international organizations over that of states, but because "it would be difficult to commit if a consulted country disagreed with his idea." Not getting prior approval for this new and apparently shocking diplomatic initiative was unconventional, and much risk was involved.

Nonetheless, Axworthy took the risk because "he knew international public opinion was supporting him." Not surprisingly, NGOs gave Axworthy a standing ovation right after his announcement about convening a treaty-signing conference. Such support "reinforced in his [Axworthy's] mind his instincts that you can work with NGOs, that you can build partnerships with NGOs, and they will be there for you and will support you."[44]

The Brussels Conference

Once Axworthy challenged transnational civil society to work together with national governments, the ICBL attempted to create text for the treaty in consultation with international lawyers and disarmament experts. The experience of trying to actually draft the treaty text gave ICBL members the opportunity to learn the complexities and problems of international law and empowered them to engage in legal dialogue later during the treaty text negotiations in Oslo.

By December 1996, the stigmatization campaign was bearing fruit. The UN General Assembly passed a resolution urging states to "pursue vigorously an effective, legally binding international agreement to ban use, stockpiling, production, and transfer of antipersonnel landmines with a view to completing the negotiation as soon as possible."[45] The final vote in the General Assembly took place on December 19, 1996 and was 155 to 0 in favor, with ten abstentions and twenty states absent. Following conferences in Vienna and Bonn in February and May, respectively, a conference was held in Brussels on June 24–27, 1997. An impressive ninety-seven nations signed a declaration pledging "to pursue an enduring solution to the urgent humanitarian crisis caused by antipersonnel landmines." The delegates affirmed that the "essential elements" of such an agreement should include a comprehensive ban on the use, stockpiling, production, and transfer of antipersonnel land mines; the destruction of stockpiled and removed antipersonnel land mines; and international cooperation and assistance in the field of mine clearance in affected countries. The signatories also "affirm[ed] their objective of concluding the negotiation and signing of such an agreement banning antipersonnel landmines before the end of 1997 in Ottawa, [and] invit[ed] all other States to join them in their efforts towards such an agreement."[46] The ninety-seven signatories in Brussels included most of the mine-infested states and the key European mine producers, with thirteen of NATO's sixteen member states signing. Key states missing from the Ottawa Process at this stage included China, Greece, India, Japan, North Korea, Pakistan, Russia, South Korea, Turkey, the United States, and most of the countries of the Middle East.

The ICBL welcomed the momentum created through the Ottawa Process, but it feared that the rapid growth in the number of participants would erode the consensus that had been built among states endorsing an unambiguous ban. The ICBL made it clear that it "would rather see a simple comprehensive treaty signed by fewer countries than sell out this treaty with exceptions, reservations and loopholes simply to increase the number of signatories."[47]

Before the conference in Brussels, an unexpected development weighed in to increase the legitimacy of the Ottawa Process. On May

21, 1997, the British government announced its full participation in the Ottawa Process, fulfilling the new Labor government's campaign pledge. This decision had an unexpected impact across the Channel. Saying that it could "no longer bear to be isolated,"[48] France also announced its full participation. The British and French decisions to join the Ottawa Process added great weight because both countries were permanent members of the UN Security Council. Until their decisions, middle-power states had been leading the Ottawa Process, so Britain and France's participation greatly contributed to the legitimacy of the process. This meant that only Greece, Turkey, and the United States within NATO, and Finland and Greece within the EU, were not officially taking part in the process.

U.S. Participation and the Oslo Negotiations

The ICBL welcomed the British and French decisions but remained seriously concerned about the U.S. position. The United States had been taking confusing, ambiguous, and sometimes contradictory stances on the land-mine issue. By being the first state to declare an export moratorium in 1992, it appeared to take a leading role. However, it had demanded the exemption of self-destructing and self-neutralizing antipersonnel mines during the CCW review session. The U.S. Campaign to Ban Landmines condemned the official U.S. position as "obstructionist." In a full-page open letter to the president, fifteen retired military officials, including General Norman Schwarzkopf and former commanders of NATO and U.S. forces in Korea, suggested that antipersonnel mines were "not essential" and that "banning them would not undermine U.S. military effectiveness or the safety of [the] forces, nor those of other nations." They argued that such a ban was "not only humane, but also militarily responsible."[49] Right after the CCW failed to ban mines, President Bill Clinton expressed the intent to "launch an international effort to ban antipersonnel landmines. . . . The U.S. will lead a global effort to eliminate these terrible weapons and to stop the enormous loss of human life."[50] However, in Ottawa, the United States again expressed a preference for discussing the matter at the CD and, in January 1997, Clinton made it quite clear that the United States would not join the Ottawa Process.

Yet after a defense policy review, the U.S. government announced on August 18, 1997 that it would participate in the three-week treaty negotiation in Oslo. In a letter circulated to many governments, U.S. Secretary of State Madeleine Albright made it clear that the United States was seeking substantive changes. Specific proposed amendments included making a geographical exception of the Korean peninsula; changing the definition of antipersonnel mines; and extending the transitional period by requiring at least sixty countries, including all five permanent members of the Security Council and at least 75 percent of mine producers and users, to approve the treaty, or requiring an optional nine-year deferral period. Once the U.S. delegation joined the Oslo negotiations, Albright's letter made it plain that the delegation was "not in Oslo to negotiate a ban treaty but to bend the treaty to accommodate existing U.S. policy" and that its proposals were an integral package that could not be broken up into separate pieces.

The U.S. campaign denounced the fact that the United States had not taken any major steps to eliminate antipersonnel mines, unlike most of the other nations participating in the Ottawa Process. It also sent e-mail messages to ICBL members, alerting them of the serious consequences the U.S. decision could have on the treaty text, and it called for urgent collaboration in sending fax and e-mail messages to President Clinton. It also suggested that national campaigns around the globe try to meet the U.S. ambassadors in their countries and the national delegations attending the Oslo negotiations, to ensure that the integrity of the Ottawa Process not be compromised. The ICBL forwarded a letter to the core-group countries a day before their meeting with the U.S. delegation, in which it expressed its "extreme concern over the impact of the U.S. government's decision. . . . Regrettably, it is abundantly clear that the U.S. has not in any substantial way changed its policy. . . . Those who form the core of the Ottawa Process—as like-minded states which have come together to complete a true ban treaty in rapid fashion in response to a global humanitarian crisis—have a special responsibility to ensure that the integrity of such a treaty is maintained. . . . We urge you to send the unmistakable message to the U.S. government . . . that this is going to remain a ban treaty."[51]

The ICBL was not alone in its determination not to water down the treaty. Ambassador Jackie Selebi of South Africa, chairman of the diplomatic negotiations in Oslo, met NGO members before the beginning of formal negotiations. Indeed, the first people he met with after arriving in Oslo—except for the Norwegian hosts—were ICBL members, because "it was important to us that both governments and the NGOs demonstrate confidence in what we were doing." Selebi was well aware of how concerned NGOs were about the U.S. decision. He told ICBL members in the meeting on August 31, 1997, "[L]et us not start with suspicions. Let us work in such a way that we help each other to promote this cause."[52] Selebi met with ICBL members several times during the negotiations to keep them informed.

In addition to such informal consultations, the ICBL participated in the conference as a formal observer. This status did not allow voting, but the ICBL was able to intervene and make statements. Through its presence, the ICBL both kept itself informed about the negotiations and kept the pressure on the official delegations. These same points were true for some NGO members included in national delegations.

Diplomatic negotiations began on September 1, 1997, for what was scheduled to be a three-week process. Put simply, the negotiations in Oslo boiled down to a single factor: whether to insist on a total ban on antipersonnel land mines or to accommodate states not ready for a total ban. The existing framework, drafted during negotiations in Vienna and Bonn, called for a total ban, but a small but influential group of countries—mainly Australia, Japan, and the United States—introduced amendments and proposals that would have introduced loopholes.

Other countries—essentially those countries that supported the Ottawa Process from the initial stages—tried to develop a strong text that would establish a total ban. Members of this group developed "close working relationships with each other which provided solidarity, friendship and support for the individuals concerned in keeping their own governments on course as well as in building commitment by other governments to the achievement of the ban treaty."[53] A delegate from a middle-sized power noted that at one point, "I was more faithful to the core group countries than to my own ministry."[54] The solidarity of the core group was the key to maintaining the integrity of the treaty.

The procedures followed in Oslo were standard UN General Assembly rules, meaning that decisions could be made by a two-thirds majority vote if consensus could not be achieved. Consequently, the U.S. delegation needed to lobby countries within the larger group in order to win support. However, U.S. efforts proved to be unsuccessful, and it withdrew its proposals at the last minute. On September 18, 1997, the conference adopted the text without voting.

On December 2–4, 1997, 122 countries signed the treaty in Ottawa. Over 2,400 delegates, NGOs, and media gathered from over 150 countries. And on December 10, 1997, the 1997 Nobel Peace Prize was awarded to the ICBL and Jody Williams. The Nobel Committee noted that the Ottawa Process could be "a model for similar processes in the future," and that "it could prove of decisive importance to the international effort for disarmament and peace."[55] The ICBL called for a ratification contest, and on September 23, 1998, Burkina Faso deposited its instrument of agreement, becoming the fortieth state to do so. The treaty entered into force on March 1, 1999, just fourteen months after the signing ceremony in Ottawa.

Restructuring the Campaign: The Post-Ottawa Trials

The task of the ICBL is not over. The ultimate goal of the ICBL—the comprehensive banning of antipersonnel mines—will not be achieved until all mines are cleared from the soil and all mine victims are reintegrated into their societies. In the post-treaty period, the ICBL has undergone a structural change to keep the campaign sustainable. It adopted rules for voting on issues of importance, and Williams stepped down from her role as coordinator and was appointed an ICBL ambassador, along with Tun Channarethe and Rae McGrath.[56] Several working groups were established to concentrate on specific issues, such as widespread adherence to the treaty, victim assistance, mine clearance, legal cases against producers, and responsibility for cleanup.

One key challenge is monitoring treaty compliance. To strengthen independent monitoring mechanisms, the ICBL submitted its *Landmine Monitor Report: Toward a Mine-Free World* to the first meeting of state parties held in Maputo, Mozambique, in May 1999. With eighty researchers reporting on every country in the world, the 1,100-page report provided comprehensive information on mine use, production, trade, stockpiling, humanitarian issues, de-mining, and survivor assistance. It represented "the first time that non-governmental organizations and other elements of civil society are coming together in a coordinated, systematic and sustained way to monitor a humanitarian law or disarmament treaty, and to regularly document progress and problems."[57] The ICBL plans to publish this report annually.

One of the challenges lying ahead for the ICBL is universalizing the treaty. The ICBL is becoming increasingly global as it expands to new regions where national campaigns are nonexistent, including many nations in the former Soviet bloc, the Middle East, and Asia. These are regions where domestic civil society is not fully developed and is often left out of the international networks. Japan is one such society. The experience of the Japan Campaign to Ban Landmines (JCBL) supports the argument that the absence of mature domestic civil society limits the role NGOs such as the JCBL can play in a global agenda, particularly on security and disarmament issues. Nevertheless, this limitation also reinforces why civil society collaboration across borders is so important, because transnational networks can complement the limitations of the domestic civil society.

The Japanese Experience

On August 4, 1998, Toshihiro Shimizu, a member of the JCBL, received an unexpected phone call from Japanese Prime Minister Keizo Obuchi. The author of this chapter had an article published on the opinion page of the *Asahi Shimbun* that day, reminding the newly appointed prime minister of his responsibility to ratify the Ottawa Convention. At that point, thirty-five countries had ratified the treaty, and thirty-two of them had already deposited their instruments of accession with the United Nations. It was only a matter of time before the treaty would enter into force, and the JCBL felt that it was imperative for Japan to be one of the forty countries making the convention enter into force. Obuchi contacted the JCBL office immediately after reading the article to convey the message that his administration was putting the utmost effort into preparing domestic legislation for ratification at the earliest possible time.

The Japanese government initially planned not to sign the Ottawa Convention because a treaty "not joined by the big landmine states such as the United States, Russia, China and India is not realistic and enforceable."[58] However, in September 1997 Keizo Obuchi, then newly appointed as foreign minister, questioned the government's position when he said, "it is contradictory to contribute a large sum of money for mine clearance in Cambodia and refuse to sign the treaty."[59] Obuchi's statement became the turning point in Japan's policy on land mines. The statement surprised the public as well as government officials in Obuchi's own ministry, since it was made without going through the official ministerial review process. After nearly three months of consideration, the government decided to sign the treaty, and Obuchi himself flew to Ottawa to join the signing ceremony in December 1997.

The government's reversal resulted mainly from external pressures, such as the momentum created by the Ottawa Process, the death of Princess Diana, and the awarding of the Nobel Peace Prize to the ICBL. It had little to do with the role of domestic civil society. The Japanese government's turnaround was in response to pressure from transnational civil society and other international sources—dynamics from which Japan's own civil society, ironically, was absent.

Civil Society in Japan

The role of civil society organizations in the case of land-mine policy should be examined in the broader context of the role of NGOs and nonprofit organizations (NPOs) in Japan. The history of civil society institutions, particularly NGOs, began long after World War II. In 1960, only five organizations were identified as NGOs.[60] This number gradually increased with the rise of humanitarian organizations working in Indochinese refugee camps in the 1970s, but the total number remained under 100, and real growth waited another decade. The change came with the series of UN World Conferences, beginning with the UN Conference on Environment and Development (the Rio summit) in 1992. For this event, a number of NGOs organized themselves as a coalition group for the first time to lobby the government and took part in the NGO forum held parallel to the official UN summit. This was a real benchmark in the history of NGOs in Japan. Their short history and limited experience, as well as cultural factors such as the lack of language skills, had long hindered Japanese NGOs from being part of the international NGO community.[61]

Domestically, it took an earthquake to change attitudes and laws relating to NGOs and NPOs.[62] The Great Hanshin-Awaji earthquake in January 1995 claimed over 6,000 lives and became the turning point in Japanese civic activity. More than 1.3 million volunteers and a multitude of citizen organizations gathered to assist victims, and intense media coverage enabled the public to witness their dedicated work. In contrast, bureaucratic rules and regulations hampered the government's ability to act in the emergency, and the cumbersome bureaucratic procedures, formalities, and ministerial rivalries that dominate Japan's government were revealed to the world. A few weeks later, work began on new legislation to make it easier to incorporate as an NPO.[63] Up to that point, government agencies had complete discretion to approve or deny NGO incorporation, and applications were not even considered unless the proposed organization had assets of approximately 300 million yen and an annual budget of 30 million yen. After a long and heated debate in the Diet, the Law to Promote Specified Nonprofit Activities (the NPO law) was passed law in 1998, making incorporation much easier (although not yet providing tax incentives for contributions to NGOs).

Implications for the JCBL

The direct implication of the JCBL's not being incorporated is the same as for the 90 percent of Japanese NGOs that are not incorporated.[64] Such necessities as opening bank accounts, leasing copy machine and computers, and contracting telephone lines have to be done as individuals, not as an organization, making it necessary for groups to open new bank accounts or rerent equipment whenever an individual leaves the organization. And fund-raising is constrained. The JCBL has no access to official funds and is totally dependent on membership dues and charitable contributions from individuals to cover its project costs (all staff are volunteers). The JCBL raised over 10.9 million yen from July 1997 to June 1998, suggesting that it had gained certain public recognition in Japan. But the intake of funds decreased dramatically the following fiscal year due to declining public interest in the land-mine issue.

Undoubtedly, campaign activities have lagged behind those in Western nations. For example, there was no concerted effort to urge the government to participate in the Ottawa Process until the very last moment. The JCBL was launched in June 1997. Prior to that, a few NGOs had advocated the need for a land-mine ban, but their activities were sporadic and failed to generate public pressure. Yet the government's perception of the role of domestic civil society did shift as work progressed toward ratification of the treaty.

During the ratification campaign, the JCBL consciously began to work closely with the ICBL, relying on it for information about the progress of ratification and the means and costs of destroying stock-piled mines as mandated by the convention. Thus, the JCBL obtained credible new information well before government officials did, enabling the JCBL to pressure the government to take concrete action. The prime minister's telephone call to the JCBL—an unheard of gesture in Japan—demonstrated that the government could no longer ignore domestic civil society. Indeed, government officials testified in the Diet about the important role of transnational civil society in establishing the treaty, and they admitted that civil society organizations had been well ahead of them in obtaining up-to-date information.[65]

In the final moments before ratification, a high-ranking Ministry of Foreign Affairs official actually asked for JCBL collaboration in convincing opposition-party politicians not to obstruct the parliamentary hearing so that ratification could proceed smoothly. JCBL members were also given the official's mobile phone number so that they could exchange information on the minute-to-minute progress of the parliamentary deliberations. Ratification was completed on September 30, 1998, with Japan becoming the forty-third nation to ratify the convention.

Notwithstanding the domestic nature of civil society in Japan, the disadvantageous position of the JCBL has not completely undermined its activities. The lack of funds and official status has set limitations, but the power the JCBL gained through the transnational network outweighs such constraints. Both the transnational civil society and the domestic civil society, empowered by its affiliation to the international network, eventually influenced the government. The experience of the JCBL demonstrates that, although mature domestic civil society is vital for transnational civil society to function effectively, the very existence of transnational civil society can work to empower a domestic civil society.

A venture begun by two individuals from civil society developed into a movement that established a new international norm and produced a treaty that bans a weapon that was widely used by military forces throughout the world for decades. States such as China, Russia, and the United States argued repeatedly that a treaty not joined by problematic states, such as mine producers and exporters, was unacceptable, and even today they are seeking to establish a treaty banning the export of mines at the CD.

Notwithstanding these criticisms, the conclusion of the Ottawa treaty has made the world a better place. The nature of the land-mine problem demanded urgent action, and although a number of states— China, Russia, the United States, and others—remain outside the treaty framework, they have unilaterally instituted export moratoria. The United States has increased its funding for mine action programs, and Russia has demonstrated interest in signing the treaty.[66] Since the beginning of the Ottawa Process, 12 million mines have been destroyed, twelve countries have completely destroyed their mine arsenals, the number of countries producing antipersonnel mines has dropped to sixteen from fifty-four, and eleven major donor countries have initiated nearly 100 new mine action programs in twenty-five countries after the signing of the treaty.[67]

When the CCW failed to achieve a comprehensive ban, the ICBL quickly redirected its energy toward the Ottawa Process. ICBL members were also realistic enough to judge when compromise would be necessary to achieve its objective. In the final treaty negotiations in Oslo, the ICBL gave way on an issue such as antihandling devices. It also agreed to weaker provisions for treaty verification and compliance than it would have preferred, in order to get the largest possible number of countries to join in the ban treaty.

The ICBL made the negotiation process significantly more transparent. A few states included NGO representatives in their delegations;

this provided NGOs with detailed information on the development of negotiations and the ICBL with access to the most confidential questions addressed in closed diplomatic circles. ICBL members used such information to lobby delegates, send messages to colleagues waiting at home, and confer with the media. Modern technology and conventional communication styles facilitated the ICBL's dissemination of information and enabled campaign participants to take quick and coordinated action when necessary. At the same time, face-to-face communication built confidence and trust among campaign members. The ICBL deliberately held international conferences at different locations to produce opportunities to meet different people, expose varied audiences to its goal, and attract maximum media attention. The consistent flow of information kept the subject alive in many countries. Face-to-face communications also strengthened the sense of belonging, and the competitive spirit to excel in working toward a common goal among different national campaigns contributed, to some extent, to group cohesion.

The ICBL, as an amorphous network, never possessed a bank account or even a street address. Indeed, it was not an officially registered organization in any part of the world. It had never developed a coherent funding capacity or a central budgetary mechanism. Instead, each organization was responsible for raising its own funds, mostly from American and European foundations and regional organizations. ICBL staff members were not officially accountable to the ICBL, but rather to the NGOs that had hired them. Although there was a steering committee that made daily decisions, its responsibilities were largely logistical. Also, no single NGO played a determining role in the international campaign. There were particularly influential NGOs—those with financial resources or expertise—but none dominated the international campaign. All important decisions relating to campaign activities, tactics, and strategy were adopted at the general assembly that represented the national campaigns.

The very flexible nature of the network and the respect for national campaigns enabled the ICBL to exercise the kind of power it did as a transnational civil society in establishing a treaty, but the campaign also encountered some difficulties beneath the surface. In the early years, NGOs from mostly Western democratic countries that shared common values, interests, and political cultures represented the ICBL, but differences of opinion began to surface as it expanded to include over 1,000 NGOs from five continents. Sometimes personal disagreements and conflicts over campaign strategies threatened the cohesion of the network, as demonstrated by the widely publicized conflicts over the Nobel Peace Prize.

The ICBL established working relationships with a variety of actors —domestic politicians, several like-minded governments, and international organizations—in pursuit of the common goal of a ban treaty. All partners were vital, and the ICBL's work would have been severely restricted without any of them.

Partnership with the core group of countries provided the ICBL with specific contacts during the Ottawa Process to share the planning process for the political steps leading to the conclusion of the treaty. And "this way of working represented something qualitatively new in NGO/government relations in the evolution of international policy on arms-related issues."[68] It should be noted that it was the ICBL that helped bring about this core group by bringing pro-ban states together and creating an enabling environment for them to take concrete actions. Once these states were identified as a group, a sense of solidarity developed that proved vital to the achievement of a treaty free of loopholes.

Politicians often proved to be particularly sensitive to the demands of civil society. Senators in Belgium took the lead in preparing legislation, despite strong protests from the government. Senator Leahy in the United States took the first step to introduce the concept of an export moratorium to the world. Obuchi changed policy in Japan, and Axworthy committed to the Ottawa Process when he realized that there was enough support from transnational civil society. Axworthy summarized the changing role of civil society in the arena of new diplomacy as follows: "[O]ne can no longer relegate NGOs to simple advisory or advocacy roles in this process. They are now part of the way decisions have to be made. They have been the voice saying that governments belong to the people, and must respond to the people's hopes, demands and ideals."[69]

Jody Williams referred to civil society's changing role in the post–cold War era in this way: "They [governments] challenged the world to work openly with civil society, to perhaps show the world that we no longer had to see each other as adversaries, that actually governments and civil society should dialogue, that we actually are part of the same world community and should work together for change. . . . The post cold war world is different, and we have made it different, and we should be proud we are a super power."[70]

Notes

1. International Committee of the Red Cross (ICRC), *Anti-Personnel Landmines—Friend or Foe? A Study of the Military Use and Effectiveness of Anti-Personnel Mines* (Geneva: ICRC, 1996), p. 9.
2. Articles 51 and 35 of Protocol I (1977), Additional Protocol I to the Geneva Convention of 1949.
3. The Arms Project, a division of Human Rights Watch, and Physicians for Human Rights, *Landmines: A Deadly Legacy* (1993), p. 36.
4. U.S. State Department, *Hidden Killers: The Global Problem with Uncleared Landmines* (Washington, D.C.: U.S. State Department, 1993), pp. i, 3.
5. Thomas Gebauer, e-mail interview with the author, October 22, 1997.
6. Gebauer interview.
7. ICBL press release, October 2, 1992.
8. NGO Conference on Antipersonnel Mines, Closed Working Session minutes, p. 2.
9. Closed Working Session minutes, p. 2.
10. Closed Working Session minutes, p. 2.
11. Letter from Senator Patrick Leahy to HI, January 28, 1993.
12. Phillippe Chabasse and Jean-Baptiste Richardier, interview with the author, Lyon, May 12, 1997.
13. Phillippe Chabasse, "The French Campaign" in *To Walk without Fear*, ed. Maxwell A. Cameron et al. (Oxford: Oxford University Press, 1998), p. 61.
14. Forty-eighth session of the UN General Assembly, Resolution 48/679.
15. HI has offices in Lyon, Paris, Brussels, Geneva, and Minneapolis.
16. Senator Roger Lellemand, interview with the author, Brussels, May 15, 1997.
17. Verschvelen, interview with the author, Brussels, July 1, 1997.
18. Lellemand interview.
19. Senator Martine Dardenne, interview with the author, Brussels, May 1997.
20. Vincent Stanier, interview with the author, Brussels, April 30, 1997.
21. Pieter van Rossem, interview with the author, Utrecht, May 1, 1997.
22. Tony D'Costa, interview with the author, Dublin, June 21, 1999.
23. Celina Tuttle, interview with the author, Ottawa, May 5, 1997.
24. Rae McGrath, "Report to the 1998 Tokyo NGO Conference on Antipersonnel Landmines," p. 200.
25. Human Rights Watch Arms Project, "Exposing the Source," vol. 9, no. 2(G) (April 1997), p. 2.
26. "Exposing the Source," pp. 2–3, 4.

27. Boutros Boutros Ghali, UN General Assembly, 49th Session, A/49/357 and A/49/857/Add. 1.
28. Sadako Ogata, UNHCR, July 5–7, 1995.
29. Rae McGrath, on the definition of antipersonnel mines, March 18, 1997.
30. "CCW Failure Rate: 100%," *CCW News* (October 13, 1995).
31. Steve Goose, interview with the author, Washington, D.C., September 1997.
32. Van Rossem interview.
33. Katherine Coor, delegate from Ireland, interview with the author, June 26, 1997.
34. Although Canada was not officially invited, Bob Lawson had asked to attend the meeting out of interest.
35. E-mail from MAC to selected ICBL members, April 17, 1996.
36. David Atwood, interview with the author, Geneva, May 1997.
37. *CCW News* (Geneva edition) 12 (May 3, 1996): 2.
38. Boutros Boutros Ghali, May 3, 1996.
39. Lloyd Axworthy, Canadian minister of foreign affairs, October 5, 1997.
40. Article 2, Title I, Joint Action of October 1, 1996.
41. Article 3, Title I, Joint Action of October 1, 1996.
42. Brian Tomlin, "On a Fast Track to a Ban: The Canadian Policy Process," in *To Walk without Fear*, p. 202.
43. Ambassador Johan Molander, interview with the author, Stockholm, April 25, 1997.
44. Bob Lawson, interview with the author, Ottawa, May 6, 1997.
45. UN General Assembly, Resolution 51/54S.
46. Declaration of the Brussels Conference on Antipersonnel Landmines.
47. Jody Williams, opening statement to the Brussels Conference, June 24, 1997.
48. An official from the French Ministry of Foreign Affairs, interview with the author, Paris, September 1997.
49. Open letter to the president, April 1996.
50. President Bill Clinton, May 16, 1996.
51. ICBL letter to the core-group countries, cosigned by Jody Williams and Steve Goose, August 21, 1997.
52. Ambassador Jackie Selebi of South Africa, interview with the author, Geneva, October 20, 1997.
53. David Atwood, "Banning Landmines: Observations on the Role of Civil Society," paper prepared for the volume *Peace Politics of Civil Society*, June 1998, p. 10.
54. Interview with the author, Ottawa, December 5, 1998.
55. Nobel Peace Prize for 1997, Norwegian Nobel Institute, October 10, 1997.
56. Rae McGrath stepped down from this position in 1999.
57. Statement of the ICBL to the first meeting of state parties to the 1997 Mine Ban Treaty, delivered by Stephen Goose of HRW, head of the ICBL delegation, Maputo, Mozambique, May 4, 1999.
58. Statement by the Japanese delegation at the NGO briefing held during the Oslo conference, September 9, 1997.
59. The Japanese government has donated over $25 million for mine clearance and victim assistance through Overseas Development Assistance (*Asahi Shimbun*, September 19, 1997).

60. Japanese NGO Center for International Cooperation (JANIC), *NGO Data Book '96* [Japanese] (Tokyo: JANIC, 1996).

61. In fact, there are only fifteen NGOs with consultative status among the UN Economic and Social Council's 1,068 organizations (UN Press release ORG/1261, January 5, 1998). No Japanese NGO has a liaison office in either New York or Geneva.

62. In Japan, the term NGO refers to nonprofit organizations involved in overseas programs, and NPO refers to nonprofit organizations engaged in domestic activities. For the purpose of this chapter, both NGO and NPO refer generally to nongovernmental and nonprofit organizations.

63. For details of discussion on the NPO bill, refer to *Civil Society Monitor* vols. 1–4, Japan Center for International Exchange, at http://www.jcie.or.jp.

64. A survey conducted by JANIC in 1995 revealed that only 25 of 247 organizations had incorporated status (JANIC, *Data Book*).

65. The statements were made on several occasions during parliamentary hearing sessions by officials from the Ministry of Foreign Affairs Committee (House of Representatives Proceedings Report No. 5, September 25, 1998).

66. Russia expressed interest during the French-Russian bilateral negotiations, October 10, 1997.

67. For details, refer to the Landmine Monitor Report at http://www.icbl.org.

68. Atwood, "Banning Landmines," p. 10.

69. Address by Lloyd Axworthy, minister of foreign affairs, to the Oslo NGO Forum on Banning Antipersonnel Landmines, September 10, 1997.

70. Address by Jody Williams, coordinator of ICBL, to the Treaty Signing Conference and Mine Action Forum, December 3, 1997.

7

The Power of Norms versus the Norms of Power: Transnational Civil Society and Human Rights

Thomas Risse

Dictators on the Run?

IN OCTOBER 1998, a Spanish judge requested that Britain arrest and extradite to Spain the former Chilean dictator General Augusto Pinochet to stand trial for genocide, torture, and executions. During the 1970s, Pinochet had been responsible for some of the worst human rights abuses in the history of his country. When Chile returned to democracy in 1990, few perpetrators of human rights abuses were brought to justice. General Pinochet became a member for life of the Chilean Senate, enjoying diplomatic immunity as a former head of state. But are torture and genocide part of the job description for heads of states? The British lord judges who adjudicated the Spanish extradition request judged that Pinochet could be held accountable for torture and other abuses, but only those committed after Britain had ratified the United Nations (UN) Anti-Torture Convention.

In May 1998, Indonesia's President Suharto was forced to resign after more than thirty years of ruling his country. Most observers agreed that the Asian financial crisis, with its disastrous consequences for the Indonesian population, caused Suharto's loss of power. Widespread riots and looting, attacks on the economically powerful Chinese minority, and a crime rate that has spiraled out of control seem to corroborate this analysis. A closer look at the events in Indonesia reveals, however, that Suharto's resignation was only the culmination of a longer chain of events. East Timorese human rights activists had at least as much to do with Suharto's loss of power as brokers on Wall Street did.

What do Pinochet's arrest in London and Suharto's resignation in Jakarta portend? Are dictators on the run worldwide? Are human rights norms finally gaining ground against the interests of the powerful? And if changes really are occurring, who is responsible?

Even a superficial look at the annual reports of Amnesty International and other human rights organizations reveals that torture, disappearances, mass killings, and other atrocities have not yet substantially decreased worldwide. Although governments and other state agents may be less likely to commit human rights violations, there is an alarming rise of atrocities against human beings by nongovernmental groups such as terrorists, guerrilla movements, paramilitary and private security forces, and the like.

Nevertheless, real progress has occurred. States that want to be members of international society "in good standing" increasingly realize that they have to respect basic human rights and meet some minimum standards of behavior toward their citizens. Even China's leaders, not generally known for their concern about the rights of their citizens, recently asked the Japanese and German governments to advise them how to institute the rule of law. Fifty years after the UN General Assembly adopted the Universal Declaration of Human Rights, these norms have become standards of acceptable behavior in international society. Dictators can no longer claim "interference in internal affairs" when confronted with gross violations of human rights. This is a profound change in the underlying principles of international society.

And that progress is overwhelmingly due to the efforts of transnational civil society. Pinochet's arrest and Suharto's resignation would not have been possible without the decade-long struggles and the transnational mobilization of human rights activists around the globe and in the countries concerned. The norms these activists have created increasingly circumscribe the power of governments and have profoundly transformed our understanding of national sovereignty. International nongovernmental organizations (INGOs), churches, trade unions, and political foundations were all crucial in accomplishing two tasks. First, they helped to establish human rights standards firmly in international law and to create monitoring institutions such as the UN Commission for Human Rights. Second, they linked up with groups in the domestic civil societies of many norms-violating states to help bring about change in human rights behavior.

This chapter traces the evolution of transnational civil society in the human rights sector. It shows how the increased sophistication of international human rights law and international institutions and the growth of transnational civil society in this area went hand in hand. It also analyzes the effects of these transnational activities "on the ground," that is, achieving government compliance with human rights standards. The chapter concludes by evaluating the overall record of transnational civil society in the human rights area and laying out future challenges.

The chapter concentrates on a subset of international human rights norms, namely, civil and political rights enshrined in the 1976 Covenant for Civil and Political Rights, in particular the "freedom from" norms (freedom from torture, from detention without trial, from disappearances, and so forth). This focus is purely practical, with no implications that such rights are more important than other widely recognized rights such as social or economic ones. Rather, progress (or failure) regarding norm compliance is more easily measurable when it comes to these rights. Moreover, the mechanisms and dynamics of transnational mobilization identified in this chapter may well be generalizable across other human rights.

International Human Rights and the Mobilization of Transnational Civil Society

INGOs have long mobilized for human rights. Centuries before terms like "transnational civil society" entered the language of social scientists and political practitioners, similar movements were already active across societies.[1] Anglo-American campaigns to abolish slavery in the United States and to prohibit the international slave trade from the late eighteenth to mid-ninteenth centuries are among the earliest. The Anti-Slavery Society, founded in 1839, was probably the oldest human rights INGO.[2] From 1874 to 1911, Western missionaries, Victorian ladies in Great Britain, and Chinese reformers joined forces in the Natural Foot Society to fight the practice of foot binding in Imperial China. There is even a predecessor to recent campaigns against female genital mutilation (female circumcision). In the 1920s, the Church of Scotland Missionary Society led a transnational campaign against female circumcision among the Kikuyus in Kenya.

But these isolated campaigns do not compare either in quantity or in quality with what happened after World War II. Transnational civil society in the human rights area today encompasses not only a much larger variety of INGOs, such as Amnesty International, Human Rights Watch, and the International Commission of Jurists, but also churches, trade unions, peace movements, and foundations such as the Ford Foundation and the German Friedrich Ebert and Konrad Adenauer Foundations. Although the latter are not solely human rights groups, they often engage in promoting international human rights.

Starting near the end of World War II, these groups began to shape a broad range of human rights norms. At the Dumbarton Oaks conference in 1944, followed by the San Francisco conference that founded the United Nations in 1945, NGO lobbying was crucial in securing the inclusion of human rights in various articles of the UN Charter. NGO lobbyists worked hard to ensure that the UN Charter would contain provisions setting up a human rights commission, which was then specifically mandated in the charter. This Commission on Human Rights drafted the Universal Declaration of Human Rights, which the UN General Assembly adopted in December 1948. INGO input in this "Magna Charta of Human Rights" was significant.[3]

These documents, however, were essentially nonbinding declarations of intent. Few intergovernmental organizations (IGOs) specifically worked in this area, so no binding agreements were negotiated. The same holds true for regional agreements and organizations to protect human rights—with the significant exception of Western Europe, where the binding European Convention on Human Rights (including a Human Rights Court) came into force in 1953. In Latin America, the Organization of American States (OAS) established the Inter-American Commission on Human Rights in 1959, but this organization got legal "teeth" only when the American Convention on Human Rights went into force twenty years later. At the time, the INGO sector focusing exclusively on human rights was equally limited. In 1953, for example, only thirty-three human rights INGOs existed worldwide.[4]

In 1961, however, Peter Benenson, a British lawyer, and two colleagues founded Amnesty International. Benenson had read a newspaper article about two Portuguese who had been imprisoned because of a dinner conversation criticizing the Salazar dictatorship. He decided that something ought to be done to help these "prisoners of conscience." On May 28, 1961, the London-based *Observer* published his article "The Foreign Prisoner," which other newspapers around the world picked up immediately. Amnesty International was born. The organization quickly spread from Britain to the Federal Republic of Germany and then on to other Western European countries and the United States. In 1977, when Amnesty received the Nobel Peace Prize, it had 168,000 members in 107 countries. These members were mostly organized in local groups. Each would "adopt" three political prisoners, one each in a Western democratic, a communist, and a Third World country, and work for their release. This principle of balanced neutrality toward the various types of political regimes served to quickly establish the moral authority of Amnesty, together with its meticulous research and information-gathering activities.[5]

From the early 1970s on, the activities of transnational civil society in the human rights area grew dramatically. Seventy-nine human rights INGOs were active worldwide by 1983; this number more than doubled to 168 by 1993.[6] By 1999, Amnesty International alone had more than a million members in more than 160 states, even though half of its membership is concentrated in three countries, the United Kingdom, Germany, and the United States.[7] There are some 5,300 local Amnesty groups in more than ninety countries registered with the International Secretariat in London.

This explosion of activities emerged out of particular transnational campaigns against repressive regimes during the 1970s. Four such campaigns stand out. First, the Greek coup d'état in 1967 gave rise to human rights campaigns, particularly in Europe. When reports of widespread atrocities in Greek prisons became known, Amnesty International and others launched their first transnational campaign against torture, setting in motion a process that eventually led to the Anti-Torture Convention (see below).

Second, the repressive regime of Augusto Pinochet following his putsch against the democratically elected President Salvador Allende in 1973 led to the rise of a tremendous number of transnational activities, particularly in the United States, where the Nixon administration had actively supported Allende's overthrow. From 1974 to 1976, the U.S. section of Amnesty expanded from 3,000 to 50,000 members. Human rights organizations emerged everywhere in Latin America.[8]

Third, the antiapartheid campaign against South Africa spawned a vast number of transnational efforts.[9] The Soweto massacre in June 1976, during which police killed sixty-nine students during a demonstration, led to an international outcry against the apartheid regime. The antiapartheid movement soon became one of the most powerful campaigns in transnational civil society. Its claims resonated particularly well with and were able to "transnationalize" the demands of the civil rights movement in the United States of the 1960s.

The repressive regimes in these three regions of the world, which gave rise to the mobilization of so many people, did not commit particularly awesome crimes against humanity, at least as compared with other oppressive governments. At about the same time during the 1970s, Uganda's dictator Idi Amin ordered the systematic killing of supporters and tribal kinsmen of his predecessor, Milton Obote. He nearly committed a genocide against his own people—resulting in far less international mobilization. What Greece, Chile, and South Africa had in common, though, is the fact that the repressive regimes had either replaced democratic governments or—as in the case of South Africa—claimed to be a liberal democracy even though political rights were confined to the white minority. Thus, it was the gap between proclaimed liberal values and actual behavior that mobilized transnational civil society.

Last but not least came the 1975 Helsinki Final Act of the Conference on Security and Cooperation in Europe (CSCE). On Western European insistence, over the objections of both the United States and the Soviet Union, it included a human rights provision. The Helsinki human rights standard provided dissidents in communist Eastern Europe and the Soviet Union with a powerful tool against their regimes and had a dramatic effect on the rise of dissident movements in Eastern Europe and the former Soviet Union. Soviet and East European citizens learned quickly about the content of the Helsinki agreement through word of mouth, samizdat publications, and Western media. In May 1976, Soviet dissidents founded the Helsinki Watch Group; the Charter 77 movement was born in Czechoslovakia on January 1, 1977. Each of these and other groups legitimized their demands through reference to the Helsinki human rights document that their communist governments had signed. They then linked up with human rights organizations in Western states and in transnational civil society and provided them with regular updates on repression in the Soviet Union and Eastern Europe. As a result, human rights concerns became a regular feature of the CSCE follow-on meetings in Belgrade (1977–78) and Madrid (1980–83). Thus, the "Helsinki effect" led to substantial human rights mobilization in Eastern Europe, and this mobilization contributed significantly to the fall of the Berlin Wall and the end of the Cold War in 1989.[10]

The ordeal of the dissident groups in Eastern Europe and the Soviet Union also led in 1978 to the creation of Helsinki Watch, an American NGO. Arthur Goldberg, former Supreme Court justice and U.S. representative at one of the CSCE follow-on conferences, was concerned about the limited media coverage of human rights violations in the communist bloc and convinced the Ford Foundation to become active in this area. The president of the Ford Foundation approached Robert Bernstein, an activist among American publishers, to start a human rights campaign focusing on communist Eastern Europe and the Soviet Union. Bernstein founded Helsinki Watch in the United States—alluding to the Moscow group with the same name. Although Helsinki Watch originated from the initiative of a U.S. government official, it quickly asserted its independence. In 1981, Bernstein founded America Watch to investigate human rights abuses by right-wing dictatorships in Latin America that were supported by the Reagan administration. Over the next years, Bernstein and others created more regional "watchdog" organizations, such as Africa Watch and Asia Watch. Ten years later, Human Rights Watch (HRW) became the umbrella organization of the regional watchdogs and a main competitor as well as ally of Amnesty International among human rights INGOs. Although HRW originated as a U.S.-based organization, it mushroomed into a truly global INGO during the 1990s.[11]

At the same time that transnational civil society was mobilizing in these campaigns, it was also benefiting from the emergence of international legal standards that went beyond the broad goals of the Universal Declaration. In 1976, the Covenant for Civil and Political Rights, as well as the Covenant for Economic and Social Rights went into force. During the same year, the New York–based UN Human Rights Committee started its activities.

The strengthening of the international legal framework for human rights protection directly affected the growth of INGOs and other groups operating in transnational civil society. It did so through the authority of international law as opposed to just moral convictions. There is quite a difference between, say, arguing that female circumcision constitutes an immoral atrocity against human dignity and the right to one's own sexuality, on the one hand, and being able to pinpoint an international legal prohibition against genital mutilation, on the other. In the latter case, advocacy groups not only have a moral case against the particular human rights violation; they can also argue that the norm violator puts itself outside the community of civilized nations and often is violating standards it has agreed to.

The other side of this coin concerns the influence of transnational civil society on the creation of these norms themselves. As argued earlier, INGO activities during the 1940s had a significant impact on the UN Charter and the Universal Declaration of Human Rights. In the absence of sustained campaigns and lobbying efforts by INGOs and particular individuals, probably not a single human right would have been written into international law. The history of the 1984 UN Convention against Torture and Other Cruel, Inhuman, or Degrading Treatment or Punishment provides an instructive example.[12] It began with the 1967 Greek colonels' putsch against the democratically elected government in Athens. Amnesty International, together with several Scandinavian countries, accused the junta of torture and other violations of human rights and brought the case to the attention of the European Human Rights Convention and its organs. At the time, this convention contained the only legally binding provision against torture worldwide. The Greek case triggered worldwide protests, as a result of which Amnesty International decided to launch a global campaign against torture in 1972. Sweden, the Netherlands, Austria, Costa Rica, and others then used the Amnesty campaign to raise the issue of torture in the UN General Assembly one year later. The Chilean coup d'état only added oil to the fire of the antitorture campaign. In 1974, the

General Assembly mandated that experts begin working on a declaration against torture.

Amnesty and other INGOs started petition campaigns and mobilized public opinion to influence the attitude of their national governments. Amnesty's peculiar structure of national sections together with an international secretariat was helpful in organizing this campaign. The experts' draft, considerably influenced by lawyers working for Amnesty, became the basis for negotiations in the UN Human Rights Commission on an antitorture convention.

Various governments, including the Netherlands, France, and Australia, rejected some of the legally binding provisions as intrusions into their national sovereignty. At this point, Amnesty and other INGOs not only worked closely with the UN Human Rights Commission to influence the drafting of the convention but also increasingly lobbied national governments. This campaign concentrated on the weakest link in the chain of Western resistance to the convention— the Netherlands. Amnesty's ability to act both globally as an INGO and simultaneously through its national chapters greatly facilitated carrying out parallel global and national campaigns. When the Dutch government changed its position in 1980, Amnesty successfully persuaded the French and Australian governments to change course too. In December 1984, ten years after its first activities on the issue, the UN General Assembly passed the Anti-Torture Convention. It went into force in 1987.[13]

This case in many ways typifies how transnational civil society goes about creating international norms. First, Amnesty International and other groups were decisive in putting the question of torture on the international agenda. Such agenda setting is quite common. Recent examples concern the rights of indigenous peoples and women's rights.[14]

Second, nongovernmental actors participated in the negotiations and working groups drafting the international agreements, both indirectly as members of expert groups and directly as members of official national delegations. In other words, transnational civil society is involved in treaty making. In this role, INGOs are not necessarily opposing national governments. Rather, groups of states are closely cooperating with INGOs and relying on their expertise and knowledge. In the case of the Anti-Torture Convention, national governments such as

Sweden worked closely with Amnesty and aligned with INGOs against other groups of states.

Third, transnational civil society does not operate solely within the frameworks provided by international organizations such as the UN. Rather, the effectiveness of human rights INGOs depends on their grounding in domestic civil societies. The successful conclusion of the Anti-Torture Convention was possible because Amnesty and other INGOs sat in the negotiating chambers and, at the same time, their activists lobbied local, regional, and national communities to become active toward their national governments.

Finally, the case demonstrates the power resources available to transnational civil society. By any material standard, transnational civil society is weak. There is no antitorture army and no wealthy human rights multinational corporation. Amnesty, the giant among the human rights INGOs, has an annual budget of about $29 million.[15] A survey of NGOs working in the human rights area identified financial limitations as by far the most significant organizational obstacle facing transnational civil society in this area.[16] The mean annual budget of human rights NGOs was $ 1.6 million, with a huge gap between the annual revenues of Northern and Southern NGOs (average income of the latter was $400,000).

The influence of transnational civil society in the human rights area stems from the power of moral authority and legitimacy, on the one hand, and the accepted claim to authoritative knowledge, on the other. These two aspects—moral authority and knowledge—go together and cannot be separated.

Moral authority is directly related to the claim by transnational civil society that it somehow represents the "public interest" or the "common good" rather than private interests. This is a crucial condition. INGOs can quickly lose their credibility if they become identified with some special economic or political interests. It took HRW quite a while, for instance, to lose its initial reputation as an instrument of U.S. human rights policy. The ability to act as credible speakers for the oppressed with no other concern than to promote their inalienable rights is what makes the transnational human rights organizations so powerful, even if compared with and pitched against major states or private firms.

This rather idealist picture must be tempered somewhat. Human rights belong to the core identity of the community of liberal and democratic states, which also happen to be the most powerful states in terms of economic and other resources. Although human rights INGOs do not simply represent Western interests (they have been fighting Western policies for too long for such a claim to be credible), their moral authority is not totally disconnected from political, economic, and even military power in the global system.

Even so, moral authority by itself does not explain the impact of transnational civil society in human rights. It goes hand in hand with a widely accepted claim to knowledge. Today, Amnesty International, HRW, and the Lawyers Committee for Human Rights *define* what constitutes a human rights violation. Other groups, INGOs, and even states might provide the information and disseminate it. But only if Amnesty, HRW, or the Lawyers Committee "approves" of this information as being correct does this constitute a human rights violation in the eyes of the international community. Many Western governments, including the United States and Germany, often use information provided by Amnesty or HRW almost verbatim when they write their own human rights reports.[17]

The authoritative claim to knowledge enjoyed by INGOs today did not fall from heaven. Very strict information-gathering rules were necessary to establish such credibility. Amnesty International, for example, uses only information that at least three independent sources have corroborated. Moreover, while information gathering itself may be decentralized, Amnesty headquarters in London strictly controls the spread of news about particular rights violations in a given country. HRW uses similar rules of information gathering, but its use of the information in particular campaigns appears to be more strategic and more strongly geared toward raising media attention.

INGOs can then use their moral authority and their information to convince other actors—particularly governments and international organizations, but also the general public in many countries—that they have an obligation to act. When dealing with Western states, they usually remind these governments that liberal democracies, by definition, are supposed to be concerned with protecting human rights and the rule of law. In a liberal democratic state, why would a government place national sovereignty, economic gains, or strategic interests over human rights? Shaming strategies are used to highlight the gap between a country's proclaimed liberal identity, on the one hand, and its unwillingness to conduct its foreign policy accordingly, on the other.[18]

INGOs also rely on shaming when dealing with human rights–violating governments. Shaming in such a case serves the purpose of putting the government on notice that its actions place it outside the international community. In the South African case, for example, the transnational campaign against apartheid portrayed the country as a pariah state outside the community of "civilized" nations.[19] Some repressive governments might not care. Others, however, are deeply offended, because they want to belong to the "civilized community" of states. In many cases, leaders of countries care what leaders of other countries think of them. Shaming implies a process of persuasion, since it convinces leaders that their behavior is inconsistent with an identity to which they aspire. When transnational civil society accused Moroccan King Hassan II of serious human rights abuses in 1990, for example, he felt insulted, since the national identity of Morocco was at stake: "Our history, thanks to the creative spirit which illustrates a large contribution to the sciences, the arts, to civilization, and to the law, shows that our country has always seen itself as living in a civilized society next to the developed states and nations."[20]

Ultimately, then, human rights norms, and the transnational civil society agents that promote those norms, have become such powerful devices in international relations because they help define a category of states—"liberal states." Sovereignty has always depended on mutual recognition. Now, to be recognized as a state in good standing is moving beyond the old standard of effective and exclusive control of territory. In some cases, these liberal "clubs" are quite specific—in the case of the European Union, for example, only democratic states with good human rights records can join the club. In the inter-American system, such norms are just now emerging. The OAS Managua Declaration of 1993, for example, includes explicit statements about what kind of states are welcome in the club. The OAS members declare "the need to consolidate, as part of the cultural identity of each nation in the Hemisphere, democratic structures and systems which encourage freedom and social justice, safeguard human rights, and favor progress."[21]

Norm Spirals and Boomerangs: The Domestic Impact of Transnational Civil Society

Is the international human rights talk just cheap talk? What about the continual atrocities and human rights violations all over the world, as reported in the yearly statements of Amnesty International, the U.S. Department of State, and other monitoring institutions? What about the contribution of transnational civil society and its norm-creating activities on the ground, that is, in the domestic implementation of human rights standards?[22]

To estimate that impact, the study on which this chapter is based looked at paired cases of countries with serious human rights situations from five regions of the world—northern Africa, sub-Saharan Africa, Southeast Asia, Latin America, and Eastern Europe. In addition to the well-publicized "success stories" such as Chile, South Africa, the Philippines, Poland, and the former Czechoslovakia, we examined a series of more obscure and apparently intractable cases such as Guatemala, Kenya, Uganda, Morocco, Tunisia, and Indonesia. We explored the influence that transnational mobilization and campaigns had in a wide variety of states with very different cultures and institutions. On the basis of these country cases, we developed a dynamic model of human rights changes that links international law and the mobilization efforts of transnational civil society to opposition and dissident activities in the domestic societies of norm-violating countries.

Various studies on the impact of human rights norms in Latin America have emphasized how domestic and transnational social movements have united to bring pressure "from above" and "from below" to compel governments to abide by human rights standards. Margaret Keck and Kathryn Sikkink referred to this process as the "boomerang effect."[23] A boomerang pattern of influence exists when domestic groups in a repressive state bypass their government and directly search out international allies to bring pressure on their states from outside. National opposition groups, NGOs, and social movements link with foreign members of the transnational network, which then convince international organizations, donor institutions, or great powers to put pressure on norm-violating states. Transnationally operating INGOs provide access, leverage, information, and often money to struggling domestic groups. International contacts "amplify" the demands of domestic groups, pry open space for new issues, and then echo these demands back into the domestic arena (see figure 7.1).

To understand the full dynamics of transnational civil society in ensuring the implementation of human rights, we have to go beyond this boomerang model, which shows static snapshots of the linkages among local and transnational actors. In reality, the evolution of human rights practices resembles not a single boomerang throw but a whole spiral of boomerangs repeatedly crossing national borders. This dynamic approach reveals how governments are likely to respond to transnational pressures, what can be expected at various stages, and, most important, why transnational civil society is essential to bring-

FIGURE 7.1   THE BOOMERANG EFFECT

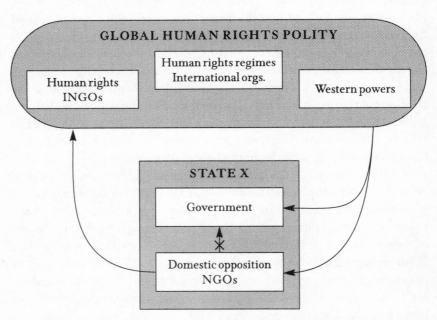

Source: From Thomas Risse and Kathryn Sikkink, "The Socialization of Human Rights Norms into Domestic Practices: Introduction," in *The Power of Human Rights: International Norms and Domestic Change*, ed. Thomas Risse et al. (Cambridge: Cambridge University Press, 1999), p. 19.

ing about change in national human rights practices. In short, the spiral keeps spiraling only if transnational civil society makes it happen (see figure 7.2).

The spiral is a dance with many partners: transnational civil society (composed of INGOs, churches, trade unions, political foundations, and the like) loosely connected to officials working for intergovernmental organizations or for national governments. The international institutions are primarily the human rights bodies of the UN and the various human rights treaties that have been drafted and ratified under UN auspices, but they also include some regional institutions, such as the Inter-American Commission and Court of Human Rights.

Phase I: Repression and Activation of Transnational Civil Society

The spiral starts with a repressive situation in some country—the target. Struggles over political power are almost always the main reason for human rights abuses by repressive governments. In the Philippines, for example, President Marcos proclaimed martial law in 1972 to get rid of domestic armed opposition. Tens of thousands of Filipinos were arrested and tortured.[24] In Indonesia (1965), Morocco (1971–72), and Kenya (1982), repressive regimes committed human rights abuses to fight off coups d'état. The levels of repression vary greatly among countries, from extreme repression bordering on genocide (as in the cases of Uganda and Guatemala) to much lower levels of repression (as in the case of Tunisia).[25] This phase of repression might last for decades, since many oppressive states never make it onto the agenda of transnational civil society. Unfortunately, the degree of repression may even determine whether transnational INGOs can acquire information about human rights conditions in a country. When the genocide in Rwanda took place in 1994, for example, information gathering was next to impossible, since all humanitarian organizations had fled. In the case of the Chilean coup d'état in 1973, however, it took Amnesty International and the International Commission of Jurists just three days to send a cable to the OAS's Inter-American Commission on Human Rights requesting its intervention.[26] In Indonesia, a small legal foundation started operating in 1971 and then began exchanging

FIGURE 7.2   THE SPIRAL MODEL OF HUMAN RIGHTS CHANGE

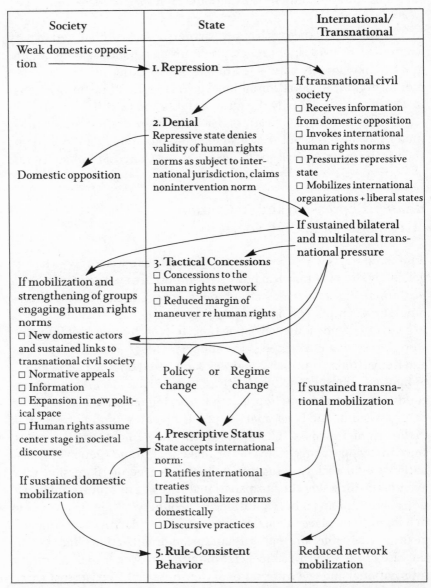

Source: Modified from Thomas Risse and Kathryn Sikkink, "The Socialization of Human Rights Norms into Domestic Practices: Introduction," in *The Power of Human Rights: International Norms and Domestic Change*, ed. Thomas Risse et al. (Cambridge: Cambridge University Press, 1999), p. 20, fig. 1.3.

information with Amnesty, the International Commission of Jurists, and others, thus throwing a first boomerang and linking with transnational civil society.[27] At this stage, transnational mobilization is a necessary condition for moving the process further.

Phase 2: Norms Denial

The second phase of the spiral puts the norm-violating state on the international agenda, almost always through the efforts of transnational civil society. Human rights violations in South Africa during the 1960s and 1970s, and in Chile and the Philippines during the 1970s, created an environment in which such consciousness-raising could take place and were thus crucial for the emergence of transnational civil society in the human rights area. These transnational groups could then be reactivated during the early 1980s, when they started lobbying Western powers and international organizations. Even in Poland and Czechoslovakia, where repression under communism had always been a concern for Western governments, it was transnational pressure that put human rights on the Western agenda in the late 1970s.[28] Helsinki Watch, among others, amplified the concerns of dissidents in Eastern Europe and the Soviet Union toward Western public opinion.

The initial activation of transnational civil society often results from a particularly awful violation of human rights, such as a massacre. When news about systematic torture and the disappearance of many opposition leaders reached the West after Pinochet's coup in 1973, transnational civil society quickly mobilized.[29] INGOs usually compile and disseminate information about human rights practices, often with the cooperation of human rights organizations in the repressive state. In the Chilean case, for example, the Catholic Church and its Vicariate of Solidarity provided the crucial link between national human rights organizations and transnational civil society. The transnational groups then start lobbying intergovernmental human rights organizations as well as Western states, where they target both public opinion and national governments. These lobbying activities might lead to some pressure on the repressive government to improve its human rights conditions.

Norm violators almost always react by denying the initial charges of human rights abuses. Denial goes further than simply objecting to particular accusations. The norm-violating government claims that the criticism constitutes an illegitimate intervention in the internal affairs of the country. For years, the communist regimes in Eastern Europe argued that Western accusations of human rights abuses constituted an intervention in internal affairs, even after the Helsinki accords had come into effect.[30] The government may even succeed in mobilizing some nationalist sentiment against foreign intervention and criticism. Kenya's arap Moi and Indonesia's Suharto used similar anticolonial rhetoric to reject charges of human rights violations made by Amnesty International. As a quasi-official Indonesian statement put it in 1978, "Amnesty still suffers from a 'moral arrogance' of the West which has been deplored by the Third World at large . . . [A]ll their efforts and objectives will be just counterproductive."[31]

Thus, the first boomerang throw often appears to be counterproductive, because it allows the repressive regime to solidify domestic support. The presence of a significant armed insurgent movement can dramatically extend this stage by heightening domestic perceptions of threat and fear. Any success of insurgent movements appears to validate the government's claim that the order or the very integrity of the nation is at stake, and it isolates domestic human rights organizations and international pressures by identifying these groups as conscious or unconscious accomplices of terrorism. But governments that publicly deny the authority of international human rights law as interference in internal affairs are at least implicitly aware that they face a problem in terms of their international reputation.

The denial stage can last for quite a long time. Some repressive governments care little about international pressures. They might also kill off or buy off the domestic opposition while it is still too weak to mount a major challenge to the regime. Therefore, the transition to the third phase constitutes the biggest challenge. This transition depends primarily on the strength of transnational mobilization in conjunction with the vulnerability of the norm-violating government to international pressures.[32] Almost all human rights campaigns involve particular kinds of material pressures, for example, when foreign aid becomes conditional on human rights performance. But the vulnerability of repressive governments may also come from a country's tradition of accepting normative commitments. Chile's Pinochet, for example, never denied the validity of international human rights norms. Given Chile's democratic tradition, he could not simply claim the principle of noninterference. Pinochet even accepted visits by the Inter-American Commission on Human Rights and by Amnesty International, while he continued to torture political prisoners.[33]

In the Indonesian case, the local Catholic church gathered most of the information on human rights abuses in East Timor and disseminated it abroad via organizations such as Pax Christi (a Catholic peace movement) and Asia Watch. This information then reached various UN bodies as well as the Non-Aligned Movement. At the same time, transnational civil society managed to activate members of the U.S. Congress and the European Parliament on the situation in Indonesia. When the UN Commission on Human Rights started criticizing the Indonesian government in the mid-1980s, the government responded by opening the previously closed province to outside observers. This tactical concession backfired, because more information about human rights abuses reached the international community, and transnational civil society disseminated it widely. The turning point was reached in 1991. When the UN special rapporteur on torture visited Dili, East Timor, he witnessed a massacre of civilians who had peacefully demonstrated against the regime. The Dili massacre, immediately reported by the international media, mobilized transnational civil society in a comprehensive way against human rights abuses of the Suharto regime. International and domestic NGOs now changed course and brought together the previously unrelated activities of the East Timorese networks and human rights groups in Indonesia proper. Responding to INGO pressure, Canada, Denmark, and the Netherlands froze their economic aid to Indonesia, while the United States, Japan, and the World Bank threatened to do so. The international reaction to the Dili massacre moved Indonesia toward the next phase in the process.[34]

Phase 3: Tactical Concessions

If transnational civil society manages to escalate the pressures, the norm-violating state is likely to seek to pacify international criticism. At this point, the repressive government makes concessions to regain military or economic assistance or to lessen international isolation.

Although the government might then temporarily improve the situation—for example, by releasing prisoners—human rights conditions do not improve all that much. The more sustained period of international concerns, however, allows the initial "rally around the flag" effect to wear off. The minor improvements give the repressed domestic opposition new courage and space to mount its own campaign of criticism against the government.

In case after case, transnational pressure turns out to be the single most important cause of change toward initial concessions by the norm-violating government, even more important than pressure from other governments. In some cases—Indonesia, Kenya, Guatemala, Chile, and (to a lesser extent) the Philippines—the advocacy coalitions managed to convince some Western governments to institute sanctions, which can help but are not always needed. In the South African case, which entered the tactical concessions stage after the Soweto massacre in 1976, international sanctions emerged only gradually in response to the massacre and were not fully effective until the mid-1980s.[35]

Developments in Indonesia provide a good example of the dynamics of this phase.[36] In response to the international outcry following the 1991 Dili massacre, President Suharto speedily appointed a National Investigating Commission, which, surprisingly, issued a rather critical report of the events. This concession accomplished its goal in the sense that foreign donors resumed economic aid to Indonesia. But Suharto was no longer in control of the situation. INGOs worked hard to bring together the previously disconnected domestic human rights groups in East Timor and in Indonesia proper. They did so by convincing East Timorese leaders that they should focus on human rights violations rather than the question of self-determination. In the early 1990s, "human rights" proved to be an effective rallying cry, both unifying the domestic opposition and ensuring broader international support for its goals. The Indonesian opposition then used human rights violations in East Timor to criticize repressive practices of the Suharto regime in general. As East Timorese opposition leader and 1996 Nobel Peace Prize winner José Ramos-Horta put it, "the fate of East Timor and the democracy movement in Indonesia are intimately linked, each supports the other.... The more pressure that is focused on Suharto about East Timor, the more space there is for the opposition to push for change in Indonesia."[37] Suharto's tactical concessions opened political space for civil society in Indonesia to mobilize. In 1992, and again with the help of resources provided by transnational civil society, activists founded independent trade unions, an association of journalists, and new political parties tolerated by the regime. In 1993, the (International) Lawyers' Committee for Human Rights published a special report on Indonesia, "Broken Laws, Broken Bodies," condemning the widespread practices of torture. In March of the same year, the UN Human Rights Commission adopted a critical resolution that was supported by the U.S. government. In response to the increasing domestic and transnational pressures, and anticipating criticism of his country at the upcoming World Conference on Human Rights in Vienna, Suharto instituted a national human rights commission in 1993 that published rather critical reports. This move, of course, legitimized human rights claims of the opposition even further. In 1996, the human rights causes in East Timor and Indonesia in general gained further international legitimacy when Ramos-Horta and Bishop Ximenes Belo received the Nobel Peace Price. By then, transnational civil society mobilization had succeeded in changing Indonesia's international image from that of a stable and reliable power in East Asia to that of a corrupt and oppressive dictatorship.

Yet human rights conditions in Indonesia did not improve. On the contrary, the Suharto government combined tactical concessions to relieve the pressure with continual crackdowns against the opposition. But the regime had long since lost control over the domestic situation, which became obvious when the economic crisis hit the country in late 1997. Since transnational civil society and the domestic opposition had successfully damaged Suharto's reputation—pointing to the lack of public accountability, systematic human rights violations, and widespread corruption—the crisis gained a different meaning than in Thailand or South Korea. It served as a catalyst for change, and mass protests ultimately led to Suharto's resignation in June 1998. Although the political situation in Indonesia is far from stable, it is quite remarkable that President Jusuf Habibie, Suharto's successor, continued on the path to establish the rule of law in the country. The fierce power struggle between the Indonesian military and the civilian leadership is far from over and has resulted in atrocious human rights abuses in East Timor (which is now de facto an international protectorate) and elsewhere in the country. Yet Indonesia's new president, Abdurrahman Wahid, has proceeded with the human rights policies of his predecessor.

198 | THE THIRD FORCE

There is remarkable similarity between the processes of change in Indonesia and events in totally different corners of the world during the phase of tactical concessions. Morocco, Kenya, South Africa, Guatemala, Chile, the Philippines, Poland, and former Czechoslovakia all experienced stages whereby transnational and domestic civil society aligned and put the repressive regimes under increasing pressure. Almost always, norm-violating governments responded with a combination of tactical concessions and continued repression. Almost always, they lost control over the domestic situation. They then faced two choices: change or run. Among the eleven countries investigated for this study, only the late Moroccan king picked the first choice and embarked on a process of sustained political liberalization. Today, the Islamic monarchy of Morocco is the most liberal state in the Maghreb region. In most other cases, human rights violators eventually had to go (though sometimes through negotiated transitions), as in South Africa, many Latin American countries, and Eastern Europe.

The most important effect of transnational mobilization against a determined government is not so much to change the behavior of the government but to facilitate social mobilization in the domestic arena of the repressive state. The focus of activities is now likely to shift from the transnational to the domestic level. Transnational mobilization in this stage empowers and legitimates the demands of the domestic opposition. It also protects the physical safety of many activists on the ground. It accomplishes these goals by:

- Spreading information about the domestic situation in the country around the globe.

- Lobbying key Western governments, parliaments, and international organizations to toughen their stance toward the norm-violating government.

- Providing financial resources and training in human rights issues to domestic NGOs and other opposition groups.

- Confronting the norm-violating government in a continuous debate regarding its human rights practices.

This is the most precarious phase of the spiral model. It moves the process forward toward enduring change in human rights conditions only if domestic opposition and civil society are able to use the boomerang provided by the transnational coalitions to mobilize inside the country. If a government responds with unrelenting repression of activists, it can temporarily break the upward spiral process. At the beginning of phase 3, the domestic human rights movements are often small and dependent on a handful of key leaders. Arresting or killing these leaders decapitates the movement, and the resulting fear paralyzes it. This is what happened during the 1989 demonstrations in Tiananmen Square in Beijing. But the additional repression is costly to the government in terms of its domestic legitimacy, and it may validate international criticism by revealing more clearly the coercive power of the state.

If the cycle is not delayed, the domestic opposition is likely to gain strength. The fully mobilized domestic NGO networks, linked to the global human rights coalitions, can be activated at any time. Toward the end of the tactical concession phase, norm-violating governments are no longer in control of the domestic situation.

Phase 4: Prescriptive Status

We reach the fourth phase of the spiral if and when national governments completely accept the moral validity of human rights norms and start institutionalizing the norms in the domestic legal context. The binding nature of human rights norms is no longer controversial, even if the actual behavior continues violating the rules. The process by which human rights ideas gain prescriptive status is decisive for their sustained impact on political and social change. Governments accept the validity of human rights norms if and when:

- They ratify the various international human rights conventions, including the optional protocols.

- They institutionalize the norms in the constitution or domestic law.

- They create an independent commission or provide some mechanism for individual citizens to complain about human rights violations.

- They publicly acknowledge the validity of the human rights norms irrespective of the (domestic or international) audience, no longer denounce criticism as interference in internal affairs, and engage in a dialogue with their critics.

Governments reach this stage after they have been confronted by fully mobilized domestic opposition groups and transnational INGO coalitions. At this point, either liberalization from above or a regime change is likely to occur. The move toward enduring human rights improvements in Poland, Czechoslovakia, South Africa, Chile, Guatemala, the Philippines, Indonesia, and Morocco resulted from the pressures of a full-fledged and well-organized domestic opposition linked with transnational civil society. In the cases of South Africa, Chile, Guatemala, the Philippines, and Indonesia, Western powers and major allies of the respective states finally joined the INGOs in their opposition against the norm-violating regimes and helped to move them "over the top." But they almost always followed rather than led the opposition. The Reagan administration ceased supporting the Marcos regime only when it had convinced itself that Marcos would be toppled anyway. The same holds true for the Clinton administration's decision ten years later to stop cooperating with Suharto one day before he resigned.[38] In other words, it is the interaction between transnational civil society and domestic opposition groups that brings countries to the phase of prescriptive status, rather than the (usually minimal) pressures exerted by Western governments or international organizations.

Uganda, the Philippines, and South Africa reached full prescriptive status immediately after the regime change, when the new governments began ratifying international agreements, institutionalizing them into domestic law, and fully embracing human rights norms in their communicative behavior. In Uganda, for example, the National Resistance Movement under the leadership of Yoweri Museveni took over power and ousted the Obote regime in 1986.[39] The new government immediately ratified the various international human rights conventions and transposed its provisions into domestic law, particularly the prohibition against torture. The government also established two procedures for individual complaints by citizens. In 1995, the new constitution instituted the Uganda Human Rights Commission with far-reaching legal competences. It has regularly issued reports on the Ugandan human rights situation that criticized the government. In 1997 alone, the commission dealt with more than 350 individual complaints.

Ratification of this or that international human rights agreement may constitute a tactical concession rather than the full acceptance of its precise normative content. Nevertheless, empirical case studies provide ample evidence that the acceptance of international norms through treaty ratification is not inconsequential. Governments entangle themselves in an international and domestic legal process that they subsequently find harder and harder to escape. The Helsinki human rights norm and its consequences for domestic change in Eastern Europe are a particularly striking example.[40] This process of rhetorical "self-entrapment" usually begins when a government is forced to make tactical concessions. Over time, however, a true dialogue frequently develops about concrete improvements in human rights conditions on the ground involving transnational civil society, international organizations, domestic groups, and the government of the target state.

The notion of prescriptive status describes developments in individual countries. But if prescriptive status were the result of primarily domestic factors, one would expect human rights norms to achieve this status in different countries at different times. Yet, in most of the countries we investigated, governments accepted the validity of international human rights norms around the same period—in the decade from 1985 to 1995. These countries are so different with regard to other aspects of their domestic politics, institutions, and socioeconomic conditions that the convergence around this period is puzzling, unless we incorporate global developments. There is no obvious reason why this happened at this time—the basic norms in the Universal Declaration of Human Rights and the main international institution, the UN Human Rights Commission, have been around since 1948, and the main treaties have been in force since 1976. The end of the Cold War might provide an explanation. But it is itself part of the story of the "power of norms," since the Helsinki human rights provision played a substantial part in ending communist rule in Eastern Europe and the former Soviet Union.[41] Another possible explanation is that all pieces of the domestic-transnational spiral model need to be firmly in place so that the international norm can have domestic effects on the ground. Not until the mid-1980s were all the components of this international and transnational structure fully formed, with the growing number of human rights treaties, international organizations, and INGOs; increased funding by political foundations for human rights work; and key countries now including human rights in their bilateral and multilateral foreign policies.

Phase 5: Rule-Consistent Behavior

Once human rights attain this prescriptive status, there is still a major role for transnational civil society in ensuring that deeds match words. Governments might accept human rights norms but still continue to torture prisoners or detain people without trial and the like. Sometimes, national governments are not fully in control of their police and military forces, which commit the human rights violations. The Ugandan, Philippine, and Indonesian cases are instructive.[42] Political violence escalated in the Philippines in the late 1980s, and counterinsurgency operations by the army led to increasing human rights abuses. Human rights conditions in the Philippines saw real improvement only after 1992, when the government negotiated peace agreements with various rebel groups.

In the Ugandan case, guerrilla activities in the north of the country have hindered the sustained improvement of human rights conditions.[43] Despite a consistent commitment to human rights by the new government under Yoweri Museveni, the police and the military continued to abuse human rights. While most of transnational civil society lost interest in the case, Amnesty International engaged the government in a continuous dialogue that included missions to Uganda and detailed proposals on how to improve prison conditions. Since the mid-1990s, international human rights organizations have increasingly focused on abuses and repression by Sudan-based rebel groups that conducted a systematic "war against children." UNICEF and other organizations, including the U.S. government, started paying attention to the situation in northern Uganda. This has become a rather peculiar case, whereby transnational civil society, Western states, and international organizations side with the government, which has proved its commitment to human rights, against guerrilla groups known for their widespread atrocities.

It is crucial for this phase that the domestic-transnational coalitions keep up the pressure in order to achieve sustainable improvements in human rights conditions. The particular difficulty in this phase is that gross violations of fundamental human rights actually decrease, so international attention declines, too. Although some INGOs try to keep the spotlight on actual behavior, international institutions and Western states are sometimes satisfied when rulers merely say the right things. This is particularly problematic when there has been a regime change, bringing into power a coalition that includes human rights activists. Nevertheless, conditions will improve in a sustainable way only when transnational civil society and domestic groups continually push national governments to live up to their claims. Only then can the final stage in the spiral model be reached, whereby governments comply with international human rights norms in a habitual way and the rule of law enforces compliance.

This does happen. Each of the seven countries included in our sample that reached full prescriptive status also experienced a subsequent, sustained, and drastic improvement in human rights conditions. Poland, Czechoslovakia, South Africa, Chile, Uganda, the Philippines, and Guatemala all matched words with deeds eventually.

Evaluation and Future Challenges

The Power of Transnational Civil Society

Transnational civil society has affected human rights at both the global and the national levels. At the global level, it has contributed in three ways. First, transnational civil society originally put human rights on the international agenda and kept it there. Thanks to the activities of INGOs lobbying international organizations, national governments, and domestic civil society, human rights are among the most densely regulated international norms. Second, transnational civil society provides credible information to the global community about human rights violations in various corners of the world. Third, thanks to transnational civil society lobbying national governments and mobilizing public opinion, many Western governments and international organizations such as the World Bank have incorporated human rights into their foreign policies or operational guidelines. Foreign offices all over the world have now instituted human rights desks and special human rights officers to monitor the issues and collaborate with transnational civil society.

As to improving human rights conditions on the ground, transnational civil society serves three purposes:

1. It puts repressive governments on the international agenda and raises moral consciousness.

2. It empowers and legitimates the claims of domestic opposition groups against their norm-violating governments, and it partially protects the physical integrity of such groups from repression.

3. It challenges norm-violating governments by creating a transnational structure pressuring such regimes simultaneously from above and from below.

In sum, transnational civil society has established the power of norms against the norms of power. This does not mean that INGOs always win their struggles against norm violators (consider the People's Republic of China, Colombia, and Myanmar). In some cases, it has taken decades to achieve substantial human rights improvements. But the world would have far fewer established international human rights norms, and probably far fewer improvements in human rights practices in many countries, were it not for the constant efforts of activists in transnational civil society.

The Sustainability of INGO Power: Lessons

Although the activities of transnational civil society are necessary to bring about a sustained improvement in human rights conditions on the ground, there are limits to their influence. First, INGOs need to link up with domestic civil society in norm-violating states in order to be effective. "Free-floating" pressure is unlikely to bring about change. The stronger the links between transnational civil society and fully mobilized domestic opposition groups and social movements, the more likely it is that repressive governments wil be forced to change course. Second, the spiral takes time to develop the necessary momentum. In cases such as South Africa and Indonesia, transnational pressure had to be sustained for several decades.

Third, transnational civil society needs the cooperation of states and national governments. To create robust and specific human rights standards, INGOs must convince enough states that international law needs to be strengthened. Sometimes, they do this by directly lobbying national governments. Sometimes, they change human rights policies of states by mobilizing domestic public opinion. Transnational civil society also needs states for the effective improvement of human rights conditions on the ground. Only states are able to guarantee the rule of law, and the rule of law is a necessary condition for the improvement of human rights on the ground. This presents a dilemma. On the one hand, the repressive state apparatus needs to be weakened in order to bring about human rights change in the first place and create political space for civil society to flourish. On the other hand, transition governments frequently lack the capacity to control their own repressive apparatus and enforce the rule of law.

Fourth, difficult challenges lie ahead. The most serious of these concerns human rights violations in situations of civil war and the like, where legitimate authorities with a monopoly on the use of force—that is, "states"—no longer exist. In Rwanda, Burundi, Liberia, Uganda, and Colombia, it is no longer national governments that commit the worst human rights violations but private armies, guerrilla troops, mercenaries paid by cartels of drug dealers, and others. The spiral model and the boomerang effect do not operate in these cases. International pressures and sanctions rarely work, since many of these groups are vulnerable to neither moral nor material pressures.

Fifth, this chapter concentrated on civil and political rights, which can be guaranteed only by states implementing the rule of law. When it comes to social and economic rights, however, states are often not the appropriate targets for INGO activities. Rather, private actors such as multinational corporations and domestic firms may become the targets of mobilization. Most recently, for example, INGOs have started targeting multinational corporations to prevent them from exploiting child labor. Campaigns against the Nike and Nestlé corporations are cases in point. These campaigns have resulted in innovative agreements involving INGOs, states or international organizations, and private corporations to ban child labor. This example points toward a fruitful avenue of future activities, particularly in the area of social and economic rights—the underdeveloped agenda of the human rights area.

Another challenge concerns the links between transnational civil society and domestic civil societies, particularly nationally operating NGOs. In many countries, NGOs have become so dependent on external funding and other resources provided by the transnational community, such as foundations, that they tend to lose their domestic base. According to a worldwide survey of human rights NGOs, 60 percent of them relied on foundation grants, while more than 50 percent received funding from national governments or international organizations.[44] Of course, in the early phases of the spiral, external support is often needed to enable domestic NGOs to mount a challenge to their governments at all. But INGOs and political foundations need to be sensitive that they do not create new structures of dependency, this time between transnational and domestic civil societies. In the case of Kenya, for example, competition for funding increased among local NGOs when a growing number of international human rights organizations targeted the country during the late 1980s and early 1990s.[45]

These remarks finally lead to the question of how desirable the power of transnational civil society is in the human rights area. Of course, one can hardly argue against the role of transnational civil society in documenting gross human rights abuses and in condemning as well as preventing torture in many regions of the world. Yet questions of legitimacy and democratic accountability of transnational civil society arise as its activities touch on highly controversial questions of economic and political rights. Take the most recent example of the failed meeting of the World Trade Organization (WTO) in Seattle. Many human rights INGOs mobilized against the WTO's millennium round alongside environmental groups and (American) trade unions. Yet the relationship between free trade and human rights improvements is far from clear. It is at least an unsettled question whether opening up a country's economy to the outside world might also enable the domestic-transnational linkages necessary to unfold the dynamics of the spiral model. Many countries in the developing world have started to resent the unholy alliance of Western protectionist sectors (business and labor alike) with human rights advocacy coalitions. The latter need to be aware that their moral authority and knowledge as prime sources of normative power can easily be captured by private interests, even if these interests are highly legitimate (such as labor).

Notes

A draft of this chapter was presented at the Japan Center for International Exchange workshop and Global ThinkNet conference in Paris, March 16–19, 1999. I thank the members of the Project on Transnational Civil Society for their comments and input. Ann Florini in particular provided extremely helpful criticism. Moreover, I have greatly benefited in my work on human rights from cooperating with Sieglinde Gränzer, Anja Jetschke, Stephen S. Ropp, Hans-Peter Schmitz, and Kathryn Sikkink. I also thank Alison Weston for research assistance. Finally, I am grateful for the generous support of the Japan Center for International Exchange and the German Research Association (*Deutsche Forschungsgemeinschaft*).

1. Margaret Keck and Kathryn Sikkink, *Activists Beyond Borders: Transnational Advocacy Networks in International Politics* (Ithaca, N.Y.: Cornell University Press, 1998), chap. 2.
2. William Korey, *NGOs and the Universal Declaration of Human Rights: "A Curious Grapevine"* (New York: St. Martin's Press, 1998), pp. 117–19.
3. For details, see Keck and Sikkink, *Activists Beyond Borders*, pp. 84–86; Korey, *NGOs and the Universal Declaration*, chap. 1; John P. Humphrey, *Human Rights and the United Nations: A Great Adventure* (Dobbs Ferry, N.Y.: Transnational Publishers, 1984).
4. Data in Keck and Sikkink, *Activists Beyond Borders*, p. 11; Jackie Smith, "Characteristics of the Modern Transnational Social Movement Sector," in *Transnational Social Movements and Global Politics: Solidarity Beyond the State*, ed. J. Smith et al. (Syracuse, N.Y.: Syracuse University Press, 1997), p. 47.
5. Korey, *NGOs and the Universal Declaration*, chap. 7.
6. Keck and Sikkink, *Activists Beyond Borders*, p. 11.
7. According to Korey, *NGOs and the Universal Declaration*, pp. 301–2; for data, see http://www.amnesty.de/facts.
8. Keck and Sikkink, *Activists Beyond Borders*, p. 90.
9. David Black, "The Long and Winding Road: International Norms and Domestic Political Change in South Africa," in *The Power of Human Rights: International*

Norms and Domestic Change, ed. Thomas Risse et al. (Cambridge: Cambridge University Press, 1999), pp. 78–108; Audie Klotz, *Norms in International Relations: The Struggle Against Apartheid* (Ithaca, N.Y.: Cornell University Press, 1995).

10. Daniel C. Thomas, *The Helsinki Effect* (Princeton, N.J.: Princeton University Press, forthcoming).

11. Korey, *NGOs and the Universal Declaration*, pp. 237–39, chap. 14.

12. Hans-Peter Schmitz, "Nichtregierungsorganisationen (NRO) und internationale Menschenrechtspolitik," *Comparativ* 7 (1997); Virginia Leary, "A New Role for Non-Governmental Organizations in Human Rights: A Case Study of Non-Governmental Participation in the Development of International Norms on Torture," in *UN Law/Fundamental Rights: Two Topics in International Law*, ed. A. Cassese (Alphen aan den Rijn: Sijthoff & Noordhoff, 1979), pp. 197–210; Korey, *NGOs and the Universal Declaration*, pp. 171–80.

13. The United States declared a reservation against the Anti-Torture Convention because of its position on the death penalty.

14. Korey, *NGOs and the Universal Declaration*, chap. 12; Alison Brysk, *From Tribal Village to Global Village: Indian Rights and International Relations in Latin America* (Stanford, Calif.: Stanford University Press, 2000).

15. 1998 figure; see http://www.amnesty.de/facts.

16. Jackie Smith et al., "Globalizing Human Rights: The Work of Transnational Human Rights NGOs in the 1990s," *Human Rights Quarterly* 20, no. 2 (1998): 392.

17. Of course, when it comes to strategically important countries such as the People's Republic of China, Western states rarely quote human rights INGOs anymore.

18. On these and other "strategic constructions," see Keck and Sikkink, Activists Beyond Borders; Martha Finnemore and Kathryn Sikkink, "International Norm Dynamics and Political Change," *International Organization* 52, no. 4 (1998): 887–917.

19. Black, "Long and Winding Road"; Klotz, *Norms in International Relations*.

20. Quoted from Sieglinde Gränzer, "Staatliche Menschenrechtsdiskurse in Marokko," manuscript, European University Institute, Florence, 1998.

21. Viron P. Vaky and Heraldo Munoz, *The Future of the Organization of American States* (New York: Twentieth Century Fund, 1993), p. III.

22. This section reports results from a German-American research project that systematically investigated the domestic impact of international human rights norms (see Risse et al., *Power of Human Rights*). This part of the chapter draws on Thomas Risse and Stephen C. Ropp, "International Human Rights Norms and Domestic Change: Conclusions," in *Power of Human Rights*, pp. 234–78, along with Thomas Risse and Kathryn Sikkink, "The Socialization of Human Rights Norms into Domestic Practices: Introduction," in *Power of Human Rights*, pp. 1–38.

23. Keck and Sikkink, *Activists Beyond Borders*; Alison Brysk, "From Above and Below: Social Movements, the International System, and Human Rights in Argentina," *Comparative Political Studies* 26, no. 3 (1993): 259–85; Brysk, *From Tribal Village*.

24. Anja Jetschke, "Linking the Unlinkable? International Norms and Nationalism in Indonesia and the Philippines," in Risse et al., *Power of Human Rights*, pp. 134–71.

25. Sieglinde Gränzer, "Changing Discourse: Transnational Advocacy Networks in Tunisia and Morocco," in Risse et al., *Power of Human Rights*, pp. 109–33.
26. Stephen C. Ropp and Kathryn Sikkink, "International Norms and Domestic Politics in Chile and Guatemala," in Risse et al., *Power of Human Rights*, p. 175.
27. Jetschke, "Linking the Unlinkable," p. 140.
28. Daniel C. Thomas, "The Helsinki Accords and Political Change in Eastern Europe," in Risse et al., *Power of Human Rights*, pp. 205–33; Thomas, *Helsinki Effect*.
29. Ropp and Sikkink, "International Norms."
30. Thomas, "Helsinki Accords."
31. Quoted from Jetschke, "Linking the Unlinkable," p. 141.
32. See Keck and Sikkink, *Activists Beyond Borders*; Kathryn Sikkink, "Human Rights, Principled Issue Networks, and Sovereignty in Latin America," *International Organization* 47, no. 3 (1993): 411–41.
33. Ropp and Sikkink, "International Norms," p. 179.
34. Jetschke, "Linking the Unlinkable," pp. 146–47, 155–56.
35. Black, "Long and Winding Road."
36. See Jetschke, "Linking the Unlinkable," pp. 155–62.
37. Quoted from Jetschke, "Linking the Unlinkable," p. 156.
38. Jetschke, "Linking the Unlinkable."
39. Hans-Peter Schmitz, "Transnational Activism and Political Change in Kenya and Uganda," in Risse et al., *Power of Human Rights*, pp. 39–77.
40. See Thomas, "Helsinki Accords"; Thomas, *Helsinki Effect*.
41. Thomas, *Helsinki Effect*.
42. Schmitz, "Transnational Activism"; Jetschke, "Linking the Unlinkable," pp. 162–65.
43. Schmitz, "Transnational Activism," pp. 67–71.
44. Smith et al., "Globalizing Human Rights," p. 410.
45. Schmitz, "Transnational Activism," p. 76.

8

Lessons Learned

Ann M. Florini

THE PREVIOUS SIX CHAPTERS have provided an in-depth examination of how transnational networks arise and operate and what they accomplish. This chapter evaluates the answers they provide to the questions outlined in chapter 1: how powerful the networks are, whether the sources of their power are sustainable, and what role for transnational civil society is desirable.

Growing Power

If the previous six chapters make any one thing clear, it is this: the growing attention to transnational civil society is not mere hoopla. It reflects a real, and considerable, increase in the number and effectiveness of transnational nongovernmental networks. The power of transnational civil society manifests itself at virtually every stage of policy making, from deciding what issues need attention to determining how problems will be solved to monitoring compliance with agreements.

These cross-border networks are particularly good at getting otherwise-neglected issues onto the agendas of national governments, intergovernmental organizations, and, increasingly, corporations. Fredrik Galtung's chapter shows that international corruption was not high on the international agenda, despite the example of the U.S. Foreign Corrupt Practices Act, until Peter Eigen created Transparency International. Motoko Mekata points out that no one was seriously considering a ban on antipersonnel land mines prior to the creation of the International Coalition to Ban Landmines (ICBL). Sanjeev Khagram demonstrates that despite its huge investment in dam projects, the World Bank had not seen fit to evaluate whether the projects were working as intended until intense pressure from transnational coalitions made concerns over dams a high priority for the institution. According to Rebecca Johnson, the nuclear weapon states showed little propensity to take seriously the demands of other governments for a comprehensive nuclear test ban treaty, but the complementary if uncoordinated activities of Greenpeace boats, the Nevada-Semipalatinsk Movement, and behind-the-scenes work by arms-control groups made the issue impossible to ignore. Chetan Kumar makes it clear that the Zapatistas would be one more minor footnote to history instead of an international cause célèbre were it not for the transnational network that mobilized in their defense.

Transnational coalitions do much more than force governments, nongovernmental organizations (NGOs), and corporations to talk about specific issues, however. They influence those discussions, shape the agreements that result, and monitor whether and how well parties are complying with the terms. It is clear that there would be little or nothing in the way of international human rights standards were it not for the determination of what has now become a large and entrenched transnational community of human rights activists. The influence of those human rights activists now goes far beyond setting pious aspirations. As Thomas Risse's chapter argues, they helped create the situation in which Indonesian president Suharto was peaceably ousted, contributed to the nonviolent end of the Cold War through the Helsinki effect, and continue to exert a surprising and largely unheralded degree of influence over the actual behavior as well as rhetorical commitments of governments around the world. Third-sector groups not only induced nuclear weapon states to start talking about a test ban; they caused those states to recalculate the costs and benefits of retaining the option of nuclear testing—a startling degree of influence on core state security interests. It is widely acknowledged that there would be no treaty banning land mines today had the ICBL not existed, but the land-mine campaign's effect has gone beyond bringing the treaty into existence. Even mine-producing countries that are not party to the treaty have imposed moratoria on the export of mines. Around the world, fewer mines are being laid, and more are being cleared, than was the case before the ICBL. And monitoring of compliance with the treaty is in the hands of an offshoot of the ICBL.

Some civil society groups are moving beyond the role of advocate and monitor, providing services directly, implementing governmental policies, or otherwise taking on roles traditionally reserved to governments and intergovernmental organizations (IGOs).[1] Most of these, in essence, are acting as subcontractors to governments, which increasingly are channeling funds for service provision, development projects, and humanitarian relief through NGOs. For the most part, such subcontractors are not the same groups as those involved in the advocacy coalitions or form only one element of a coalition. But in some cases, governments are turning significant official responsibilities over to advocacy coalitions.

Limits to Power

There are clear limits on the ability of transnational civil society networks to induce governments, IGOs, and corporations to hew to their demands. For one thing, there is no single, coherent transnational civil society agenda. The vast array of third-sector actors involved in efforts to control nuclear weapons found themselves sharply divided over the Non-Proliferation Treaty extension. Moreover, it is not enough to accomplish the relatively straightforward goal of getting governmental negotiators to sign a treaty. Since the 1996 conclusion of the Comprehensive Test Ban Treaty, India and Pakistan have conducted their first nuclear weapons tests, and the U.S. Senate has voted against ratification. Transparency International's ability to bring about an antibribery convention will matter only if that convention actually reduces the incidence of bribery.

Those limits are inherent in the nature of the power of transnational civil society. It works indirectly, by persuading others. The effectiveness of that persuasion often depends on finding a sympathetic ear in high places. The ICBL found that changes in governments mattered enormously, as first Canada's Lloyd Axworthy and then the British Labour Party came into office. High-level support is not always necessary—Greenpeace's activities, for example, were aimed at raising public consciousness—but usually little is accomplished without at least some of it.

More broadly, the networks remain powerful only as long as they retain their credibility. And sometimes civil society gets it very wrong indeed. Humanitarian relief organizations found their credibility badly damaged in 1996 by what turned out to be their greatly exaggerated reports of suffering and death among refugees from Rwanda. Although the organizations insisted that they were doing the best they could in a situation in which information was scarce, making reasonable assumptions about supplies of food and water in camps they could not enter, journalists who had reported the false figures "relished the opportunity to debunk the apocalyptic warnings of the humanitarian agencies."[2] To the extent that transnational civil society networks provide inaccurate or misleading information (whether deliberately or inadvertently), they undermine their effectiveness.

When transnational civil society forgets that its power is soft, not hard, it not only fails to achieve its immediate objectives but also undermines the moral authority that is its real claim to influence. Rebecca Johnson's account of Greenpeace demonstrates this vividly. Greenpeace has a long and successful track record of using its boats to spotlight and harass nuclear testers and whalers. But at some point, Greenpeace seems to have begun believing that it could physically prevent a nuclear test from taking place. Up against the coercive power of a determined French government, Greenpeace stood no chance. And its public internal recriminations over the fiasco frittered away some of its high public standing.

And it is important not to exaggerate the global acceptance of the moral authority of civil society groups. Virtually every national government and international organization has at one time or another raised objections to what was characterized as the illegitimate usurpation of governmental authority or prerogatives, and governments and IGOs retain considerable power to fight back. Even IGOs such as the World Bank and the United Nations, which have been relatively welcoming, often seek to keep civil society groups "in their place"—providing services but not included in formal decision-making processes. NGOs have begun encountering serious setbacks in their efforts to expand, or even maintain, their access to intergovernmental meetings and negotiations. Such access is critical if civil society groups are to influence decision makers and monitor proceedings.

For example, at the United Nations, the path to greater access has lately become rocky. Under the UN Charter, the Economic and Social Council (ECOSOC) sets the rules for NGO access. In 1993, responding to the growing prominence of civil society at the UN conferences of the 1980s and 1990s, ECOSOC opened intergovernmental negotiations on expanding NGO rights.[3] But, as one account argued,

> behind a rhetoric of enthusiasm for NGOs lurked profound disquiet. Delegations feared changes that might weaken or even eventually sweep away nation-state's monopoly of global decision-making. . . . Many governments in Africa, Asia, and Latin America found the proddings and exposés of the human rights NGOs to be annoying or even a threat to their sovereignty, while powerful governments in Europe, North America, and East Africa were not particularly keen on NGOs that pressed for economic justice, disarmament and global democracy.[4]

Nonetheless, after three years of negotiation, ECOSOC adopted two resolutions—one broadening consultative status, and the other calling on the General Assembly to consider the possibility of wider NGO representation throughout the UN system.

Then the trouble started. The General Assembly's working group set up to consider NGO access conveniently avoided agreeing even on its own mandate. In 1997, the conservative U.S. Congress, among its many demands for UN reform as a precondition for payment of U.S. dues, included a requirement that the UN stop holding the expensive global conferences that had done so much to increase NGO access, and Secretary-General Kofi Annan acquiesced.

By 1998, a full-scale movement to roll back NGO access was in swing, triggered by several nasty incidents. In one, an accredited civil society group included in its numbers at the Commission on Human Rights a large bloc of unaffiliated people, many of whom turned out to be anti-Castro Cuban emigrés who sharply criticized the Cuban government. Cuba took exception and proposed limits on the NGO accreditation process. In another, an Indian delegate happened to run into an NGO representative in the delegates' lounge at UN headquarters in Geneva and recognized him as the head of an Indian separatist group that had recently taken credit for kidnapping her nephew.[5] Even traditionally supportive governments began proposing restrictions. The Non-Aligned Movement issued a communiqué, including a statement of opposition to NGO access to the General Assembly. At both the UN Commission on Human Rights and the UN Conference on Disarmament, civil society groups found their access increasingly restricted. Clearly, governments retain the power to shut civil society out of the traditional fora for international problem solving.

To what degree this governmental backlash against NGO access will matter in the long run to the power of transnational civil society remains unclear. For Transparency International and the coalitions around big dams, the ability to be heard in IGOs such as the World Bank is a significant element of their influence. For many others, however, such access is irrelevant. The Ottawa Process negotiations on land mines took place outside of traditional arms-control venues. Although the human rights network uses UN channels extensively, it also has other instruments available. Many campaigns, such as the pro-democracy networks, do not need access to IGOs at all.

Businesses, increasingly the direct target of transnational civil society activities, find it even harder than governments do to keep civil society at arm's length. One recent study showed that BurmaNet and other Internet-based networks working in opposition to the current government of Myanmar (Burma) have induced Western multinationals to stop doing business there.[6] Groups such as Greenpeace have had much to do with the European public's reaction against genetically modified foods.[7] Although businesses that market directly to consumers have been most affected by transnational civil society campaigns, other types of businesses are increasingly finding themselves forced to change their practices. Oil, gas, and mining companies operating in developing countries have found themselves under intense pressure from human rights and environmental groups, often working in close collaboration with local peoples.[8]

Accounting for the Power Shift

Are the case studies and other similar cases flukes? Is the current prominence of transnational civil society merely a temporary coincidence of favorable factors? Or is there evidence of an enduring change in the pattern of global politics?

Skeptics see the current period as a temporary interregnum, going so far as to describe this as the "interwar period" between the end of the Cold War and the beginning of some new Great Power conflict that will inevitably dominate global affairs. That view assumes that even if transnational civil society is having a significant impact, this merely reflects a temporary unipolar moment, with a hegemonic leader—the United States—that happens to be peculiarly susceptible to the persuasive powers of civil society.

It is certainly true that the end of the Cold War loosened the international system and offered NGOs more space in which to speak out and be heard. Transparency International was able to create an anti-corruption movement in part because corrupt officials could no longer count on automatic external support from their superpower patrons. The comprehensive test ban became possible because there was less perceived need for, and hence legitimacy of, nuclear testing.

But a less jaundiced view can discern broad trends that seem likely to foster a strong role for transnational civil society for the foreseeable future, trends that would be affected but not dissipated by the renewal of ideological disputes between states. Those trends are the strong growth of domestic civil society, technological changes, the growing number of focal points around which transnational civil society can coalesce; the availability of funding, and the ability of transnational civil society coalitions to learn from and build on previous efforts.

Domestic Nodes

As the case studies indicate, transnational civil society cannot float free in a global ether. It must be firmly connected to local reality. Sanjeev Khagram's comparison of the effectiveness of transnational efforts to reform or halt dam projects in various countries illustrated that the strength of domestic civil society within the targeted countries was crucial. Dam projects in China and Lesotho, where domestic civil society is weak, were far less likely to be reformed or halted than projects in India or the United States. With the notable exception of Japan, governments were far more influenced by domestic civil society campaigns in favor of a land-mine treaty than by anything the ICBL did. The efforts of human rights international NGOs to change the behavior of repressive governments had little effect unless the domestic civil societies in those countries were able to act, at least to provide the credible information on which the transnational campaigns depended. If a significant, organized domestic constituency is lacking, external actors usually can accomplish little.

In most regions of the world, increasingly vigorous domestic civil societies provide the nodes for transnational networks. With democratization has come the beginning of a broader acceptance of the desirability, or at least the inevitability, of a strong civil society. The wave of democratization that swept through Eastern Europe, Latin America, and Africa in the 1990s opened the way for strengthened domestic civil societies that could participate in transnational networks. Even in the Middle East, largely bypassed by the trend toward democratization, some 70,000 NGOs existed as of the late 1980s.[9]

The growth of civil society does not automatically follow from democratization. As Motoko Mekata's account of the travails of the Japan Campaign to Ban Landmines shows, the lack of a hospitable legal environment can cripple domestic civil society, restricting its participation in transnational networks. In many regions, governments are beginning to make it easier for civil society organizations to form and to act. The most striking change has appeared in the countries of the former Soviet Union and Eastern and Central Europe. The former communist governments had stifled civil society, allowing it to exist mostly in the form of government-controlled mandatory "voluntary" activities, although a few Eastern European countries managed to keep at least a rudimentary form of civil society alive. Since 1989, however, the growth of NGOs and other elements of civil society in several of those countries has been nothing short of spectacular, reflecting both democratization and the strong support of Western donors, both of which have led to pressures on the new governments to allow independent civil societies to function. But governments in other parts of the world have also begun to change their attitudes toward, and their laws governing, civil society. Japan, for example, passed a law in 1998 easing what had been onerous financial requirements for the registration of NGOs.

A major question is whether domestic civil society will continue to grow. To some degree, the future of domestic civil society depends on the same trends that will influence the future of transnational civil society—information technology, the availability of funding, and evolving ideas about the legitimacy of civil society's participation in governance. These are discussed later. But perhaps the most important, and largely unanswerable, question about the future state of domestic civil society in various regions around the world relates to the broader progress of democracy.

It is possible to have a form of democracy without a vibrant domestic civil society; for example, Japan, France, and Spain have democratically elected governments but relatively few independent civic groups.[10] It is also possible for a country to develop a rich associational life without developing democratic and liberal values, as Weimar Germany apparently did.[11] But far more often, democratization and the development of a strong civil society go hand in hand. Indeed, as Thomas Risse's and Sanjeev Khagram's chapters show, domestic civil society groups often organize themselves in response to specific types of abuses by governments. Those groups then become involved in broader democratization processes within their societies, helping to open up political space for a greater flowering of civil society. Whether Risse's spiral will continue to operate and spread, or whether the future of democracy is more bleak, is a question beyond the scope of this book, but undoubtedly the future of civil society and the future of democracy are intertwined.

Growth in domestic civil society reflects the fact that over the past few decades, the whole idea of civil society has taken on greater legitimacy among the general public in most parts of the world, leading not only to acceptance of its right to speak but also to an ever-larger pool of potential recruits. Particularly in Western countries, where polls show decreasing levels of trust in government, people seem to find data obtained and provided by nongovernmental sources more trustworthy than information from governments. Numerous studies have shown declining levels of trust in government and falling levels of satisfaction with regime performance in the United States and Western Europe over the past four decades.[12] By contrast, publics seem to invest civil society groups with moral authority.

Technology

Transnational civil society has already benefited greatly from the wide dissemination of information technology and the growing ease of international travel, developments driven by market forces but very useful for activists trying to organize themselves and influence the opinions of others. States have long used information as an instrument of power by issuing convincing propaganda, withholding information, or stifling the flow of information. Likewise, civil society groups have long used information as a tool to influence public opinion and decision makers. But the information revolution has meant that civil society groups have significantly more data and more means to disseminate it than ever before. This trend, coupled with the proliferation of NGOs in developing countries, has vastly expanded the reach of civil society networks. With contacts that extend from New York to Bangkok and from parliaments to the grassroots, civil society networks have access to unprecedented amounts of timely information, which they disseminate quickly and widely. Ever-cheaper communication and transportation technologies are making people in very different parts of the world aware that they share common interests and values and enabling them to act together to realize common goals.

Although attention tends to focus on computers and the Internet, equally revolutionary for much of the world is the potential of telephone access. The Grameen Bank in Bangladesh, which has reaped accolades for its millions of highly successful microenterprise loans to poor Bangladeshis in more than half the country's villages, is now tackling the lack of telephone access in rural areas, providing an important model for how to integrate the poor into this crucial element of the information age. Grameen Phone provides cellular phone service. In rural areas, it provides loans to villagers so that they can buy phones and begin selling calls. As of late 1999, more than 200 village phones were in operation, and Grameen Phone had 25,000 customers nationwide, with plans to expand to at least 300,000 subscribers by 2001.[13]

The availability of information technology and the growing number of domestic nodes interact in ways that amplify the power of transnational networks. In the late 1980s and early 1990s, Brazil faced criticism over the continuing invasions of Yanomami reserves by gold miners. Brazil loudly trumpeted its dynamiting of the miners' airstrips as the ultimate solution to the problem. But the Brazilian government found that external protests continued, because Brazilian network members faxed evidence to their U.S. counterparts that miners had rebuilt the airstrips.[14]

These older technologies explain much of the success of transnational civil society to date, but it is the connectivity available through the Internet that may solidify and expand the power of transnational civil society beyond all previous experience. The Internet makes it much easier for political activism to take place outside the territorial control of governments. As Chetan Kumar's chapter shows, even matters that once fell firmly under the aegis of domestic authorities now appear under the transnational spotlight. Web sites posting information from the Zapatistas can be found from Ireland to Australia.

As information technology becomes cheaper and more widely available, what are rapidly becoming the basic tools of e-mail and Internet access will enable transnational civil society to incorporate a vastly greater range of people than ever before possible. As of 1998, the Internet became a truly global network, with virtually every country in the world having some sort of connection.[15] There are now 43 million Internet host computers in 214 countries.[16] Although relatively few people currently have Internet access, the growth rate is phenomenal. In 1995, less than 1 percent of the world's adults (over age sixteen) made at least weekly use of the Internet. By 1998, that number was 3 percent, and it was expected to climb to nearly 6 percent by 2000 and to almost 12 percent by 2005.[17] As is well known, North America and Western Europe are disproportionately represented among Internet users. But by 2005, projections are that nearly 16 percent of the adult population of Eastern Europe will be on the Internet at least weekly, 5 percent of the Asia-Pacific population, and 10 percent of the South and Central American population. Even the Middle East and North Africa, perennially the also-rans in such matters, will see nearly 3 percent of their adults accessing the Internet every week.

These do not seem like huge percentages, but they add up to

significant numbers of people. While only 44 million people were on-line weekly in 1995, that will jump in a decade to 765 million—over 200 million each in North America and Western Europe, nearly 200 million in the Asia-Pacific region (where usage is growing the fastest), and some 30 million to 60 million in each of the remaining regions of the world. Given that the active participants in most transnational civil society networks are counted in the mere thousands, the potential for growth through the new information media seems clear.

Although access to information technology remains highly unequal both within countries and across regions, even the existing unequal access gives citizens of the world's poorer regions far more opportunity to have a voice than they ever had before. Moreover, there is no shortage of projects under way aimed at redressing the imbalance. A group of Silicon Valley executives has called for the creation of a nonprofit organization called ClickStart, which would use federal subsidies to help connect low-income Americans to the Internet.[18] The United States Information Agency, now part of the U.S. Department of State, established Global Technology Corps (GTC), a public-private partnership that recruits high-tech volunteers for short-term projects on everything from web design to e-commerce to information technology as part of humanitarian assistance. In the flowery language of the GTC web site, "By supporting activities that integrate computing technologies into the culture and character of local communities, GTC volunteers help build a future in which the global information network is not a luxury of the privileged but a resource for all."[19] Such development assistance efforts are increasingly common, sponsored not only by aid agencies but also by private organizations such as George Soros's Open Society Institute. Volunteers in Technical Assistance (VITA) announced a partnership in late 1999 with Wavix of Maryland and Surrey Satellite Technology, Ltd., of Guilford, England, to bring low-cost e-mail services to rural areas of developing countries by sharing a low-earth-orbit satellite. Many IGOs support specialized networks.

Conversely, governments may try to make life more difficult for activists using the Internet. The Internet, and particularly the exponential rise in the number of Internet users, poses a dilemma for governments. Although governments may want the business opportunities that enter their countries via the Internet's cross-border information highways, those new highways also bring many unwanted travelers and ideas. In China, "Hactivists" have infiltrated government web sites boasting progress in human rights, replacing official statements with claims that "China's people have no rights at all, never mind human rights."[20]

According to the French-based watchdog group Reporteurs sans frontieres, forty-five countries restrict their citizens' access to the Internet, usually by requiring them to subscribe to a state-run Internet service provider, and twenty of those countries heavily filter that access.[21] China's efforts to restrict access have attracted particular attention. Internet users have increased from 2 million in 1998 to nearly 9 million in 1999. There are also approximately 35.6 million e-mail accounts. Given the burgeoning number of people connecting to the Internet, the Chinese government is striving to promote the advance of information technology, on the one hand, and maintain direct control over the information flow in and out of the country, on the other.

On January 26, 2000, the Chinese government issued official regulations intended to control the release of information on the Internet. Although much of what is forbidden, specifically the dissemination of "state secrets,"[22] was already illegal under existing law, the government approved the legislation after Internet monitoring revealed extensive leaks. Under this new law, the Computer Information Systems Internet Secrecy Administrative Regulations, all content going onto the web from China must be approved by the state. This includes operators of chat rooms, personal web sites, and e-mail. The basic principle of the law is that "whoever puts it on the Internet assumes responsibility."[23]

The latest content regulation law is not the only attempt by the Chinese government to control e-information. Another law, adopted in late 1999, required all users of encryption software to register with the government by January 31, 2000, and forbids the use of foreign encryption software.

Consequences of Internet regulation have already been felt in China. A computer technician who provided 30,000 Chinese e-mail addresses to dissidents abroad was sentenced to two years in prison. On the flip side, however, farmers from the Anhui province in central China used the Internet and e-mail to expose a corrupt local Communist Party chief.[24]

Enforcement of the new Internet regulation law will be difficult, as there are several loopholes. Anyone can register and set up overseas web sites with Chinese content and e-mail their friends in China, telling them to read those sites. Blocking sites is an ineffective means of information control. It takes approximately two months to track down the relay server of a site and block access, while sites can change their addresses the next day. Most Chinese analysts see the regulation as more of a scare tactic than a true limitation on the Internet.[25] The Chinese government's attempts to keep control of the type and flow of information are unlikely to succeed. And if they do succeed, it will be at such a cost to the Chinese economy that pressures for reform will quickly arise.

Technological changes have undoubtedly contributed to the flowering of transnational networks. Technology by itself can never be more than an enabling condition for the development of cohesive transnational civil society coalitions. As Motoko Mekata points out in the chapter on the land-mines campaign, e-mail mattered, but without the hard work of scores of national-level campaigns, the e-mail coordination would have meant little. But as it becomes easier to exchange information and plan logistics with counterparts thousands of miles away, the opportunities for vigorous coalition activities will grow.

Focal Points

Globalization itself—the increasing integration of economies and societies—is providing an ever-larger number of focal points around which transnational networks can coalesce. First, more people are recognizing that they have common problems. In some cases, entrepreneurial activists are creating institutions around which a network can form, as Peter Eigen did in creating Transparency International. In other cases, such as the land-mines and dams cases, the networks arise when domestic groups become aware that others are involved in similar activities elsewhere.

Just as important, transnational groups are taking advantage of the organizational infrastructure created by states and IGOs attempting to promote and grapple with the consequences of globalization. The IGOs themselves provide handy targets around (or against) which transnational civil society can coalesce. Much of the work of the human rights networks aims at taking specific cases to the United Nations or tries to strengthen the UN's human rights machinery. As described in Sanjeev Khagram's chapter, the antidam campaigns found the World Bank a useful target.

Even in the absence of a formal, physical international organization to provide a focal point, transnational civil society finds other targets of opportunity. International negotiations are particularly useful (and often result from the demands of transnational civil society coalitions, such as the Ottawa Process that led to the land-mines treaty and the comprehensive test ban negotiations). Scores of treaties and declarations specify that it is not all right to torture one's citizens, enslave one's workers, dump pollutants on unsuspecting neighbors, deliberately target civilians in wartime, or rely on weapons of mass destruction. Such agreements, signed by most of the world's governments, establish standards against which transnational civil society can, and does, loudly and publicly compare the actual behavior of states and corporations. As the former Warsaw Pact countries found after they signed the Helsinki accords, including the famous Basket Three on human rights, the lack of any intention to live up to such agreements provides little defense in the court of world opinion.

Governments and IGOs have frequently, if unwittingly, provided particularly useful breeding grounds for civil society networking by sponsoring international conferences. Perhaps most important were the United Nations conferences on global issues that began in the 1970s, which both reflected and spurred the development of a stronger, more integrated transnational civil society. NGOs appeared in force at the 1972 UN Conference on the Human Environment, with accredited NGOs outnumbering governmental delegations two to one. NGOs gathered at many more conferences over the subsequent two decades, on issues ranging from population to women to food.[26] Most dramatic was the 1992 UN Conference on Environment and Development (UNCED) in Rio de Janeiro, Brazil. NGOs had a striking influence over the agenda and outcome. In fact, NGOs vastly outnumbered governments by some 650 to 178, not counting the thousands of participants in the parallel nongovernmental forum.[27] The UNCED deliberately promoted the participation of these civil society bodies, and in its final report, Agenda 21, it called on the UN system and all intergovernmental fora to find ways to incorporate the expertise and views of NGOs.

And so they did. At the 1994 Cairo Conference on Population and Development, for example, NGOs were everywhere—as members of the delegations of such countries as the United States and Japan, as negotiators in the informal negotiating sessions where the real work got done, as participants in the informal parallel nongovernmental conference that has become a feature of all the UN conferences, and as producers of the newsletter that kept everyone informed about the daily activities of the complex and sprawling negotiations. Cairo's final report, a sixteen-chapter document, allotted one full chapter to a discussion of facilitating and formalizing NGO participation.[28] By the time of the Beijing conference on women, this enormously expanded role for NGOs had come to seem so normal that an uproar ensued when the Chinese government exiled the parallel nongovernmental forum to a site far from the official conference.

The heyday of UN mega-conferences is over, done in by budget constraints, general exhaustion, and, not least, the feeling on the part of some governments that civil society's role in them was getting out of hand, as discussed earlier. But the transnational networking made possible by the conferences has created or reinforced nongovernmental linkages involving all sorts of groups in a wide range of countries.

However, if governments and IGOs do not provide handy focal points, at least some sectors of transnational civil society seem quite able and willing to create their own. In February 1997, more than 2,000 people from 112 countries came together for what in many ways resembled a UN mega-conference, right down to the heads of state droning on past the end of their allotted speaking time. But the organizer was an ad hoc coalition of NGOs, not the UN. And the goal was not to negotiate an intergovernmental treaty or final statement. It was "to launch a global movement" aimed at promoting the provision of microcredit: extremely small loans to very poor people who lack access to more traditional forms of credit and thus have no means of financing the microenterprises that could lift them out of destitution.[29]

In short, the existence of intergovernmental efforts to address transnational issues has helped spur the development of transnational civil society coalitions. As states form more and more IGOs and undertake more and more negotiations on everything from investment to money laundering to the protection of dolphins, transnational civil society finds itself with a plenitude of convenient focal points for its efforts. And as transnational civil society grows, it seeks new issue areas for which it demands intergovernmental negotiations and organizations, creating additional avenues to draw in more of civil society.

More broadly, the processes of globalization will themselves ensure plentiful targets for a growing transnational civil society. The protests in Seattle described in chapter 1 were just one in what will certainly be a long series of mobilizations around issues and institutions connected with economic integration across borders. The world is still working out the rules for trade and finance, as well as the connections between these issues and others, such as the environment and human rights. Transnational civil society is demanding a major role in these decisions. Seattle was not unique; it was not even the first major battle. As Khagram's chapter makes clear, transnational activism has spotlighted the World Bank for two decades. But the campaign that epitomizes what lies ahead for global economic rule making may be the one against the once-obscure Multilateral Agreement on Investment.

In the early 1990s, as levels of foreign direct investment soared, the Western industrialized countries agreed that a multilateral framework was needed to bring order to a system then based on some 1,600 bilateral investment treaties.[30] Negotiations began at the Organization for Economic Cooperation and Development in May 1995. For nearly two years, no one paid much attention as the negotiators came up with a draft treaty that focused on the rights of foreign investors, prohibited governments from favoring local investors, and required that benefits provided to investors from one country be extended to investors from all countries. It was never clear whether governments would actually reach agreement, given the number of exemptions sought and the lack of consensus on various points. But when someone leaked a copy of the draft text to an American NGO called Public Citizen in February 1997, Public Citizen posted it on the web, and a full-scale campaign to stop the treaty was launched. Opponents claimed that the treaty would strip governments of the ability to do anything that could conceivably impede an investor's ability to make a profit, including environmental, health, or workers' rights laws.[31] By the time the negotiators gave up in December 1998, the campaign had sparked public protests, letter-writing campaigns, widespread media coverage, and parliamentary hearings.[32]

As long as economic integration continues, rules to govern it and institutions to manage it will be needed. That means there will be no shortage of targets around which transnational civil society can coalesce. These will include not only the specific international organizations charged with fostering and overseeing such integration, such as the World Trade Organization and the International Monetary Fund (IMF), but also the vast complex of corporations and national government agencies involved in economic activity. Related campaigns already exist. The Jubilee 2000 campaign, which calls for the cancellation of the crippling debts owed by the world's poorest countries, is now a coalition stretching across sixty-four countries that has racked up some remarkable successes. The American, British, and Canadian governments have already promised to cancel the debts of many of the most heavily indebted poor countries, and the World Bank, the IMF, and the G-7 governments agreed under pressure to a fundamental review of the Bank's heavily indebted poor country initiative.[33]

Funding

Transnational civil society is relatively low-cost, especially in the advocacy field. Volunteers do much of the work, and those who are paid usually earn less than they would in comparable private-sector or government jobs. Nonetheless, the salaries, office expenses, computer networks, and frequent international travel have to be financed somehow. Figures on how much they spend and who funds them are notoriously hard to come by.[34] It is difficult to find overall figures on how much money transnational civil society networks are receiving, but the trend appears to be upward. In general, and in sharp contrast to the usual perception of civil society as a realm autonomous from the state, NGOs depend heavily on government funding. In North America and Europe, that dependency is growing. Britain quadrupled its official funding of NGOs in the decade from the early 1980s to the early 1990s.[35] In the Netherlands, Canada, and the Scandinavian countries, it is common to find NGOs that receive 50 to 90 percent of their funding from their governments.[36]

The trend is similar for official funding flowing from rich-country governments to developing countries: although overall aid is declining, both the relative share and the absolute amount of the aid being funneled through NGOs rather than to governments is growing, and more and more of it is flowing directly to Southern NGOs rather than through Northern intermediaries.[37] U.S. foundations became far more active overseas in the 1990s. From 1990 to 1994, funding of overseas recipients soared 74 percent, growing five times faster than funding of U.S.-based international programs.[38] Such funding shifts are strengthening the domestic nodes of transnational civil society beyond the well-developed bases in North America and Western Europe.

Beyond these broad generalities, however, not much is known, in large part because the organizations involved in the networks rarely make it easy to investigate their funding. Transparency International lists its funders on its web site, but few other organizations do. Amnesty International merely provides its budget and a statement that it accepts no government funding, while the ICBL says nothing about its funding at all. This is not necessarily an attempt to be secretive. The ICBL is a coalition of groups, many of which do provide information on their sources of income. Indeed, because few transnational civil society coalitions are as centralized as the anticorruption network, it would be difficult for even a determined network to provide a good sense of the amount of money flowing into and out of its coffers.

The troubling point remains the heavy dependence of many networks on Northern funding sources. The widespread land-mines campaign mythology is that the campaign was run on e-mail from a log cabin in Vermont; on the contrary, the ICBL efforts were well-financed by groups such as the Vietnam Veterans of America, enabling campaign leaders to shuttle around the globe and organize a highly visible mass-media blitz. The Climate Action Network owes its origins in significant part to generous early support from the German Marshall Fund. Unless and until this funding pattern changes, to the extent that particular coalitions need significant funding, their future will depend in part on the continued willingness of Northern governments and foundations to provide the money.

Learning from Experience

Success is breeding success. Two years after the signing of the land-mines treaty, some of the same NGOs that participated in the ICBL created the International Action Network on Small Arms to push for strong international controls on the light weapons (machine guns, rifles, grenades, mortars) that are responsible for the vast majority of deaths in the civil wars plaguing much of the world.[39] This network consciously models itself on the ICBL.

The ICBL is not the only source of inspiration. The Zapatista network draws heavily on the work of activists involved in fighting U.S. policy toward Central America in the 1980s (indeed, some analysts see it as the last gasp of that network). The Jubilee 2000 campaign mentioned earlier compares itself to the slave-trade abolitionists. The campaign's web site introduction argues:

> One of the closest parallels to the debt crisis is the Atlantic slave trade. It, too, was a system of international oppression accepted for generations as a normal and necessary part of trade and life. ... But in 1833 the slave trade was abolished in all British possessions. It was not because of one powerful individual or institution, but because of the concerted effort of thousands of people. ... In the same way, the oppression of the debts of the poorest countries could be ended by the year 2000.[40]

All these factors amount to trends, not inevitabilities. People will be able to form networks across borders with ever-greater ease, but nothing will compel them to do so. Some issues will draw effective networks around them, but others will not. Some governments and corporations will change under the influence of or deliberately choose to work with various transnational civil society coalitions. Other governments and corporations will fight tooth and nail and at least some of the time will win. This does not make for a smooth and orderly process. To the extent that the world relies on transnational civil society for its global governance, it will get a series of ad hoc muddlings through.

Desirability

Now we come to the hardest of the three questions. If transnational civil society is both strong and sustainable, is this good or bad? Or, to render the question more properly nuanced, what is good and bad about its emerging role, and what can be done to encourage the good and alleviate the bad?

Transnational civil society networks are often quite effective at portraying themselves as doers of good. Coalitions claim to represent the broader, longer-term collective interests of humanity. Transparency International, human rights groups, antinuclear activists, the ICBL, and the coalition against big dams have all claimed to be working in the global public interest. The transnational coalitions described in Chetan Kumar's chapter focus on a single country rather than the world as a whole, but they too claim to be acting on behalf of the public interest. By and large, advocacy networks espouse broad goals that are hard to object to: protecting the environment, raising the living standards of the poor, promoting democracy and governmental accountability, reducing the threat of catastrophic war.

But there is nothing inherent in the nature of civil society—local or transnational—that ensures representation of a broad public interest. The neo-Nazi hate groups that exchange repugnant rhetoric over the Internet are just as much transnational civil society networks as are the human rights coalitions. Moreover, once coalitions move from broad goals to specific campaigns with specific strategies and tactics, it can become much less clear what interest is actually being represented. In summer 1994, for example, a coalition of agriculture and trade groups torpedoed America's imminent ratification of the Biodiversity Treaty agreed at the UNCED in 1992, claiming that the treaty could destroy U.S. agriculture. It later turned out that much of their opposition grew out of a misinformation campaign conducted by a far-right fringe group. Greenpeace came under heavy criticism in 1995 for its successful campaign to prevent the Royal Dutch/Shell Group from disposing of the Brent Spar oil rig by sinking it in the North Sea—a campaign Greenpeace continued even after independent analyses showed that the environmental consequences of the sinking would be insignificant.[41]

In one respect, the question of the desirability of transnational civil society is unanswerable in any objective manner. To victims of land mines, to villagers threatened with displacement and pauperization by massive dam projects, to business executives tired of being shaken down for bribes, to people struggling for democracy and equity within their countries, transnational civil society may appear a very good thing indeed. Without networks like the ICBL, the coalition around big dams, Transparency International, or the Haitian and Zapatista networks, few of these people would have redress for their complaints. But to governments trying to protect national security through weapons programs they deem proper, to owners of dam-building firms who believe they are providing a major public benefit through the development of needed infrastructure, to societies trying to reform themselves from the inside, transnational civil society can seem disruptive, narrow-minded, and above all unaccountable.

Legitimacy and Accountability

Even for those who share the goals of particular networks, troubling questions about legitimacy and accountability remain. Transnational civil society networks by definition operate at least in part beyond the reach of the specific governments, businesses, and individuals they most affect. They often consist of people in one place claiming to speak on behalf of people in another. To date, most have remained relatively immune to the growing pressure for transparency on the part of governments and the private sector. There are no easy means of imposing accountability—by its very nature, transnational civil society is not subject either to elections or to market tests. Yet to leave the issue unaddressed is to threaten the long-term legitimacy of an important contributor to global governance.

Specific transnational civil society coalitions do indeed tend to pursue narrow mandates, often lacking mechanisms for reaching broad agreements across peoples and issue areas. After all, their raison d'être is usually a single issue or group, and they induce contributions from both their own members and outsiders by claiming that their cause has the highest claim on those resources. Such claims can serve as a force for fragmentation. Being relieved of the burden of accountability to diverse constituencies means that NGOs and their networks often can avoid the messy trade-offs among issues that constitute the heart of governmental politics; rarely are they asked to amalgamate anywhere near as many interests as governments must. Instead, they can focus on a narrow mandate, which helps to focus passion and energy around either a moral issue or a clear goal. But the lack of accountability that gives civil society organizations such freedom of action could allow more constrained governmental or corporate actors to paint civil society organizations as irresponsible, ignorant trouble-makers or as nefarious plotters hiding a secret agenda.

There are several bases on which transnational civil society claims the right to do what it does. The most common are superior knowledge, delegation, and representativeness. Knowledge claims appear in many of the case studies. As Thomas Risse's chapter shows, human rights organizations such as Amnesty International, which spent decades carefully checking out reports of specific abuses in all regions of the world, have acquired a global reputation for accuracy and political neutrality. Transparency International's annual corruption index has influence in large part because the information on which it is based comes not from governments but from polls of businesspeople all over the world about their perceptions of the level of corruption in various countries. TI has also spent considerable time and effort on encouraging and disseminating research that demonstrates the pervasiveness and costliness of international corruption. Those opposed to large dam construction claim superior knowledge about the true costs and benefits of the projects. Motoko Mekata's account of the land-mine campaign reveals the degree to which on-the-ground experience in mine-infested countries gave organizations within the campaign credibility in arguing for a ban on land mines.

A second source of legitimacy for some elements of transnational civil society is a seal of governmental approval. Most formal domestic and international NGOs have some government's implicit approval through the legal recognition extended to such organizations. As described earlier, some elements of civil society are going beyond such acceptance of governmental authority to work far more closely with governments as subcontractors or as full partners. But relying on government as the source of civil society authority is highly questionable. To the extent that civil society's moral authority depends on the perception that it is promoting worthy causes in opposition to concentrations of power, governmental approval may even undermine the broader legitimacy of the coalitions.

Perhaps the trickiest basis for claiming legitimacy is representativeness. This is, after all, the basis of legitimacy of elected governments, which are expected to comply with widely recognized standards for holding free, fair, and regular elections to ensure that government officials who fail to represent the wishes of their constituents can be

234 | THE THIRD FORCE

removed by those constituents. For transnational civil society coalitions, even defining who the constituents are can be difficult, and few
processes exist for democratic selection of representatives. Most often,
contentions about the illegitimacy of transnational civil society focus
on allegations that the coalitions claim to be representing the poor and
downtrodden of the world, largely in the South, but are made up primarily of the relatively wealthy and educated and espouse Northern,
not global, values.

Although this has been a valid criticism in the past, it is becoming
increasingly outdated as civil society nodes grow in most parts of the
world and as Northern nodes learn from experience about the importance of treating Southerners as partners, not victims.[42] Sanjeev Khagram's account of the evolution of the anti–multilateral development
bank campaign shows that what began as an effort to address Northern civil society concerns quickly broadened. One recent study found
that more than a third of all international human rights NGOS are
headquartered in the global South.[43] Indeed, direct South-South networking is on the rise. Much of it began with Northern support, but it
is increasingly independent.[44] The problem of unequal participation
in the coalitions remains significant, but Northern dominance of
transnational civil society is neither as monolithic nor as insuperable
as it is often portrayed.

Part of the problem of legitimacy is the lack of obvious means for
holding transnational civil society accountable. Governments that fail
to represent their citizens can be voted out of office in democracies, or
overturned. Corporations that fail to serve their employees, customers, or shareholders can suffer high turnover, declining sales, or
stockholder revolts. But when Transparency International publishes a
survey indicating that some countries are hopelessly corrupt, and aid
to those countries is then slashed on the basis of their corruption,
what is their redress?

This is a real problem, but one that is easily, and frequently, exaggerated. All civil society advocacy stands or falls on the persuasiveness
of the information it provides. Over time, groups whose facts and arguments prove unfounded discredit themselves. The deliberately dishon-
est and the merely incompetent can certainly do short-term damage,
but they are unlikely to have significant, long-lasting influence.

As transnational civil society grows, it is evolving some of the self-correcting mechanisms that have arisen in democracies with flourishing domestic civil societies. Groups begin to hold one another accountable for the accuracy of their arguments. Government agencies and corporations learn how to respond to attacks they consider unjustified—and they also learn how to fend off attacks that may be very well justified. For all the accomplishments of civil society coalitions, the balance of power still favors governments and corporations, whose resources will always vastly outweigh those available to the advocacy element of the third sector.

Future Directions

Like all trends, the trends that have contributed to the extraordinary growth of transnational civil society cannot be extrapolated indefinitely. Information and communications technologies seem sure to continue their dizzying advance, but whether they will truly become widely accessible in the poorer parts of the world is unclear. The powerful growth in domestic civil societies may prove an unstoppable juggernaut—or we may be in for a period of harsh clampdowns. The power of example may continue to inspire, unless some network embroils itself in a major fiasco that discredits the whole sector.

Most likely, however, transnational civil society is here to stay. But it will not necessarily continue to look like the older networks in the human rights or nuclear disarmament field. Two significant changes are under way. First, networks are increasingly bypassing governments altogether and targeting, or partnering with, the private sector. This is happening in the human rights field, as Risse mentions, but it is particularly evident in the environmental field. As Khagram's chapter shows, civil society has been linking up across borders on environmental issues for decades, forming particularly strong connections in opposition to such targets as the World Bank's environmental practices and the environmental impact of big dam construction. Transnational environmental activism grew to a frenzy in 1992, in connection with the UNCED in Rio de Janeiro. Up to that point, activism tended to be of the standard sort: lobbying governments and IGOs to change rules and laws. But by the time of the 1997 UNCED review conference, many of the transnational civil society participants were convinced that this approach was failing. Not only were the environmental problems identified at Rio not being solved, things were getting worse. As a result, groups are turning their attention to a more direct approach. Rather than trying to persuade governments to adopt laws and negotiate treaties that will regulate the environmental practices of their citizens (including corporations), environmental groups are addressing consumers and producers directly. The environmentalists are engaging in collaborations with businesses, helping them find ways to make a profit at lower environmental costs. They are promulgating codes of conduct to which they ask businesses to adhere. They are mounting protest campaigns against particular practices by specific multinationals. And they are buying stock in the companies they wish to target, enabling them to use shareholders' meetings to put pressure on managers.[45]

Second, civil society's role in global governance is changing from that of gadfly to that of direct participant in the management of global issues. Transparency International works closely with the World Bank in the anticorruption campaign, as the ICBL did with the Canadian government. The dams case provides a potentially useful model for managing other transnational issues. The World Commission on Dams has brought together transnational civil society, governments, and the private sector in a common effort to achieve a consensus assessment of big dams and their alternatives, along with criteria for the making and decommissioning of dams. This is no easy task. The commission includes both people who see big dams as essential providers of irrigation water and electrical power for poor countries that desperately need them, and people who see big dams as gigantic despoilers of the environment and destroyers of local livelihoods. If the commission succeeds, it could provide a powerful model for new approaches to global governance.

Transnational civil society *can* serve humanity well. Because the networks claim to speak on behalf of the global future, they provide a kind of competition for the public conscience. That competition prods government officials to consider broader perspectives than the immediate bureaucratic turf battle or the next election or even the immediate national interest; it pushes corporate officials to consider more than the next quarter's bottom line. It also helps keep attention on pressing transnational issues that worsen slowly and incrementally, the sort of barely perceptible change that ordinarily does not register on the political radar screen. Like the proverbial frog in the pot of water, if the temperature is raised slowly enough, nothing triggers the frog to jump out, or the government to take action, until the water has boiled the frog to death.

Transnational civil society may be creating the basis of a global polity: not a world government, but something of a common culture with broadly shared values. Some of these are already widely recognized, such as the universality of basic human rights and the need for economic development to be environmentally sustainable. The insistence of transnational civil society on these values holds governments and the private sector to international standards that are high aspirations, not the lowest common denominator of acceptable international behavior.

Since globalization is increasingly leaving all of us susceptible to the actions of others far away, it seems fitting that transnational civil society provides a mechanism for people everywhere to have some say about those actions. For the large number of people whose governments are less than fully democratic (or less than fully responsive to the needs of citizens unable to make large campaign donations), transnational civil society can provide the only meaningful way to participate in decision making.

For all these reasons, it is highly desirable to find means to deal with the drawbacks of transnational civil society without unduly hampering its strength. Because there is no easy, one-size-fits-all measure for determining which of the thousands of clamoring voices are pursuing noble goals (or even which goals are truly noble), those means should not constrain the sector's vaunted flexibility. No one model serves for all of transnational civil society, just as no one model serves for all of the private sector.

The one very broad means that transnational civil society should adopt is the same one that governments and businesses are increasingly being pressured to adopt in the name of good governance: transparency. Civil society organizations are by and large quite poor at providing information about their personnel, operations, funding sources, and expenditures, and even sometimes their purposes. Sometimes that opacity is a deliberate effort to conceal nefarious misdeeds. More often, it merely reflects the natural human tendency to see getting on with the job as more important than reporting on one's activities. But if transnational civil society networks are to flourish as significant contributors to the management and resolution of global problems, they will have to do better. There is a role for governments here to require reporting on funding sources and expenditures. But it is up to civil society itself to make the case for itself, by being as open and honest about its own purposes and activities as time and resources will permit.

Notes

1. For example, one survey found that 56 percent of the responding human rights INGOs had assisted an intergovernmental agency in implementing human rights policy. See George Lopez, Ron Pagnucco, and Jackie Smith, "Globalizing Human Rights: The Work of Transnational Human Rights NGOs in the 1990s," *Human Rights Quarterly* 20 (1998): 379–412.
2. Michela Wrong, *Financial Times*, November 25, 1996, quoted in Nik Gowing, "'Dispatches from Disaster Zones': The Reporting of Humanitarian Emergencies," paper prepared for Conference on New Challenges and Problems for Information Management in Complex Emergencies, London, May 27–28, 1998, p. 31.
3. The following discussion is based primarily on James A. Paul, "NGO Access at the UN," July 1999, at www.globalpolicy.org/ngos/analysis/jap-accs.htm.
4. Paul, "NGO Access."
5. Elizabeth Olson, "A Challenge to Immunity of Lobbyists at the UN," *New York Times*, August 8, 1998, p. 4.
6. Tiffany Danitz and Warren P. Strobel, *Networking Dissent: Burmese Cyberactivists Promote Nonviolent Struggle Using the Internet* (Washington, D.C.: United States Institute of Peace, 1998).
7. Control Risks Group, *No Hiding Place: Business and the Politics of Pressure* (London: Control Risks Group, 1997).
8. Control Risks Group, *No Hiding Place*.
9. Michele N. Ferenz, "Review of Civil Society in the Middle East," *Nonprofit and Voluntary Sector Quarterly* 28, no. 1 (March 1999): 83–99.
10. Thomas Carothers, "Civil Society," *Foreign Policy* 117 (winter 1999–2000): 18–29.
11. Sheri Berman, "Civil Society and the Collapse of Weimar Germany," *World Politics* 48, no. 3 (April 1997).
12. See Joseph Nye, "In Government We Don't Trust," *Foreign Policy* 108 (fall 1997); Pippa Norris, ed., *Critical Citizens: Global Support for Democratic Governance* (Oxford: Oxford University Press, 1999).
13. L. Jean Camp and Brian L. Anderson, "Grameen Phone: Empowering the Poor Through Connectivity," *Information Impacts Magazine* (December 1999), at www.cisp.org/imp/december_99/12_99camp.htm.

14. Margaret Keck and Kathryn Sikkink, *Activists Beyond Borders: Transnational Advocacy Networks in International Politics* (Ithaca, N.Y.: Cornell University Press, 1998), p. 21.

15. Ben Petrazzini and Mugo Kibati, "The Internet in Developing Countries," *Communications of the Association for Computing Machinery*, June 1999.

16. Toni Rutkowski, "Bottom Line: The Net—You Either Get It or You Don't," *Communications Week International*, March 1, 1999.

17. Computer Industry Almanac (December 1999), at www.c-i-a.com/199908;v.htm.

18. Katie Hafner, "We're Not All Connected, Yet," *New York Times*, January 27, 2000.

19. www.globaltechcorps.org/aboutthegtc.htm.

20. Amy Harmon, "'Hactivists' of All Persuasions Take Their Struggle to the Web," *New York Times*, October 31, 1998, p. A6.

21. "The Twenty Enemies of the Internet," press release, August 9, 1999, at www.rsf.fr/uk/alaune/ennemisweb.html.

22. The definition of "state secret" is incredibly broad. For example, if the details regarding the age or health of a Communist Party leader have not been published, dissemination of that information is a leak of state secrets.

23. Elizabeth Rosenthal, "China Issues Rules to Limit E-Mail and Web Content," *New York Times*, January 27, 2000.

24. Rosenthal, "China Issues Rules."

25. "China's Internet Clampdown Will Lose Sting in the Long Run: Analysts," *Inside China Today*, January 27, 2000.

26. Steve Charnovitz, "Two Centuries of Participation: NGOs and International Governance," *Michigan Journal of International Law* 18, no. 2 (winter 1997): 261–62.

27. Charnovitz, "Two Centuries of Participation," p. 265.

28. Charnovitz, "Two Centuries of Participation," p. 265.

29. "The Microcredit Summit: NGOs Host a World-Class Meeting," *One Country* 8, no. 4 (January–March 1997): 4–6.

30. Stephen J. Kobrin, "The MAI and the Clash of Globalizations," *Foreign Policy* 112 (fall 1998): 98.

31. Kobrin, "MAI," p. 102.

32. Peter (Jay) Smith and Elizabeth Smythe, "Globalization, Citizenship, and Technology: The MAI Meets the Internet," paper presented at the annual meeting of the International Studies Association, Los Angeles, March 17, 2000.

33. Larry Elliott, "G7 Look at Plans for Debt Relief," *Guardian*, February 19, 1999.

34. The most comprehensive study of civil society to date measures all nonprofit activities country by country, including nonprofit hospitals and universities. This gives an impressive sense of the global scope of nonprofit activity but no guidance about how much transnational civil society networks are spending. See Lester Salamon et al., *Global Civil Society: Dimensions of the Nonprofit Sector* (Baltimore: Johns Hopkins Center for Civil Society Studies, 1999).

35. Overseas Development Institute, "NGOs and Official Donors," *Briefing Paper* No. 8, 1995, at www.oneworld.org/euforic/odi/odi8_gb.htm.

36. Michael Edwards and David Hulme, "Too Close for Comfort? The Impact of Official Aid on Non-governmental Organizations," *Current Issues in Comparative Education* 1, no. 1 (1998), p. 2.

37. For various estimates, all showing the same trend, see Mary Jennings, "New

Challenges for Northern NGOs," *Trocaire Development Review* 10, pp. 13–27, at http://oneworld.org/euforic/trocaire/tdrjen_r.htm; INTRAC, Direct Funding from a Southern Perspective, *INTRAC NGO Management and Policy Series* No. 8, 1998; Edwards and Hulme, "Too Close for Comfort?"; Overseas Development Institute, "NGOs and Official Donors."

38. Foundation Center, "New Report Documents Striking Changes in International Grantmaking by US Foundations," at http://fdncenter.org/about/news/pr_9801a.html.

39. Paul Eavis, "Awash with Light Weapons," *World Today* 55, no. 4 (April 1999): 19–21.

40. www.jubilee2000uk.org/about.html.

41. P. J. Simmons, "Learning to Live with NGOs," *Foreign Policy* 112 (Fall 1998): 82–96.

42. See Julie Fisher, *The Road from Rio: Sustainable Development and the Nongovernmental Movement in the Third World* (Westport, Conn.: Praeger, 1993), on the proliferation of Southern NGOs.

43. Lopez, Pagnucco, and Smith, "Globalizing Human Rights," p. 387.

44. Many Southern networks developed among groups that had initially been brought together by Northern nongovernmental or global intergovernmental organizations. Institutions such as the Organization for Economic Cooperation and Development (OECD), the Food and Agriculture Organization (FAO), and the United Nations Environment Program (UNEP) have funded conferences, workshops, surveys, and training to bring together Southern NGOs. See Julie Fisher, "International Networking: The Role of Southern NGOs," in *Organizational Dimensions of Global Change: No Limits to Cooperation*, ed. David L. Cooperrider and Jane E. Dutton (Thousand Oaks, Calif.: Sage Publications, 1999), p. 217.

45. Peter Newell, "Environmental NGOs, TNCs and the Question of Governance," in *International Political Economy Yearbook on the Environment*, ed. V. Assetto and D. Stevis (Boulder, Colo.: Lynne Rienner, forthcoming).

Annotated Bibliography
Prepared by Yahya A. Dehqanzada

"Are NGOs Overrated?" *Current Issues in Comparative Education* 1, no. 1 (November 1998).

The articles in this special issue provide a theoretical overview of the issues and questions surrounding the dramatic rise in the number and influence of nongovernmental organizations (NGOs) in development: What should the role of NGOs be? What are the consequences of foreign funding of NGOs? And what sort of relationships should NGOs maintain with state governments?

Arnove, Robert F., and Rachel Christina. "NGO-State Relations: An Argument in Favor of the State and Complementarity of Efforts."

Although it is true that NGOs can generally respond to local needs with greater flexibility and ease, they certainly cannot replace state governments, as case studies of Nicaragua, Papua New Guinea, and Palestine clearly demonstrate. Most NGOs lack both the human and financial resources to bring about significant change. Much of NGOs' time is spent raising funds, and NGOs must often respect the wishes of their dominant funders. Therefore, for best results, NGOs and states must coordinate their efforts, despite the danger this poses to NGO legitimacy.

Edwards, Michael. "Are NGOs Overrated? Why and How to Say 'No.'"

Development NGOs can claim legitimacy through either representation or results. The former path requires NGOs to increase the demand for development, as well as secure financial independence in order to minimize undue donor influence. Development NGOs have had little success in bringing this about. The latter path requires NGOs to demonstrate their results. NGOs often have no idea what their results are, or what can be attributed to their own interventions. Consequently, a lack of accountability, transparency and the inability to learn from previous experiences have diminished the legitimacy of development NGOs.

Edwards, Michael, and David Hulme. "Too Close for Comfort? The Impact of Official Aid on Nongovernmental Organizations."

In recent years, bilateral and multilateral donor agencies have accepted a New Policy Agenda driven by two assumptions: (1) free economies and private-sector initiatives are the best mechanisms for achieving economic growth, and (2) democratic systems of government are essential for healthy economies. To these ends, donor agencies have channeled large amounts of funds to NGOs, resulting not only in drastic increases in the number of both Northern and Southern NGOs but also in overdependence of most NGOs on official aid. But this heavy reliance may not be good for development or for NGOs. NGOs are not always more efficient or effective than governments. Accepting foreign funds may diminish the legitimacy of NGOs in general and advocacy NGOs in particular and may lead to co-optation of some NGOs. To avoid such problems, NGOs should try to raise a larger portion of their funds locally and to increase their organizational transparency. Moreover, donor funds could be channeled to NGOs via an independent public institution rather than foreign governments. Most importantly, NGOs must always remain clear about the overall direction of the organization and its function within society.

Ilon, Lynn. "Can NGOs Provide Alternative Development in a Market-Based System of Global Economics?"

NGOs are generally better equipped than governments to address the local needs of the people. But in the profit-driven economic system, NGOs face two distinct difficulties: (1) community-based funding is frequently weak and unreliable relative to funding driven by profit, and (2) when multilateral or bilateral organizations become primary funders of NGOs, the goals of the local NGOs may change to better accommodate the agendas of the donor organizations. NGOs can avoid all pitfalls by focusing on increased service delivery rather than increased market share and funds. This can be done only if the NGO (1) has a goal that is non-market based and maintains that goal; (2) builds power, influence, and size based on knowledge; and (3) reinvests in human resources rather than market strategies.

Stromquist, Nelly P. "NGOs in a New Paradigm of Civil Society."
NGOs perform three major functions: (1) service delivery (for example, relief, welfare, basic skills); (2) educational provision (for example, basic skills and often critical analysis of social environments); and (3) public policy advocacy (for example, lobbying for international assistance for specific purposes and monitoring or promoting pertinent state policies). NGOs' close ties to the local populations, sensitivity to local needs, flexibility of action, and experience render them better suited to perform certain tasks. It is also true that NGOs represent the disempowered who have no possibility of electing their own representatives. But this does not mean that NGOs can or want to replace governments. Instead, NGOs generally try to hold states accountable for their actions, as well as for their failures to act. The diminished role of the state is caused not by the growth in the number of NGOs but primarily by the forces of globalization and structural adjustment programs.

Baitenmann, Helga. "NGOs and the Afghan War: The Politicisation of Humanitarian Aid." *Third World Quarterly* 12, no. 1 (1990): 62–85.
As the number of Afghan refugees relocating to Pakistan has increased, NGO participation in both refugee relief programs and Afghan politics has increased as well. During this period, NGO activities have primarily been confined to three sectors: (1) provision of aid to Afghan refugees in Pakistan, (2) cross-border assistance to Afghans, and (3) lobbying foreign governments for greater support for Afghan refugees and rebels. Although NGO actions have been critical to the prevention of widespread famine, disease, and other extreme hardships, they have

been vulnerable to a high degree of politicization. Given that the United States has been the biggest financial supporter of NGO programs, many NGOs have adopted policies that accommodate the American anti-Soviet agenda. By so doing, many NGOs—especially those involved in cross-border and lobbying activities—have consciously buttressed the Afghan insurgency while ignoring the humanitarian needs of those Afghans who live in government-controlled areas.

Bebbington, Anthony, and Roger Riddell. "The Direct Funding of Southern NGOs by Donors: New Agendas and Old Problems." *Journal of International Development* 7, no. 6 (1995): 879-93.

This article offers a theoretical analysis of the potential problems associated with direct funding of Southern NGOs (SNGOs) by international donors. Such funding is often justified on the basis that SNGOs not only are better performers and more cost-effective than local governments but also can strengthen civil society in their respective countries. Although these generalizations are often true, donors must be careful when contemplating direct funding of SNGOs. If funds intended for local governments are diverted to SNGOs, this will inevitably weaken state governments. The evidence suggests that NGOs tend to be more effective when the state is relatively healthy. Additionally, in the absence of reliable information on the effectiveness of individual NGOs, direct funding of SNGOs will continue to be a risky investment. Even more troubling is the possibility that direct funding of SNGOs may in some cases lead to co-optation. Therefore, donors must first be clear on what their primary objectives are; only then can they determine whether direct funding of Southern NGOs offers the best prospects for success. It may often be the case that other initiatives —nurturing state-NGO partnership, promoting freedom of expression and association, encouraging contributions to the voluntary sector— are more appropriate for achieving the desired results.

Boli, John, and George N. Thomas, eds. *Constructing World Culture: International Non-Governmental Organizations Since 1875*. Stanford, Calif.: Stanford University Press, 1999.

This book provides a comprehensive overview of the history of international nongovernmental organizations (INGOs), interpreted through the framework of a sociological theory known as world-polity institutionalism. Half of the eight case studies examine social movement sectors (environment, women, Esperanto, and the International Red Cross). The other four look at technical, scientific, and development sectors. The book concludes with John Boli's analysis of a core theoretical problem raised by the case studies: How can INGOs exercise influence given their lack of resources and coercive enforcement capabilities? He argues that INGOs' authority is legitimated by their structures, their procedures, their purposes, and the credentials and charisma of their members.

Boulding, Elise. "The Old and New Transnationalism: An Evolutionary Perspective." *Human Relations* 44, no. 8 (1991): 789-805.

This article introduces the concept of axial ages–periods when peoples formerly isolated from one another begin significant contact– and explores how global social change organizations (GSCOs) can facilitate dialogue among civilizations. With growing state inability to meet the needs of local populations, GSCOs are gaining greater prominence as agents of socioeconomic change. GSCOs are innovative, future-oriented organizations that are not limited by either national interests or international boundaries. These organizations can open up the two-way learning process between the North and the South by creating and maintaining transnational information channels, lobbying for the adoption of constructive policies by nation-states, providing training and educational opportunities, and offering valuable problem-solving expertise.

Burbidge, John, editor. *Beyond Prince and Merchant: Citizen Participation and the Rise of Civil Society.* New York: PACT Publications, 1997.

What is the present status of the global civil society? What are the signs of a healthy civil society? What role can civil society play in a world where governments and corporations have reigned supreme for over 350 years? Citing examples from Algeria, Egypt, Ethiopia, the former Yugoslavia, India, the Palestinian entity, Romania, and the United States, contributing authors to this volume discuss these questions. The case studies illustrate that civil society is sprouting in all regions of the world, regardless of the religious, ethnic, economic, and historical backgrounds of the local populations. In some places civil society groups are empowering the masses at a grassroots level; in other places, they are reforming state institutions; and in others, they are providing services that local governments are unwilling or lack the resources to provide. But clearly, civil society in different parts of the world has not reached the same level of maturity. Important elements of a healthy nongovernmental sector—a high number of civil society organizations, freedom from government influence and oppression, the ability to oppose state policies and hold local authorities account-able for their actions, and the existence of an independent media—are frequently absent in different regional settings. However, as the global civil society matures, it will become a critical actor in shaping human-ity's future. Unlike governments and other large bureaucracies, civil society is all-inclusive, flexible, innovative, visionary, enthusiastic, and willing to experiment with risky ideas. These traits will allow civil society to find novel approaches to remedy the gravest problems facing the planet and those who inhabit it.

Carothers, Thomas. "Civil Society." *Foreign Policy* 117 (Winter 1999–2000): 18–29.

In the post–Cold War period, civil society has become synonymous with the white knights of the nongovernmental sector crusading against the evils of corruption, intolerance, poverty, and environmen-tal degradation and fighting for the rights of the world's weak and the disenfranchised. This article challenges this view, arguing that civil society is really a complex amalgam of good and evil forces (including everything from parent-teacher associations to militia groups in Mon-tana seeking the downfall of the U.S. government) advancing not only worthy and altruistic but also nefarious and self-serving ends. National civil society can be an agent of positive change, demanding accounta-bility from governments and promoting economic growth. But a ro-bust civil society is neither necessary nor sufficient for the emergence of democracy in previously autocratic societies or for greater eco-nomic success in impoverished countries. Nor can it replace a func-tioning government. More porous international borders, the spread of democracy, better information and communication technologies, and lower transportation costs have allowed civil society groups to tra-verse national frontiers, but these transnational groups for the most part still advance the agendas and values of the West. Moreover, just as in the case of national civil society groups, transnational civil society will carry with it not only the messages of the pacifists and the philanthropists but also those of the wretched and the hate-mongers.

Charnovitz, Steve. "Two Centuries of Participation: NGOs and International Governance." *Michigan Journal of International Law* 18, no. 2 (winter 1997): 183–286.

This article traces the surprisingly extensive history of NGOs in international affairs. Far from being new, NGOs have been active on the international scene since at least 1775. Over the past two centuries, NGOs have tackled such diverse issues as abolition of slavery, free trade, human rights, promotion of peace, women's rights, protection of the environment, and disarmament. The power and influence of NGOs have waxed and waned, depending on (1) the degree to which governments and intergovernmental organizations choose to draw on NGOs, and (2) the ability of NGOs to exert influence, which varies over time in terms of political freedom, internal leadership, expertise, size of membership, reliable funding, and communications technology. The end of the Cold War and the information revolution may pave the way for NGOs to play a far more visible role in international governance in the future.

Clark, Ann Marie. "Non-Governmental Organizations and Their Influence on International Society." *Journal of International Affairs* 48, no. 2 (winter 1995): 507–25.

NGOs are playing an increasingly prominent role in international politics for several reasons, including their intense focus on a very small set of issues, a membership that is dedicated to those issues, and a commitment to principle-based ideas. As examples from human rights and environmentalist advocacy groups demonstrate, NGOs have typically influenced governmental decisions by participating in intergovernmental fora and joining transnational issue networks. However, some evidence suggests that NGOs may be far less proficient at finding effective long-term solutions to global problems. NGO memberships have generally been motivated more readily by perceptible threats than by the pursuit of agendas designed to bring about structural change. Similarly, funding sources have favored projects that promise observable short-term results rather than those that require longer-term attention.

Clark, John. *Democratizing Development: The Role of Voluntary Organizations.* West Hartford, Conn.: Kumarian Press, 1991.

The author cites numerous examples from the Third World, particularly South Asia, to advocate a new role for NGOs in redefining the concept of development. Development strategies promoted by Northern governments and intergovernmental organizations (IGOs) and pursued by Southern regimes have thus far cast millions of people into abject poverty, created inconceivable wealth gaps between individuals as well as nations, devastated the environment, and drained the resources of developing countries. In the meantime, development NGOs have, for the most part, focused on their individual community-level projects, delighted by their ability to create "islands of relative prosperity within an increasingly hostile sea" (p. xi). This is clearly not enough. If sustainable development is to be achieved and poverty eradicated, a new approach based on development of infrastructure, economic growth, poverty alleviation, equity, natural resource base protection, democracy, and social justice (DEPENDS) is needed. NGOs should promote this new approach by mobilizing international public support, advocating policies that genuinely benefit the poor, experimenting with alternatives for achieving sustainable development, and monitoring the economic, social, and environmental impacts of government and IGO projects. But to do so, NGOs must overcome their isolationist tendencies and form networks with other Southern and Northern NGOs. This will allow them to significantly expand the scope and impact of their individual programs, get support from a broader constituency, improve the quality of their projects, exert greater pressure on Southern and Northern governments as well as IGOs, and secure some level of protection from hostile groups. Finally, governments are the primary agents of change. NGOs cannot be the sole advocates of DEPENDS.

Clark, John. "The State, Popular Participation, and the Voluntary Sector." *World Development* 23, no. 4 (April 1995): 593–601.

There are many benefits to involving NGOs in government activities. NGOs may be more cost-effective, they can deliver services to hard-to-reach segments of a population, they tend to be more innovative, and they can get people more involved in the decisions that affect them the most. However, because NGOs cannot offer realistic alternatives to the policies of states, they must maintain a healthy and collaborative relationship with governments. Such collaboration is possible only if (1) states and NGOs stop representing opposing camps and begin fostering trust, (2) states include NGOs in policy formulation and debate, (3) NGOs are willing to abandon their organizational isolationism, (4) donors and NGOs adequately involve local governments in their activities, and (5) donor agencies are willing to use policy dialogues to improve state-NGO relationships.

Clough, Michael. "Reflections on Civil Society." *The Nation* 268, no. 7 (February 1999): 16–18.

This article provides a theoretical analysis of the roles of governments and civil society in international governance. It finds that although states are still strong actors in the international scene, nonstate groups have dramatically increased their power and influence. However, the belief in the primacy of state governments has prevented nongovernmental entities from taking a more central role in finding appropriate solutions to global problems. Instead, NGOs have often sought to pressure national governments to come up with the right answers. In time, some other form of governance may replace the current nation-state system; but until that happens, states must learn to collaborate more closely with the independent sector, and the independent sector must learn to act more responsibly.

Edwards, Michael. "International Development NGOs: Agents of Foreign Aid or Vehicles for International Co-operation?" *Discourse: A Journal of Policy Studies* 2, no. 1 (summer 1998): 1–12.

What is the future for development NGOs that work internationally but are based in and governed from the industrialized world? Do these international NGOs still perform a legitimate function, or are they doomed to irrelevancy by economic globalization, decreased funding from donor agencies, and the growth of an independent Southern NGO community? This article traces how Northern NGOs have carried out their missions in the past and outlines how they can continue to remain important agents for economic progress in the twenty-first century. The author finds that in order to persevere, Northern NGOs must fundamentally alter their modus operandi. They need to stop competing with one another for service delivery contracts and instead coalesce around common goals and cooperate for the advancement of shared values. They need to work primarily within their own communities to build a strong domestic constituency while supporting like-minded NGOs throughout the world. According to this approach, impact comes not from the efforts of individual NGOs, regardless of their size or influence, but rather from the multiplier effect of many NGOs–both Northern and Southern–working together and exerting pressure from many different nodes.

Edwards, Michael. "International NGOs and Southern Governments in the 'New World Order': Lessons of Experience at the Program Level." In *Governance, Democracy and Conditionality: What Role for NGOs?* Edited by Andrew Clayton. London: INTRAC, 1994.

This essay highlights the activities of Save the Children Fund (SCF-UK) in Uganda, Mozambique, Gambia, Brazil, and Honduras to examine the role of international NGOs in promoting development throughout the Third World. Four broad conclusions are reached. First, NGOs cannot and therefore should not either ignore governments or try to replace them. Only states have the capacity and the legitimacy to oversee the legal, institutional, and economic frameworks within which all other institutions operate; ensure access by all segments of the population to essential resources and benefits; and maintain standards of quality in the provision of goods and services. Second, international NGOs are not well positioned to directly challenge the policies of foreign governments. External NGOs have no legitimacy in representing grassroots views and therefore can easily be dismissed. Instead, international NGOs should support local NGOs, which in turn can advise and pressure their own governments. In the meantime, international NGOs can continue to provide financial, technical, and logistical assistance to foreign governments in order to improve their capabilities and their effectiveness in addressing the needs of their citizens. Third, a deciding factor in the success of working with governments is always the wider environment in which cooperation takes place. Official donors and international NGOs must recognize and appreciate these differing conditions and avoid applying a standardized approach to all cases. Finally, working within the frameworks set up by governments is often difficult. However, a synergistic and persistent effort by both local and international NGOs can produce positive outcomes. The key is to be prepared to work with governments over the long term and not to expect quick results.

Edwards, Michael, and John Gaventa, eds. *Global Citizen Action: Perspectives and Challenges.* Forthcoming.

This book explores the potential for citizens to be active in world politics at the global level, focusing on four areas: history and overarching frameworks, influencing the international financial institutions (World Bank, International Monetary Fund, World Trade Organization), case studies of global campaigns (environment, the women's movement, land mines, debt, trade, children's rights, participation), and lessons learned and future challenges (accountability, accuracy, North-South links).

Edwards, Michael, and David Hulme, eds. *Beyond the Magic Bullet: NGO Performance and Accountability in the Post–Cold War World.* West Hartford, Conn.: Kumarian Press, 1996.

In recent years, it has become common for Western donor agencies to channel development funds through NGOs instead of inefficient and often corrupt Third World governments. This book analyzes the effects of this new policy agenda on NGO performance and accountability. Citing examples from Bangladesh, East Africa, India, and Sudan, the study finds that direct aid to NGOs may reorient accountability toward the donor agencies and away from the grassroots. NGOs that receive a significant portion of their funding from a small number of sources may be tempted to redefine their missions to ensure the continuity of funding, thus curtailing NGO flexibility and innovation. It may be prudent, therefore, to provide funding to NGOs through intermediary institutions to protect them from excessive donor influence. In the meantime, NGOs themselves should take steps to maintain their legitimacy as serious and independent agents of economic development. NGOs should create a system of multiple accountability in which they are answerable not only to their donors but also to those they endeavor to assist. In addition, NGOs should make an effort to gain greater expertise in their areas of interest, conduct regular self-evaluations, and learn from past mistakes.

Falk, Richard. "The Infancy of Global Civil Society." In *Beyond the Cold War: New Dimensions in International Relations*. Edited by Geir Lundestad and Odd Arne Westad. Oslo: Scandinavian University Press, 1993.

The challenges facing humanity—ranging from freedom from oppression and respect of basic human rights to poverty alleviation and protection of the environment—cannot be addressed by states, whose capacity to meet the needs of their populations has eroded over the years as a result of globalization, or by intergovernmental organizations, which essentially represent the interests of a few major powers. The hope of world citizenry rests, therefore, on the continued growth of social forces dedicated to human rights, democracy, and sustainable development. International civil society has already made remarkable progress in institutionalizing respect for human rights and protection of the environment; it must now extend its reach to the domains of sustainable economic growth and international security.

Fisher, Julie. *Nongovernments: NGOs and the Political Development of the Third World*. West Hartford, Conn.: Kumarian Press, 1998.

This book examines how Third World governments have responded to the growing power of NGOs; what strategies have been used by NGOs to achieve their social, economic, or political objectives; and, most importantly, how NGOs have contributed to the process of political development in Asia, Africa, and Latin America. Whereas service NGOs have generally been welcome in developing countries, advocacy NGOs —especially human rights NGOs—have often been the victims of government suspicion and repression. Relatively secure governments have shown a greater tendency to tolerate different types of NGOs, but less stable regimes have often tried to either co-opt or discredit such organizations. Still, NGOs have made significant contributions to the political development of the Third World. By breaking up excessively narrow concentrations of power, protesting government abuses, and challenging government repression, NGOs have empowered the masses to demand greater responsiveness from their political officials. Moreover, through *devolution*—a process that leads to decentralization of decision making, along with greater accountability by decision makers to local communities—NGOs have gained the ability to influence political development at both the local and national levels.

Fisher, Julie. *The Road from Rio: Sustainable Development and the Non-governmental Movement in the Third World.* Westport, Conn.: Praeger Publishers, 1993.

Evidence from the Third World clearly demonstrates that NGOs have much to contribute to sustainable development in Asia, Africa, and Latin America. Poverty, population growth, environmental degradation, and incompetent governments and self-serving power monopolies are the primary constraints to sustainable development in the poorer regions of the world. NGOs can play a central role as the promoters of sustainable development. Grassroots organizations (GROs), membership groups formed by people within communities to solve local problems, and grassroots support organizations (GRSOs), the regional or national support organizations that usually provide the conduit for foreign funds, need to work together. GROs have the local legitimacy and knowledge; GRSOs have the organizational capacity. Together, they can break up existing power monopolies, empower and organize the indigent and the voiceless to demand greater accountability and responsiveness from their government officials, educate the masses—especially women—about the need to limit population growth, and discover more innovative and more cost-effective strategies for promoting sustainable development. But NGOs must first improve their own institutional capabilities. First, GROs and GRSOs must form horizontal and vertical networks with other GROs and GRSOs to learn from one another and to scale up their efforts. Second, NGOs must learn from past mistakes. And third, NGOs must maintain their organizational autonomy. This often requires that NGOs diversify their sources of funding to minimize dependence on foreign donors and attract local participation to reduce costs. Foreign donors should realize that sustainable development in the Third World can succeed only if Southern NGOs are involved in every step. Limiting or excluding Southern NGOs from project design and implementation inevitably results in failure.

Fowler, Alan. *Striking a Balance: A Guide to Enhancing the Effectiveness of Non-Governmental Organisations in International Development.* London: Earthscan Publications, 1997.

This book, written primarily as a guidebook for members of the nonprofit community, provides insights on how to improve the effectiveness of development NGOs. Although it is generally accepted that

NGOs have much to contribute to development both at the micro (providing services to the poor) and macro (trying to modify state policies) levels, they could do better. First, the most important asset of any NGO is its credibility. Therefore, NGOs must protect their reputation and integrity by seeking financial and political independence, demonstrating effective performance, and not exaggerating their capabilities. Second, NGOs must stop concealing their failures—because of the fear that failure may result in reduced funding—and instead begin to embrace them and learn from them. Third, NGOs clearly do not have the resources to independently improve the quality of life of the world's destitute. They should move beyond the project-centric approach and gain leverage over the larger forces that keep poor people poor. NGOs need to experiment with both direct (policy advocacy, demonstrations, political lobbying, monitoring compliance with past agreements, and propagating new ideas) and indirect (informing and supporting other community organizations and social movements) strategies for producing change.

Fowler, Alan, and Kees Biekart. "Do Private Agencies Really Make a Difference?" In *Compassion and Calculation: The Business of Private Foreign Aid.* Edited by David Sogge, Kees Biekart, and John Saxby. London: Pluto Press, 1996.

This chapter challenges the commonly held belief that NGOs are altruistic organizations capable of alleviating poverty and empowering the masses on a global scale. On the contrary, as the four impact studies and several examples demonstrate, NGOs are more often driven by commercialism and the availability of donor funds than by a genuine commitment to philanthropy, and they lack both the competence and the capacity to generate real, sustainable, or long-term positive results. This is so for three reasons. First, NGOs often do not understand the roots of serious global problems; therefore, their projects are designed to address only the most obvious symptoms. Second, NGOs do not learn from past failures; instead, they try to conceal them in order to prevent the loss of donor funds. And third, NGOs tackle issues that are typically too complex; they are too small and weak to affect the larger systemic forces that strive to maintain the status quo.

Fox, Jonathan A., and L. D. Brown. *The Struggle for Accountability: The World Bank, NGOs, and Grassroots Movements*. Cambridge, Mass.: MIT Press, 1998.

For nearly twenty years, NGOs, including environmental, development, and human rights groups, have tried to pressure the World Bank into modifying some of its practices. This book traces the complex history of World Bank–NGO interactions to explore two overarching questions: What effect, if any, have NGO criticisms and protestation had on World Bank policies? To what degree have these advocacy campaigns, often led by Western NGOs, represented the people most directly affected by World Bank projects? The study finds mixed results. The World Bank has sometimes altered its practices as a direct result of NGO activities and public scrutiny, with NGOs being successful in bringing about change when they have been able to garner the support of dissidents inside the World Bank. But for most projects, social impact, participation, and environmental sustainability criteria are still not built into Bank project design. With regard to the question of whose interests Western NGOs represent, the study finds that transnational organizations have in fact become more accountable to their local partners in the Third World. However, most North-South alliances tend to be "fragile fax-and-cyberspace skeletons" that lack any long-term strategic direction. In the past, Northern organizations have formed advocacy coalitions that included their Southern brethren mainly to shield themselves from outside challenges to their legitimacy.

Higgott, Richard A., Geoffrey R.D. Underhill, and Andreas Bieler, eds. *Non-State Actors and Authority in the Global System*. London and New York: Routlege, 2000.

This edited volume uses a wide range of case studies to evaluate the changing relationships of states and nonstate actors in the international arena. After two theoretical chapters on collective action and the civil society empowerment model of development, the book includes fourteen case studies divided into three groups. The first set looks at the influence of multinational companies on the establishment of international rules. The second assesses multinational companies and the international restructuring of production. The third covers both intergovernmental and nongovernmental organizations from think tanks to the environmental movement, with particular attention to the relationship between the two.

James, Estelle, ed. *The Nonprofit Sector in International Perspective: Studies in Comparative Culture and Policy.* New York: Oxford University Press, 1989.

While focusing on the activities of national and international NGOs in a large array of countries, the contributing authors reach general conclusions on such issues as donor-NGO relations, state-NGO interactions, and short- and long-term performance of nonprofit groups. Western government subsidies make up the bulk of NGO resources, but overreliance on foreign funding may undermine NGO autonomy and flexibility of action. NGOs can limit donor influence by diversifying their sources of income, developing political leverage over donor governments, and acquiring unique and specialized expertise in their respective fields. In most of the Third World, service NGOs are often welcomed, but advocacy and human rights NGOs are commonly repressed. Advocacy NGOs can insulate themselves by garnering strong, high-level domestic and international support (for example, human rights NGOs in Chile). This strategy works if the regime in power is concerned about its international image and would like to maintain a semblance of respect for democracy and freedom of expression. It is common to assume that the nongovernmental sector is more efficient, more flexible, and more cost-effective mainly because it bypasses much of the bureaucracy and red tape that characterize governments. Although this assumption may hold true in the short term, there is little reason to believe that it will be equally true in the longer term. As donations fall, as donor agencies impose new performance standards, and as the better-informed and more committed volunteer labor force is gradually replaced with professional staff members, NGOs' comparative advantage will suffer.

Kakabadse, Yolanda N., and Sarah Burns. "Movers and Shapers: NGOs in International Affairs." Washington, D.C.: World Resources Institute, 1994.

This article highlights the significance of the 1992 United Nations Conference on Environment and Development in strengthening the role of NGOs in sustainable development, where over 1,400 accredited NGOs participated directly in the conference and thousands more attended preparatory meetings, regional discussions, and parallel negotiations. The progress made at Rio can be preserved only if states, the United Nations, and NGOs reform some of their practices:

- States must accept NGOs as full partners in devising and implementing national sustainable development strategies. States should also provide the conditions that are most conducive to the growth of the nonprofit sector.

- The United Nations should simplify its accreditation process in order to facilitate the involvement of a greater number of NGOs. Moreover, the international standing requirement for accreditation should be revised to allow national NGOs with unique qualifications and experiences to participate.

- NGOs should take steps to improve their own capabilities. They should familiarize themselves with the UN system and should create networks to maximize their power and influence.

Keck, Margaret E., and Kathryn Sikkink. *Activists Beyond Borders: Advocacy Networks in International Politics.* Ithaca, N.Y.: Cornell University Press, 1998.

International advocacy networks are informal associations organized to promote specific causes, principled ideas, and norms. The book addresses four questions: What is a transnational advocacy network? Why and how do they emerge? How do they work? Under what conditions can they be effective? It provides detailed case studies on three such networks—human rights advocacy networks in Latin America, environmental advocacy networks, and transnational networks on violence against women—along with short accounts of early networks. These demonstrate that although domestic and international NGOs often play a central role in all advocacy networks, they clearly are not the only groups involved. In addition to various NGOs, advocacy networks may include local social movements, foundations, members of the media, churches, experts, parts of regional and international intergovernmental organizations, and even parts of executive or parliamentary branches of governments.

International advocacy networks are most likely to emerge around issues when channels of communication between governments and peoples are blocked, activists believe that networking will help them get better results more quickly, and various forms of international contact facilitate the creation and strengthening of networks. Networks commonly create change through information politics—the ability to generate accurate information quickly; symbolic politics—the ability to make sense of a situation by calling on symbols, actions, or stories; leverage politics—the ability to call on more powerful actors for support; and accountability politics—the ability to hold actors accountable to their previous promises. Of course, the presence of an advocacy network does not guarantee success. Success depends on the sensitivity of the target to domestic and international pressure. Networks are most often effective when the issues involve bodily harm to vulnerable individuals or legal equality of opportunity.

Keohane, Robert O., and Joseph S. Nye, Jr., eds. *Transnational Relations and World Politics.* Cambridge, Mass.: Harvard University Press, 1971.

Classic state-centric theories of global politics assume that states are the only significant actors on the world stage and that nongovernmental groups affect international relations only through their influence on governments. *Transnational Relations and World Politics* represents one of the earlier major works that challenge this traditional view. Citing examples from multinational business, the nonprofit sector, revolutionary movements, trade unions, scientific networks, and international cartels, this volume maintains that although states are indeed central to the study of international politics, their role should not be overemphasized. Growing interdependence among nation-states, the disappearing divide between high and low politics (that is, the politics of military security as opposed to the politics of economic or environmental issues), and advances in transportation and communication technologies have fostered an atmosphere in which various nongovernmental entities can increasingly participate more directly in the policy-making process. Thus, state-centric theories of international relations are no longer accurate representations of reality. A more realistic view would have to take into account the considerable impact of the nongovernmental sector.

Korten, David C. *Getting to the 21st Century: Voluntary Action and the Global Agenda.* West Hartford, Conn.: Kumarian Press, 1990.

This book questions the practical and normative arguments favoring the widely accepted growth-centered models of economic development, calling instead for a people-centered alternative. The growth-centered doctrine is flawed primarily because it equates higher levels of gross domestic product (GDP) with economic progress, blames poverty on inadequate economic growth, and assumes that market forces and the state redistribute all benefits justly among different segments of the population. Experience has proved these assumptions false. Hence, what is needed is a people-centered strategy that emphasizes not only economic development but also the process through which such development is achieved. A people-centered strategy would take notice of the earth's finite resources, the unsuitability of the market mechanisms to equitably distribute the benefits of economic growth, and the inability or unwillingness of domestic governments to properly address the needs of the poor and the politically disenfranchised. Many of the book's recommendations are directed at the industrialized world and international organizations, as well as the NGO community. Recommendations relevant to civil society include that aid to nondemocratic states for the alleviation of human suffering should be channeled through NGOs to ensure that it does not strengthen the position of authoritarian regimes. NGOs should extend their activities beyond relief work and begin addressing the root causes of poverty. NGOs should build alliances and networks to catalyze systemic changes. Such alliances can better resist injustices, advocate policy changes, monitor agreements, protest violations, build political will, and raise global consciousness.

Ku, Charlotte. "The Developing Role of Non-Governmental Organizations in Global Policy and Law Making." *Chinese Yearbook of International Law and Affairs* 13 (1994–1995): 140–56.

This article provides a brief description of the long history of NGOs, the factors behind the recent growth in their numbers, the variety of activities undertaken by them, and the unique characteristics that render them an invaluable addition to the international development and policy-making arenas. Three case studies—attempts to strengthen the Convention on the Rights of the Child, efforts to maintain women's issues on the global agenda, and success in reforming the lending practices of the World Bank—are used to illustrate how NGOs are increasingly able to exert influence on governments and intergovernmental organizations, coordinate and mobilize the public, and supplement and complement the efforts of many national and international institutions. Traditional NGO strengths such as commitment, flexibility, cost-effectiveness, and understanding of local conditions, coupled with the networking made possible by advances in communications technologies, allow the voluntary sector to bring about significant change. Nevertheless, future successes will depend on the ability of NGOs to protect their reputations as well as their grassroots ties.

Lipschutz, Ronnie D. "Reconstructing World Politics: The Emergence of Global Civil Society." *Millennium: Journal of International Studies* 21, no. 3 (winter 1992): 389–420.

This article discusses the conditions that have facilitated the rise of global civil society. The cumulative effect of the emergence of a norm-based international system, the inability of states to cope with the socioeconomic needs of their citizenry, the crumbling of old forms of political identity centered on the state, and advances in the fields of information technology and transportation has encouraged the growth of a powerful international civil society that will undoubtedly challenge the behavior and actions of nation-states in a variety of issue areas. However, two points need to be borne in mind. First, the rise of international civil society does not mark the fall of the nation-state system. Nation-states will surely become weaker, but they can never be entirely replaced. Second, the growth in the prominence and influence of the international civil society is not necessarily good. Such power shifts could produce a healthier, more prosperous, and more peaceful world, but "a neo-medieval world with high levels of conflict and confrontation" could also result.

Mathews, Jessica T. "Power Shift." *Foreign Affairs* 76, no. 1 (January 1997): 50–66.

In most regions of the world—except where either culture or authoritarianism have prevented the proper development of a strong civil society—the role and power of nonstate actors have increased relative to those of state governments. Driven primarily by advances in the computer and telecommunications industries, the nonstate sector in general and NGOs in particular have been able to influence the decisions of the most powerful governments (such as the United States during the NAFTA negotiations) while compelling weaker states to significantly modify their behavior (such as Mexico during the Chiapas rebellion). The pattern suggests that the relative power of states will continue to decline. This power shift may enhance the ability of the international community to address pressing needs. But it may also raise problems. First, NGOs' limited capacity prevents them from undertaking large-scale endeavors. Second, in trying to expand their financial base, NGOs may compromise their operational independence. Finally, given that NGOs are by definition special-interest groups whose sole purpose is to further their narrowly defined objectives, if such organizations begin to replace state governments, the result could be a fragmented and paralyzed society.

McAdam, Doug. "On the International Origins of Domestic Political Opportunities." In *Social Movements and American Political Institutions*. Edited by Anne N. Costain and Andrew S. McFarland. Lanham, Md.: Rowman and Littlefield, 1998.

Scholars tend to link the effectiveness of nonstate actors to the relative openness of national political structures. Citing examples from Burma (Myanmar), China, the former Soviet Union, Taiwan, and the United States, this article illustrates two important points. First, opportunities exist for NGOs to pressure governments at many different levels. The foreclosure of opportunities at the national level, for example, need not spell the decline of the movement. It simply means that the movement will need to adjust its tactics and focus its efforts at a different level. Second, and more important, both international actors and the international environment have a powerful impact on the ability of activist groups to bring about change within other nation-states. In some instances, outside support may allow repressive regimes to stymie the efforts of domestic social groups (for example, Soviet assistance to Warsaw Pact countries during the Cold War). In other instances, publicizing objectionable state actions, forging ties with domestic NGOs, and making economic and military aid contingent on greater state tolerance for civil society activities can help bring about a more hospitable environment wherein social movements can flourish and pursue their respective agendas.

McCarthy, Kathleen D., et al. *The Nonprofit Sector in the Global Community: Voices from Many Nations.* San Francisco: Jossey-Bass, 1992.

Although this book does not focus on transnational civil society, it presents an array of case studies to illustrate what factors support or impede the growth of the nonprofit sector within Western, developing, and former communist-bloc countries. The case studies suggest that (1) governments have the capacity to both facilitate and impede the growth of the nonprofit sector within the territories under their control; (2) funding must be available, but foreign funding of local NGOs raises the suspicion that it may be politically motivated and may compromise the institutional autonomy of local NGOs, leading to government oppression of the NGO community; and (3) religious requirements for individual charity and collective responsibility for the material welfare of others have contributed to the growth of more institutionalized forms of philanthropy throughout Asia, Africa, and Latin America. This is especially evident in the Arab world, where *zakat*—the contribution of 2.5 percent of one's income to serve the poor—has been the driving force behind the formation of many relief NGOs and may in time contribute to the germination of some development NGOs.

Nelson, Paul J. *The World Bank and Non-Governmental Organizations: The Limits of Apolitical Development.* New York: St. Martin's Press, 1995.

This book investigates the World Bank's claims that NGOs have been increasingly involved in Bank project design and implementation. It finds that despite the World Bank's optimistic rhetoric, the impact of NGOs on Bank activities is inconsistent. Although the number of World Bank projects involving NGOs has grown steadily over the past two decades, with some spectacular successes, the scope of NGO involvement has, for the most part, remained limited. Data collected between 1973 and 1990 reveal that of the 304 joint projects between the World Bank and the NGO community, only 54 involved NGOs in project design. In the vast majority of cases, NGOs either played a minor role or were involved solely during the implementation phases. This poor performance results not only from a lack of coordination and cooperation among various NGOs but also from deeply rooted organizational characteristics (organizational culture, information selection mechanisms, commitment to orthodox economic growth models, and so forth) within the World Bank. If NGOs are to expand their influence over Bank policies and programs, it is essential that they push for greater openness in Bank decision making, pursue a more integrated agenda, coordinate their activities, and assign a greater role to Southern NGOs.

Otto, Dianne. "Nongovernmental Organizations in the United Nations System: The Emerging Role of International Civil Society." *Human Rights Quarterly* 18 (1996): 107–141.

This article highlights the deficiencies of the current system for UN-NGO interactions and recommends reforms. Two main problems exist. First, Article 71 of the UN Charter limits NGOs to a consultative role, and only with the UN Economic and Social Council (ECOSOC). Second, the 1968 UN Resolution 1296 (XLIV) places severe restrictions on the types of NGOs that can participate in the UN system. These requirements prevent formal NGO contacts with UN bodies aside from ECOSOC. They provide states with the ability to obstruct the participation of boisterous and controversial NGOs. And they favor Western-dominated international NGOs at the expense of the less powerful and more impoverished Third World NGOs. NGOs should be given the right to participate in more UN organs, including the Security Council. The requirement of international standing should be revised in order to facilitate the inclusion of national and Third World NGOs in the UN system. The ability of states to veto or expel NGOs from consultative status should be restricted. Regionalization of many of the UN functions should be considered to make NGO access easier. Methods of ensuring the protection of civil initiatives in hostile states should be given greater consideration.

Peterson, M. J. "Transnational Activity, International Society and World Politics." *Millennium: Journal of International Studies* 21, no. 3 (1992): 371–388.

This article refutes both state-centric theories of international relations and theories predicting the end of the Westphalian system. For the foreseeable future, states will continue to need civil society groups to advance their foreign policy agendas and contribute resources that individual governments either lack or would find difficult and costly to duplicate. Similarly, civil society will continue to rely on governments to provide minimal security, guarantee property rights, and help enforce contracts.

Of particular interest is the section of the article that discusses the various strategies available to civil society groups to influence the behavior of states. When possible, societal actors can use direct links to government leadership to bring about change (insider strategy). In other circumstances, groups can apply pressure through media campaigns and by mobilizing public opinion (outsider strategy). Civil society groups can even alter the behavior of foreign governments by directly lobbying those states' officials, by reinforcing the efforts of like-minded groups in those societies, and by convincing their own governments to press for reforms in the target states. However, the effectiveness of any strategy depends on the political structure of the target state, as well as its social and cultural norms and beliefs.

Rieff, David. "The False Dawn of Civil Society." *Nation* 268, no. 7 (February 1999): 11–16.

This article disputes the notion that the growing power of civil society may in time produce better governance than the nation-state system. Since the end of the Cold War, the inability of states and international organizations to manage some global problems has become quite apparent. However, this by no means leads to the conclusion that civil society in general and NGOs in particular will succeed where states and other international agencies have failed. Moreover, civil society is not necessarily a force for good. NGOs are undemocratic institutions that are accountable to no one except their members and their funders. In short, people may be "better off with honest and effective governments and legal systems, and with militaries that stay in their barracks, than with denser networks of local associations, which may stand for good values or hideous ones."

Risse-Kappen, Thomas, ed. *Bringing Transnational Relations Back In: Non-State Actors, Domestic Structures and International Relations.* Cambridge: Cambridge University Press, 1995.

This book revives the debate on transnational relations that began in the 1970s but waned under the resurgence of state-centered theories of international relations. It examines the impact of nonstate actors (largely private sector) on world politics and on the foreign policies of states. Cases include the European Economic and Monetary Union, U.S.-Japanese transnational relations, multinational corporations in East Asia, Soviet and Russian security policy, democratization in Eastern Europe, and ivory management in Africa. The book concludes with chapters by Stephen Krasner and Thomas Risse-Kappen on the theoretical implications of the empirical findings.

Risse, Thomas, Stephen C. Ropp, and Kathryn Sikkink, eds. *The Power of Human Rights: International Norms and Domestic Change.* Cambridge: Cambridge University Press, 1999.

This book celebrates the fiftieth anniversary of the United Nation's passage of the Universal Declaration of Human Rights by illustrating how global ideas about human rights have influenced governmental practices in eleven countries around the world. Have the principles articulated in the declaration affected the actual behavior of states toward their citizens? The book describes a five-phase spiral model of socialization processes that can be broadly applied to other policy areas in which global ideas have an impact on domestic affairs. Lessons are drawn from five different world regions: northern Africa, sub-Saharan Africa, Southeast Asia, Latin America, and Eastern Europe. These lessons should prove useful to human rights practitioners seeking to bring about domestic change in countries where human rights problems still persist.

Rosenau, James N. *Along the Domestic-Foreign Frontier: Exploring Governance in a Turbulent World.* New York: Cambridge University Press, 1997.

This book provides a theoretical analysis of the enormous changes transforming the international political landscape and of the impact of different actors—states, militaries, international organizations, nongovernmental groups, and individuals—on this emerging new world. According to the author, clashes between globalizing and localizing forces—a process referred to as "fragmegration"—give rise to a political space called the *Frontier*, wherein nations' domestic and foreign policies are enmeshed. It is within this realm that the quest for control in world politics is joined and the nongovernmental sector can play an increasingly influential role. Here, the NGO community can form networks of like-minded organizations to bolster their capacity to lobby different centers of power, fill the socioeconomic gaps left behind by ailing state governments, and, ultimately, shape the direction of policies pursued by the different actors in the international system.

Salamon, Lester M. "The Rise of the Nonprofit Sector: A Global 'Associational Revolution.'" *Foreign Affairs* 73, no. 4 (July 1994): 109–22.

The dramatic rise in the number of both Northern and Southern NGOs is driven by several factors: (1) the perception that the welfare state could no longer handle the ever increasing tasks assigned to it, (2) the growth of international poverty due to the oil shocks of the 1970s and the recession of the 1980s, (3) the degradation of the environment witnessed primarily in the developing countries, (4) the failure of socialism to realize the dreams of its followers, and (5) the synergistic expansion of communication technologies, along with significant increases in education and literacy rates that have made it easier for people to organize and mobilize. These developments compelled some to form NGOs to improve their conditions—a pattern repeated throughout Eastern Europe, the former USSR, the Middle East, and Latin America. The formation of other NGOs was encouraged by Western philanthropic organizations and official aid agencies to empower the vulnerable masses in the developing world. Still other NGOs were formed with the support of governments that sought help in meeting the human needs of their constituents. Although the growth in the number of NGOs is indisputable, their effectiveness is less clear. Much depends on the ability of NGOs to forge beneficial relationships with state governments, go beyond short-term feel-good projects and begin focusing on longer-term solutions to major societal problems, and expand while avoiding the increased unresponsiveness and bureaucratization that often accompany such expansions.

Sandberg, Eve, ed. *The Changing Politics of Non-Governmental Organizations and African States.* Westport, Conn.: Praeger Publishers, 1994.

Although most of the chapters focus on individual countries (Gambia, Ghana, Kenya, Tanzania, Zimbabwe), the chapters by Eve Sandberg, Michael Bratton, Karen Jenkins, and Frederick T. Anang raise issues directly relevant to transnational civil society. Some key findings include that Western governments and aid agencies have increasingly favored local African NGOs over African governments as the primary recipients of development and relief assistance. Such collaborations are regularly justified on the basis of the local expertise, flexibility of action, and innovative nature of indigenous NGOs; the perception that money given to NGOs will actually get to the target populations; African NGO claims that they strengthen the democratic process by including local people in various projects; and the belief that NGOs strengthen the private sector rather than ill-equipped, unresponsive, and sometimes illegitimate African governments. NGOs' level of dependence on foreign funding is inversely related to their effectiveness. This is so because state governments tend to be suspicious of and prone to discredit NGOs with substantial foreign ties and because NGO activities often focus on serious global problems that require long-term initiatives; foreign donors, in contrast, tend to look for quick results and may cease funding before real achievements are made. To remain effective, NGOs must maintain clarity of mission and independence of action, resisting interference by both foreign donors and local governments.

Scholte, Jan Aart. "Global Civil Society: Changing the World?" *CSGR Working Paper* No. 31/99. Warwick, U.K.: Centre for the Study of Globalisation and Regionalisation, May 1999.

Is, as many of its enthusiastic proponents suggest, global civil society the key to future progressive politics? This paper develops a definition of global civil society and explores the circumstances that have prompted its growth. It then considers the consequences of global civil society for sovereignty, identity, citizenship, and democracy. It outlines criteria for evaluating global civil society, identifying seven areas of promise and four possible dangers. The conclusion suggests ways to maximize the benefits and minimize the pitfalls of global civil society.

Scholte, Jan Aart, Robert O'Brien, and Marc Williams. "The WTO and Civil Society." *Journal of World Trade* 33, no. 1 (February 1999): 107–23.

This article describes the status of the relations between the World Trade Organization (WTO) and international civil society and recommends ways to further strengthen existing ties. Both the WTO and the NGO community can benefit from greater cooperation. NGOs can assist the WTO in accomplishing its mission by furnishing it with valuable information, legitimizing its activities, and stimulating debate about WTO policies. Similarly, the WTO can help NGOs achieve their objectives by promoting fair, equitable, and environmentally sound trade practices. Some cooperation already exists. WTO officials have consistently acknowledged the importance of NGO participation in WTO affairs and have taken steps to broaden future cooperation. However, a number of factors have constrained WTO-NGO relations. The WTO has generally given greater access to Northern NGOs and to NGOs that support its activities. Very little dialogue has been initiated with groups that have either opposed or sought to reform WTO policies. Another constraining factor has been the shallowness of relations between the WTO and the NGO community. No permanent and institutionalized channels of communication exist between NGOs and the WTO, and the WTO has done very little to include civil society in policy making. Moreover, the WTO has firmly embraced a culture of secrecy, which has, for the most part, prevented meaningful NGO participation. Lastly, a lack of qualified personnel and adequate funding has further hampered WTO-NGO interactions. This factor has been particularly debilitating to the NGO community, which has been unable to mount fully informed and large-scale campaigns for policy change at the WTO.

Schweitz, Martha L. "NGO Participation in International Governance: The Question of Legitimacy." In Proceedings of the 89th Annual Meeting of the American Society of International Law (ASIL), New York, April 5–8, 1995.

In her speech, Martha Schweitz described the increasing role of NGOs in international governance and addressed the factors that legitimize such NGO participation. She argued that NGOs need not be *representative* to be included in the policy process. NGOs are a source of information and expertise, they deliver services to people, and they often pursue noble objectives. These factors alone legitimize NGO participation. She pointed out, "The issue is not about numbers, but about values, deep commitments, and how they need to be voiced and heard at some point in the process when relevant decisions are being taken." However, NGO legitimacy could potentially be improved if NGOs begin to adhere to some standard of conduct, enhance their capacity to self-regulate, and find better ways to have their many voices heard without overwhelming the capacity of national and international agencies to listen.

Shaw, Martin. "Civil Society and Global Politics: Beyond a Social Movements Approach." *Millennium: Journal of International Studies* 23, no. 3 (winter 1994): 647–67.

This article evaluates the influence of social movements—collective actors constituted by individuals who share common interests and who wish to defend or change society, and whose primary source of leverage and therefore power is the ability to quickly mobilize their constituents—on global politics. After a brief examination of the impact of women's groups, peace movements, and human rights organizations on international relations, the author concludes that "while [social movements] are indeed important, their influence is complex, variable, and episodic" (p. 648). Social movements lack sufficient leverage over states. The extent of their influence depends on the nature of the issue with which the movement is concerned; the movement's financial resources; the extent to which the media amplify the issue; the movement's relationship with more formal organizations of civil society, such as political parties; and the movement's relationship with the state and other international actors.

Simmons, P. J. "Learning to Live with NGOs." *Foreign Policy* 112 (fall 1998): 82–96.

Over the years, both the number and the influence of NGOs have reached unprecedented levels. Increasingly, NGOs are able to influence national governments, multilateral institutions, international corporations, and societies by (1) setting agendas—forcing leaders, policy makers, and publics to pay greater attention to specific topics; (2) negotiating outcomes—designing treaties and facilitating agreements; (3) conferring legitimacy—promoting or restricting public support for various issues, products, and institutions; and (4) implementing solutions—making sure states and other actors live up to their commitments. However, the rapid proliferation of NGOs could offer mixed results. On the one hand, NGOs can improve domestic and international governance by drawing on their expertise and resources, grassroots connections, sense of purpose, and freedom from bureaucratic constraints; on the other hand, they may do harm by distorting public opinion with false or inaccurate information, lose their sense of purpose by growing larger and more bureaucratic, or lose their organizational autonomy by increasingly relying on state funding.

Sinnar, Shirin. "Mixed Blessing: The Growing Influence of NGOs." *Harvard International Review* 18, no. 1 (1995–96): 54–57.

Since 1838, both the number and the influence of NGOs have increased significantly. NGOs have extended the scope of their activities, found novel strategies for furthering their agendas, and, in the process, gained international recognition and prominence. The end of the Cold War has facilitated international consensus building and loosened the rigidity of international foreign policy making, increasing the power of NGOs. This, coupled with NGOs' traditional advantages—organizational flexibility, small size, single focus, political independence, and grassroots involvement—has given impetus to the pervasive but dangerous image of NGOs as infallible crusaders for a better world. In reality, many NGO strengths can turn into weaknesses (for example, NGOs' narrow focus may lead to tunnel vision; NGO independence may foster recklessness, duplication, and organizational deterioration). NGO success is primarily the result of a convergence of interests between Western states and international NGOs. It is unlikely that NGOs will continue to exercise the same level of influence should changes in the international security arena create a divergence of interests between Western powers and NGOs.

Slim, Hugo. "To the Rescue: Radicals or Poodles?" *World Today* 53, nos. 8–9 (August–September 1997): 209–12.

Despite the overwhelming amount of confidence in the effectiveness of NGOs, little evidence suggests that nongovernmental entities have any sustainable impact on poverty alleviation or empowerment. Some critics argue that NGOs are used by Great Power politicians to channel resources to Southern states only to prevent mass migrations to the North. Conspiracy theorists maintain that NGOs are used by Northern powers to facilitate the recolonization of the South. Less hostile critics concede that NGOs have a significant role to play but maintain that for NGOs to be more effective, they must address concerns regarding their institutional legitimacy and accountability, their relationship with donor governments and agencies, their interactions with other NGOs, and their ability to measure their successes and learn from their failures.

Smith, Jackie, Charles Chatfield, and Ron Pagnucco, eds. *Transnational Social Movements and Global Politics: Solidarity Beyond the State.* Syracuse, N.Y.: Syracuse University Press, 1997.

This book analyzes international NGOs and the broader social movements of which they are part using the rubric transnational social movement organizations (TSMOs). It includes a history of transnational social movement activity prior to World War II and a discussion of the postwar development of TSMOs. The conceptual framework in chapter 4 draws from both sociological theory on social movements and international relations theory to set the stage for the nine case studies that follow. The case studies are divided into three groups of three cases each: mobilizing transnational resources in national conflicts, generating constituencies for multilateral policy on such issues as disarmament and the environment, and targeting international institutions. The book is aimed at an academic audience and concludes with two chapters on theoretical implications.

Spiro, Peter J. "New Global Communities: Nongovernmental Organizations in International Decision-Making Institutions." *Washington Quarterly* 18, no. 1 (winter 1995): 45–56.

A growing public awareness of issues, along with a general distrust of the policy-making elites, has significantly heightened the role of NGOs. At the international level, the nongovernmental sector enjoys both moral authority, claimed on the basis of its representative nature, and the ability to spur large segments of populations to action, thanks to greater permeability of national borders and the information revolution. Consequently, it might prove useful to integrate NGOs into the decision-making process. Such a step would make international institutions more legitimate, would increase institutional transparency, and might even improve NGO accountability by forcing all NGOs to adhere to an acceptable code of conduct.

Tarrow, Sidney. "Fishnets, Internets, and Catnets: Globalization and Transnational Collective Action." In *Challenging Authority: The Historical Study of Contentious Politics*. Edited by Michael P. Hanagan, Leslie Page Moch, and Wayne te Brake. Minneapolis: University of Minnesota Press, 1998.

Growing interactions among civil society groups in different parts of the world, coupled with increasing international interdependence, porousness of state boundaries, low-cost global transportation, and, in particular, advances in information and communication technologies, have led many to forecast the coming of a transnational civil society. This article argues that such a prediction may be premature. True transnational social movements—movements that are integrated within several societies, unified in their goals, and capable of sustained interaction with a variety of political authorities—are quite rare. Such movements take root primarily among preexisting social networks that are bound together by a long history of close, interpersonal relations characterized by trust, reciprocity, and cultural learning—conditions that cannot easily be replicated on a global scale. This is not to argue, however, that there are no important forms of transnational collective action. But virtually all these cases lack the sustainability, grassroots ties, and unity of purpose that are essential to the inception of a transnational civil society.

Wapner, Paul. *Environmental Activism and World Civic Politics*. New York: State University of New York, 1996.

Concerns over the growing rate of environmental degradation and its cumulative effects have led to a great deal of speculation among academics on how best to reverse, or at least slow down, the damage to the planet's ecosystem. Although many have advocated various state-centric (including substatist and suprastatist) approaches, little attention has been paid to non-state-centric models. Citing examples from the Greenpeace, World Wildlife Fund, and Friends of the Earth experiences, this book makes the case that nonstate actors can play a central role in preserving the environment. Activist groups can employ a wide repertoire of actions, such as lobbying state officials, participating in governmental commissions, supporting candidates for office, holding conferences, publicizing environmentally unfriendly activities, and staging citizen tribunals, to raise international awareness about the environment and bring about change in international norms and regulations. And given that nongovernmental groups are not restricted by territorial boundaries, which often limit the effectiveness of state governments, they can pursue both local and global strategies to combat environmental problems.

Weiss, Thomas G., and Leon Gordenker, eds. *NGOs, the UN, and Global Governance*. Boulder, Colo.: Lynne Rienner, 1996.

    This book uses numerous case studies to evaluate how intergovernmental organizations (IGOs) and NGOs should interact. The case studies include human rights NGOs, environmentalist NGOs, women's rights NGOs, Central American development NGOs, and AIDS activist groups. Although most IGOs, particularly the United Nations and the World Bank, and NGOs share a common vision of the future, they clearly have different competencies. Using their traditional strengths —flexibility, dedication, single focus, deep community ties, and independence of action—NGOs can mobilize public opinion either to support or to oppose state and IGO policies, generate information to promote greater accountability, establish and strengthen emerging international norms, empower world citizenry through educational initiatives, partake in dangerous or controversial activities, and offer services that state governments and IGOs are either unwilling or unable to provide. But NGOs have limits. They are usually small organizations, often duplicate one another's efforts, and are often forced to rely on foreign donors or splashy projects to raise funds. And NGOs can generally operate only with the consent of state governments. If NGO projects are perceived as harmful to the legitimacy or control of the ruling regime, states can usually discredit and cripple both domestic and foreign NGOs. IGOs are often better funded and possess both the technical and the managerial expertise to carry out more large-scale projects. Additionally, IGO officials often maintain close working relationships with senior national policy makers. But most important, IGOs cannot easily be dismissed by state governments, given their international status and their close ties to other international actors. Consequently, IGOs are better equipped to focus international attention on and address some major global problems. These distinct IGO and NGO advantages make a strong case for greater IGO-NGO cooperation. Some UN organizations have already established substantial ties with different NGOs. But greater harmonization of efforts between IGOS and NGOs, though certainly desirable, seems unlikely. Competition over scarce resources, accountability to different constituencies, as well as distinct cultures and operating styles are likely to limit IGO-NGO collaboration.

Willetts, Peter, ed. *"The Conscience of the World": The Influence of Non-Governmental Organisations in the UN System*. Washington, D.C.: Brookings Institution, 1996.

This book focuses on NGO relations with various intergovernmental organizations (IGOs), including the United Nations and the World Bank. The nine chapters provide a broad description of NGO-IGO interactions and how these interactions have led to some monumental achievements in the fields of human rights, protection of the environment, and humanitarian assistance. NGOs have nearly always made a positive contribution to IGO performance and effectiveness and, through that, to the alleviation of human suffering. The UN High Commissioner for Refugees works with some 300 nongovernmental entities to meet the humanitarian needs of displaced populations. NGOs have often used IGOs as instruments for publicizing a variety of causes or setting new international norms. Amnesty International, for example, has used its access to various UN organs to call attention to violations of human rights by state authorities, and it contributed to the preparation and eventual adoption of the Convention Against Torture and Other Cruel, Inhuman, or Degrading Treatment or Punishment. NGOs regularly monitor states' compliance with various international agreements. Following the passage of the Convention on the Rights of the Child, for example, the Gulbenkian Foundation launched the independent Children's Rights Development Unit to oversee the implementation of the convention by member states. And NGOs even force IGOs to reform. In the early 1990s, growing NGO criticisms forced the World Bank to modify some of its practices. As a result, the Bank began consulting with a variety of interested parties on a regular basis, initiated routine poverty and environmental impact assessments, and established an independent inspection panel, along with a public information center.

But despite the wide recognition of NGOs' capabilities, few IGOs have taken steps to more fully involve NGOs in their activities. State-centric constitutions and charters still restrict NGO participation in IGO activities and decision making. The people of the world might be better served if these charters and constitutions were revised to give all NGOs—national and international, Northern and Southern—greater access. At the same time, the quality and legitimacy of IGO decisions might be enhanced by greater NGO participation. Regardless of what IGOs do, NGOs will continue to influence IGO decisions. As the case studies illustrate, through lobbying government and IGO officials, holding parallel conventions, joining government delegations to various international conferences, effectively harnessing the power of the media, and improving the quality of their information as well as their own professionalism, NGOs have secured a permanent place in the international system.

Yamamoto, Tadashi, ed. *Emerging Civil Society in the Asia Pacific Community.* Rev. Ed. Tokyo: Japan Center for International Exchange, 1996.
Since the end of the Cold War, countries throughout the world have experienced a dramatic increase in the number of civil society organizations such as nongovernmental groups, philanthropic associations, and independent policy research institutions. This book surveys the status of these three subcategories of civil society in the Asia Pacific region. Although the pace within individual countries varies significantly, an analysis of trends in twelve countries in the region—Australia, China, Hong Kong (before it was turned over to China), Indonesia, Japan, Korea, New Zealand, Philippines, Singapore, Taiwan, Thailand, and Vietnam—illustrates a gradual but steady increase. This growth has been due to a number of factors, including the phenomenal economic success of many countries in that part of the world, the rise of a sympathetic middle class, the inability of governments to distribute the new wealth equitably among all segments of the population, and greater appreciation by state officials for the activities of civil society groups. But many obstacles still impede further development of the nongovernmental sector in the region. Despite some progress, many governments still view independent activist groups with great suspicion and therefore afford them no financial incentives to expand the scope of their work or legal protection from state interference. In addition, given the relatively brief history of civil society groups in the Asia Pacific region, many organizations lack the professional staff

and financial resources available to similar organizations in other parts of the world. Nevertheless, these NGOs are contributing to positive change within their respective countries and are forging alliances across national boundaries to better handle pressing transnational issues such as migration and refugees, human rights, population growth, the environment, and AIDS.

Index

Abolition 2000, 67–68
abolition caucus, 64–65, 71, 80n25
academics. *See* experts
access, 214–16
accountability, 232–35
Acronym Institute, 51, 69, 71, 72, 74, 77, 79n2
Acteal massacre, 122
AFL-CIO, 129–30
Africa, 7, 218
Africa Watch, 183
After the Guns Fall Silent: The Enduring Legacy of Landmines, 155
aid, 194–95, 228–29
Aid-Watch, 93
Albright, Madeleine, 164
Aldermaston Women's Peace Camp, 56
Allende, President Salvador, 181–82
American Convention on Human Rights, 180
American Jewish Congress, 132
American Peace Test. *See* Shundahai Network
American Rivers Conservation Act, 90

America Watch, 183
Amin, Idi, 182
Amnesty International, 47n29, 123, 133, 178, 180–81, 183
  Anti-Torture Convention, 186
  big dam opposition, 97
  funding, 229
  human rights, 192–94
  information gathering, 187, 192, 233
  legitimacy of information, 187
  torture, 184–85
  Uganda, 202
Annan, Secretary-General Kofi, 215
anticorruption movement, 11, 31–32, 38, 43, 46n23, 236
Anti-Torture Convention, 177, 181, 184–86, 208n13
apartheid, 182
Argentina, 17–18
Arias, President Oscar, 23, 25–26
Aristide, President Jean-Baptiste, 116, 128, 130–32, 134–35
Arms Control and Disarmament Agency, 69–70, 81n34
Arms Control Association, 68, 81n31

arms control/disarmament move-
    ment, 5, 9–10, 14n20, 49–79, 212, 215
  behind-the-scenes work, 72–73
  direct action, 58–63
  environmentalism, 58, 60–61, 64
  experts, 68–72
  government leaders, 72–73
  origins, 54–55
  public/grassroots campaigns, 63–68
  See also nuclear weapons
Asia Watch, 146, 183, 195
Association for International Water
    and Forest Studies, 93
Axworthy, Lloyd, 157–63, 173, 214

Bankcheck Quarterly, 93
banks, 33, 91, 220, 234. See also World
    Bank
Bazin, Marc, 128
Becker, Gary, 20
Beer, Angelika, 146
Belgium, 149–51
Beneson, Peter, 181
Berne Declaration, 90, 93, 108
Bernstein, Robert, 183
Bhutto, Prime Minister Benazir, 28
big dam projects, 2, 5–6, 11, 83–110,
    114n56, 212, 216
  alternatives, 110
  costs, 111n6
  definition, 110n1
  environmental impact, 2, 85–94, 112
    n26, 235
  management, 236
  resettlement issues, 85, 88, 95,
    97–100, 103, 112n26, 113n32, 113n41
  World Bank, 87–88, 93–103, 112n28,
    224–25
  World Commission on Dams, 83,
    95, 104–7, 236
Big Dams: Claims, Counterclaims
    (Dhawan), 111 n10
Biodiversity Treaty, 231

Blackwelder, Brent, 91
Boeing Corporation, 26
boomerang effect, 189–90, 190f
Bosshard, Peter, 108
Both Ends, 93
Boutros Ghali, Boutros, 153–54, 158–59
boycotts, 66–67
Brazil, 107
Bribe Payers Index, 29–30, 35
bribery. See corruption
British-American Security Infor-
    mation Council, 81 n31
British Labour Party, 163, 214
Brown, L. David, 108
Bunn, George, 79nn9–10
Bush administration, 56
  land mines, 148–49
  Haitian refugees, 129–30
business community, 10, 43, 211, 216,
    235
  big dam projects, 107
  corruption, 18–20
  human rights, 205–7
  land mines, 152
  public opinion, 11, 236–37
  Transparency International, 30–31,
    36
  World Commission on Dams, 107
Bvumbwe, Reverend, 36

Cameroon, 28–29
Campaign for Nuclear Disarma-
    ment, 52, 53, 57
Campaign for the NPT, 68–71, 77,
    81 n31, 81 n34
Campaign to Ban Landmines. See
    International Campaign to Ban
    Landmines
Caputo, Dante, 130
CARE, 8
Carnegie Endowment for Interna-
    tional Peace, viii
Carter Center, 144n29

Catholic Church, 117–28
  Bishop Samuel Ruiz, 119, 122–24
  human rights, 193, 195
  land mines, 154
  ccw Convention/Protocol II, 144,
    148, 153
  conference, 155–56, 158–59, 171
ccw News, 155
Cedras, General, 131
Center for Defense Information,
  81 *n*31
Cernea, Michael, 94, 100
Channarethe, Tun, 166
Chanteau, Miguel, 125
Charter 77, 182–83
Chiapas, Mexico, 115–28, 139. *See also*
  Zapatistas
Chico River dam project, 87–88, 96–97
children, 202–3, 206
Chile, 192–93, 196
  Augusto Pinochet, 2–3, 177–78,
    181–82, 194–95
  coup d'état, 184–85, 192
  human rights, 177–78, 181–82
  international norms, 194–95
China, 137–38
  elections, 144 *n*29
  human rights, 178, 208 *n*17
  Three Gorges dam project, 217–18
  web access, 222–24
Chirac, President Jacques, 62, 66–67
Christian Aid, 93
Christian Peacemakers Teams, 124
Christopher, Warren (Secretary of
  State), 32
Cirincione, Joseph, 69, 71
civil society, 218–20
  big dam projects, 106–9
  governments, 173–74
  Transparency International, 42
  See also domestic civil society;
    transnational civil society
civil wars, 205, 229–30

ClickStart, 222
Climate Action Network, 10, 229
Clinton administration, 50, 56
  Comprehensive Test Ban Treaty,
    67, 75
  Haitian refugees, 130, 132–35
  landmines, 163–64
  Chiapas, 128–29
  Indonesia, 200
coalitions, 8
  big dam projects, 88–89
  sustainability, 107–9
  Transparency International, 30–35,
    42
Coalition to Reduce Nuclear Dan-
  gers, 71, 79 *n*6
Cold War, 21, 201–2, 212, 217
Commission on Human Rights,
  179–80
Committee for National Security,
  81 *n*31
compliance. *See* monitoring
Comprehensive Test Ban Treaty, 2,
  5, 50–79, 81 *n*29, 212, 213, 217
  easy exit clause, 81 *n*32
  Greenpeace, 58–63
  origins, 55–58
  ratification, 74–75
  testing moratoria, 56, 60–64, 66,
    79 *n*9
Conable, Barbar, 98
Conference on Disarmament, 79 *n*8,
  81 *n*29, 216
  land mines, 160, 163, 171
Conference on Environment and
  Development, 101, 168–69, 225,
  235–36
  Biodiversity Treaty, 231
Conference on Population and Development, 225–26
Conference on Security and Cooperation in Europe, 183
  1975 Helsinki accords, 182

Conference on the Human Environment, 87, 225
conferences, United Nations, 215, 225–26
Congo, 136
Congressional Black Caucus, 132, 133, 135
consumers, 216
corruption, 5, 17–44, 236
  anticorruption pledges, 38
  increases, 44
  International Anti-Corruption Conference, 34–35
  Lima Declaration, 35
  market forces, 18
  public awareness, 26–30
  research, 233
  World Trade Organization, 43
Corruption Perceptions Index, 27–29, 35, 45 n2, 233
costs of big dam projects, 85, 111 n6
Council for a Livable World, 81 n31
Covenant for Civil and Political Rights, 179, 183–84
Covenant for Economic and Social Rights, 183–84
The Coward's War: Landmines in Cambodia, 146, 149
credibility, 214
Cultural Survival, 93, 97
Curitiba Declaration, 92, 104

Dahik, Alberto, 26, 31, 37
Dam Fighters Conference, 89
dam projects. See big dam projects
Dardenne, Senator Martine, 149–50
D'Costa, Tony, 151
debt, Third World, 84
decision making, 215
Demme, Jonathan, 132
democracies, 187–88
democratization, 6, 215–16, 218–20
  big dam projects, 88–89, 105–7, 109

China, 137–38
  growth of civil society, 219–20
  Haiti, 115–16, 128–35
  indigenous peoples, 116
  regional norms, 137–40
  superpowers, 135–38
  Zapatistas, 115–28
development, 8, 10, 18, 213
  anti-corruption, 21, 243
  big dam projects, 83, 105–10
  land mines, 157
  North American Free Trade Agreement, 120
  private organizations, 222
Devine, Robert, 89
Dhanapala, Jayantha, 49, 73
Dhawan, B.D., 111 n10
Diana, Princess of Wales, 168
diaspora peoples, 116, 135
  democratization, 138–39
  Haiti, 129–30, 134–35
  Hispanic Americans, 118
  Internet resources, 131–32
direct action, 45 n15, 53, 76, 133, 152
  big dam projects, 85, 98
  Chiapas, 122
  Greenpeace, 58–63
  Indonesia, 197
  land mines, 155
disarmament. See arms control/disarmament
disaster relief, 8, 169, 214–15
D'Monte, Darryl, 111 n10
Dodd, Senator Christopher, 135
domestic civil society, 186, 217–20
  big dam projects, 86–89
  governments, 218
  human rights, 189–92, 194, 198, 205
  International Campaign to Ban Landmines, 148–49
  See also transnational civil society
Dumbarton Oaks conference, 180
Dumbutshena, Enoch, 26

earthquakes, 169

Eastern Europe, 182–83, 193, 201, 218, 225

East Timor, 177–78, 195–97

Echo Park dam, 89

Ecologist, 90

Economic Development Institute, 33

economic issues, 215
  big dam projects, 84
  corruption, 18
  globalization, 120, 137, 139–40, 227
  Haiti, 128
  trade embargoes, 134

Eigen, Peter, 22–24, 30, 34, 211–12, 224

Ejercito Zapatista de liberacion Nacional. *See* Zapatistas

Ellsberg, Daniel, 51

energy sources, 83–84, 111 *n4*, 111 *n5*, 111 *n11*. *See also* big dam projects

environmental issues, 109, 216, 227
  big dam projects, 2, , 85–94, 112*n26*, 235
  business community, 108
  Chiapas, Mexico, 119
  Climate Action Network, 10
  Comprehensive Test Ban Treaty, 61
  corruption, 18–19
  Greenpeace, 58
  population growth, 3
  private sector, 235
  World Bank, 94–96, 98–99, 102–3, 112*n28*
  World Trade Organization, 206–7
  Zapatistas, 122

Environmental Defense Fund, 93, 100, 102

Environmental Policy Institute, 91, 97

Errera, Gérard, 66

European Convention on Human Rights, 180, 184–85

European Rivers Network, 90, 93, 112*n23*

European Union
  corruption, 19–20
  human rights, 188, 195
  land mines, 154, 160
  Ottawa Process, 163
  Transparency International, 32

experts, 9, 36, 118, 185–186
  arms control/disarmament, 52, 57, 59, 68–72
  Haiti, 134
  land mines, 150
  research, 34, 41
  Transparency International, 34

EZLN. *See* Zapatistas

Faso Transparence, 40

Fellowship of Reconciliation, 66–67

female genital mutilation, 180

Fifty Years Is Enough Campaign, 93

financial institutions. *See* banks

Florini, Ann, 207

Food and Agriculture Organization, 240*n44*

foot-binding, 180

Ford Foundation, 180, 183

foreign aid, 194–95, 228–29

Foreign Corrupt Practices Act, 32, 46*n16*

Foreigners of Conscience, 125

"The Foreign Prisoner" (Benenson), 181

foundations, 228–29

Fox, Jonathan A., 99, 108

free trade, 206–7

Friedrich Ebert Foundation, 180

Friends of the Earth, 93

funding, 169–70, 217, 219–20, 228–29
  arms control/disarmament, 57, 69
  human rights, 186, 206
  International Campaign to Ban Landmines, 153–54, 172
  relief projects, 8, 213–14
  Transparency International, 24, 43–44

funding, *continued*
World Bank, 101–2
World Commission on Dams, 105

Galtung, Fredrik, 5, 46n24, 211–12
Gebauer, Thomas, 145
General Electric Company, 26
genetically modified foods, 216
Gensuikin, 53
Gensuikyo, 53
German Marshall Fund, 229
German technical assistance agency
(GTZ), 23
global decision making, 215
globalization, 3, 224–28, 237
economy, 116, 120–21, 137, 139–40
Chiapas, 126
See also international norms
Global Exchange, 118, 124–25
Global Technology Corps, 222
Global ThinkNet project, viii, 207
Godeaux, Baron Jean, 36
Goldberg, Arthur, 183
Goldsmith, Edward, 91, 94, 112n23
Goodland, Robert, 94, 97
Gorbachev, Mikhail, 60, 79n9
Governance (World Bank), 21
governments, 10–11, 173–74, 200–1,
211, 214, 218, 235, 239n22
arms control/disarmament, 57–58
big dam projects, 105
Comprehensive Test Ban Treaty, 56
democracy movements, 135
funding NGOs, 228–29
globalization, 3
human rights, 181, 187–88
International Coalition to Ban
Landmines, 236
leaders' roles, 72–73
legitimacy of NGOs, 185, 233
–NGO meetings, 156–57
public interest, 231–32
relief projects, 8, 169, 214–15

Transparency International, 31–33
Treaty on the Non-Proliferation of
Nuclear Weapons, 56
web access, 222–24
Grameen Bank, 220
Grand Canyon dams, 89
grassroots movements
anti-corruption, 21–22
big dam projects, 86–89
arms control/disarmament, 63–68,
76
land mines, 152, 155
Grassroots International, 118
Gray, Clive, 133
Great Hanshin-Awaji earthquake,
169
Greek coup d'état, 181–82, 184
Greenham Common Women's Peace
Camp, 56, 60
Greenpeace, 5, 53, 47n29, 80n14, 212,
214, 216
Brent Spar oil rig, 231
Comprehensive Test Ban Treaty,
52, 55–56, 58–63
growth of civil society, 218–20
guerrilla groups, 202–3
Guidelines for National Chapters
(Transparency International),
36–37
Guillen Vincente, Rafael Sebastian,
120

Habibe, President Jusuf, 197
Hague Appeal for Peace, 10
Haiti, 107, 116, 128–35, 141–42n24
Handicap International (HI), 146,
148–50
ul Haq, Mahbub, 96
hate groups, 13–14n6, 231
health care, 9
Help the Volga River, 93
Helsinki accords, 182, 201, 212, 225
Helsinki Watch, 182–83, 193

Henry L. Stimson Center, 81 *n*31,
  81 *n*40
*Hidden Death–Antipersonnel Mines
  in Iraqi Kurdistan*, 149–50
Hildyard, Nicholas, 91, 94, 112 *n*23
Hirakud dam, 86
historic information, 8–10
  arms control/disarmament, 54–55
  big dam projects, 85–94
  human rights, 179–88
  Transparency International, 22–26
Hiti Tau, 56, 68
Hossain, Kamal, 23
humanitarian law, 144. *See also* international norms; legal issues
humanitarian relief, 213, 214
human resources, 44
human rights, 6, 11, 109, 177–209, 215,
  216, 218, 227, 234
  Augusto Pinochet, 2–3, 177–78,
    181–82, 194–95
  big dam projects, 85–86, 112 *n*26
  Catholic Church, 117–28, 193, 195
  Chiapas, 123–24
  children, 202–3
  domestic society, 189–92, 194
  free trade, 206–7
  guerrilla groups, 202–3
  Haiti, 133
  international norms, 10–11, 183–85,
    189–92, 199–202, 208 *n*22, 212
  management, 238 *n*1
  material pressure, 194–95, 196
  models of change, 190–202, 190*f*,
    191*f*
  monitoring, 124–25, 143 *n*23
  private sector, 235–36
  rule of law, 205
  United Nations, 224–25
  World Trade Organization, 206–7
  See also Amnesty International;
    United Nations Commission on
    Human Rights

Human Rights Watch, 180, 183,
  186–87
  Chiapas, 123
  Haiti, 129–30, 132
  International Campaign to Ban
    Landmines, 146, 152
hunger strikes, 133
hydropower, 111 *n*4

indigenous peoples, 109, 116
  big dam projects, 85–86, 95
  Chiapas, Mexico, 117–28
  globalization, 137
  World Bank, 96–99
Indonesia, 177–78, 192–97, 200, 212
information, 3, 10, 203, 206, 233
  growth of civil society, 219–20
  gathering, 187, 192
  "soft power," 14 *n*20
  See also technology
Institute for National Strategic
  Studies, 132
Institute for Science and Interna-
  tional Security, 68, 81 *n*31
Inter-American Commission on
  Human Rights, 123, 180, 194–95
Intermediate Nuclear Forces Treaty,
  75
International Action Network on
  Small Arms, 229–30
International Anti-Corruption Con-
  ference, 34–35
International Association of Law-
  yers Against Nuclear Arms, 64
International Campaign to Ban
  Landmines, 2, 6, 8, 143–74, 212, 218,
  229
  Canadian government, 236
  ccw Conference, 155–56, 158–59, 171
  early goals, 146
  funding, 229
  Nobel Peace Prize, 166
  Oslo negotiations, 163–66

International Campaign to Ban Landmines, *continued*
process, 171–72
structure, 172–73
International Citizen's Congress for a Nuclear Test Ban, 64
International Commission of Jurists, ⌐ 180, 192–93
International Commission on Irrigation and Drainage, 107, 114n56
International Commission on Large Dams, 94, 107, 114n56
International Committee of the Red Cross, 9, 141–42, 154
International Conference of People Affected by Dams, 104
International Dams Newsletter, 91, 92
International Fellowship of Reconciliation, 118
International Financial Corporation, 108
International Hydropower Association, 107, 114n56
international law, 9, 205
International Monetary Fund, 33, 45 n15, 157, 228
International Narmada Action Committee, 101
International Network of Scientists and Engineers Against Proliferation, 52
international norms, 10–11, 193–95, 203–4, 237
  Chile, 194–95
  democratization, 137–40
  human rights, 183–84, 185, 189–92, 199–202, 208n22, 212
  Transparency International, 42
  treaties, 225
International Peace Bureau, 64, 66
International Physicians for the Prevention of Nuclear War, 51, 52, 66

Comprehensive Test Ban Treaty, 55–56
Nevada-Semipalatinsk Movement, 63–64
international relations, 15n23
International Rivers Network, 91, 92, 102
International Service for Peace, 117
International Strategy Conference Toward a Global Ban on Antipersonnel Mines, 159
Internet, 221–22
  Chiapas, 142–43nn1–23
  democracy movements, 140
  government restrictions, 223–24
  Haiti, 131–32
  Hatewatch, 13–14n6
  Transparency International, 47 n30
  Zapatistas, 115
  See also technology
Interpol, 35
investigations, 37, 46n21
investments, 227
Izmery, Antoine, 131

Jackson, Reverend Jesse, 132
Jahangir, Asma, 125
Japan, 167–71, 175n59
Japan Center for International Exchange, *viii*, 207
Japanese Campaign to Ban Landmines, 167–71, 218
JASON Group, 71–72
Johnson, Rebecca, 5, 51, 79n2, 80n2, 80n16, 80n22, 212, 214
journalists, 36, 38, 46n21
Jubilee 2000, 230

Kazakhstan, 63–64
Keck, Margaret, 189
Kedung Ombo dam project, 106
Kenya, 194
Kerry, Senator John, 133, 135

Khagram, Sanjeev, 5–6, 212, 217–19, 227, 234, 235
knowledge. *See* information
Konrad Adenauer Foundation, 180
Kosovo, 138–39
Krepon, Michael, 68–69, 71
Kumar, Chetan, 6, 212, 221, 231

labor unions, 196–97
  Seattle, 1999, 13n5, 206–7
Landmine Monitor Report, 166–67
land mines, 2, 143–74, 212. *See also*
  International Campaign to Ban
  Landmines
land reform, 122
Langseth, Petter, 33
Latin America, 218. *See also* Chiapas; Chile
Lavalas, 128–129, 131–32
Lawson, Bob, 157, 175n34
Lawyers Alliance for World Security, 81n31
Lawyers Committee for Human
  Rights, 93, 129–30, 133, 187, 196–97
Lay, Father, 19–20
Leahy, Senator Patrick, 148–49, 173
Lee, James, 96, 97
legal issues, 9, 205, 218
  -assistance treaties, 46n20
  corruption, 24
  human rights, 178, 183–84, 189–92
  international norms, 199
legitimacy, 11, 186–88, 217, 232–35
  democracy movements, 135
  growth of civil society, 219–20
  Ottawa Process, 162–63
Lellemand, Senator Roger, 150
Lesotho Highlands Church Action
  Group, 93
Lesotho Highlands Water Project,
  88, 107, 217–18
letter-writing campaigns, 152
Lima Declaration, 35

Lloyd, Tony, 124
lobbying, 59, 67
  arms control/disarmament, 52,
  68–72
  big dam projects, 86
  Haiti, 134–35
  human rights, 193, 204
  land mines, 155
local organizations, 52, 118. *See also*
  domestic civil society
Los Alamos Study Group, 52
Lower Granite dam, 89

MacLean Abaroa, Ronald, 26
Major Dams: A Second Look (ed.
  Sharma and Sharma), 111n10
Making Democracy Work (Putnam),
  20–21
Malary, Guy, 131
Malval, Robert, 131
management
  human rights organizations, 238n1
  global issues, 236
Managua Declaration, 188
Manhattan Project II, 51–52, 71, 81n31
Manibeli Declaration, 92, 104
"Marcos," 120
Marcos, President Ferdinand, 192,
  200
market forces. *See* economic issues
Martin, Ian, 25
McCalla, Jocelyn, 134
McCully, Patrick, 101–2
McGrath, Rae, 146, 152, 166, 175n56
McNamara, Robert, 96
Médecins sans frontières, 8
media coverage
  arms control/disarmament, 53, 70,
  76
  direct action, 60–63
  funding, 229
  International Campaign to Ban
  Landmines, 147–48, 151, 155

media coverage, *continued*
  Transparency International, 27,
    35–36
medico international, 145–46
Mekata, Motoko, 6, 212, 218, 224, 233
membership organizations, 58–59,
  76
  arms control/disarmament, 52–53,
    63–68
  Transparency International, 36,
    47n29
  See also grassroots organizations
Mexican Human Rights Commis-
  sion, 122
Mexico, 2, 6, 115–28, 139
  Solidarity network, 117
microcredit, 226
Middle East, 7
military role, 10
  arms control/disarmament, 75–78
  Campaign to Ban Landmines, 158
    163
  Chiapas, 121
  death squads, 131
  Haiti, 129, 133, 134
  massacres, 143n15
  repression, 116
  rule of law, 197
Mills, Stephanie, 62
Mine Action Canada , 152, 157–58
Mines Advisory Group, 146
Minibeli Declaration, 101–2
Mitterand, President François, 61,
  149
Mkapa, Benjamin, 33
models of human rights change,
  190–92, 190f, 191f
  denial, 193–95
  international norms, 199–202
  repression, 192–93
  tactical concessions, 195–99
Mogae, President Festus, 25–36
Molander, Johan, 161

monitoring, 211–13
  elections, 144n29
  Haiti, 134
  human rights, 124–25, 143n23, 200,
    202–3
Monterey Institute for International
  Studies, 52, 72–74, 77, 81 n37
Moorea Declaration, 68, 81 n30
moral authority, 8–10, 186–88, 199, 214
moratoria
  dam building, 87
  land mines, 148–49, 154, 163, 171, 213
  nuclear testing, 56, 60–64, 66, 79n9
Morse Commission, 100
Mortgaging the Earth (Rich), 102
Moruroa, 59–61
Movement de la Paix, 53
Movimento dos Antigidos por Bar-
  ragens, 93
Muller, Bobby, 145
Multilateral Agreement on Invest-
  ment, 10, 227
multilateral development banks, 91,
  234
  See also World Bank
Multilateral Investment Guarantee
  Agency, 108
multinational corporations. *See*
  business community
Museveni, Yoweri, 200, 202
MX missile program, 75

NAFTA, 118, 119, 120, 126–27, 137
NATO, 138, 150, 163
Narmada Bachao Andolan, 87, 93,
  99, 102, 105
National Association for the Ad-
  vancement of Colored People,
  129–30, 132
National Coalition for Haitian
  Refugees, 129–34
National Commission on Human
  Rights, 125

National Indigenous Forum, 121
National Integrity Systems: The TI
 Source Book, 33, 35, 38
national organizations, 35–41, 152–53,
 185. *See also* domestic civil society
National Wildlife Federation, 97
Natural Resources Defense Council,
 56, 68, 81 *n*31, 91, 97
Nelson, Paul, 95
neoliberalism. *See* global economy
neo-Nazi groups, 231
Nestlé Corporation, 206
neutrality, 233
Nevada-Semipalatinsk Movement,
 55–56, 60, 63–64, 80 *n*22, 212
Nevada test site, 60, 63–64
New Agenda Coalition, 74
New Policy Agenda, 8, 14 *n*8
Nike Corporation, 2–3, 206
1998 ThinkNet Conference, *vii–viii*
1975 Helsinki Final Act, 182
1976 Covenant for Civil and Political
 Rights, 179
Nippon Foundation, *viii*
Nixon administration, 181–82
Nobel Peace Prize
 Amnesty International, 181
 Bishop Belo Ximenes, 197
 International Campaign to Ban
  Landmines, 143, 166, 168, 173
 José Ramos-Horta, 196–97
Non-Aligned Movement, 216
nongovernmental organizations, 3,
 9, 185, 218, 225–26
North American Free Trade Agree-
 ment, 118, 119, 120, 126–27, 137
North Atlantic Treaty Organiza-
 tion, 138, 150, 163
Novaya Zemlya, 60, 64
NPT. *See* Treaty on the Non-Prolifer-
 ation of Nuclear Weapons
Nuclear Age Peace Foundation, 64
Nuclear Control Institute, 71, 81 *n*31

nuclear weapons testing, 2, 56,
 60–64, 66, 79 *n*9, 80 *n*17, 81 *n*29.
 See also arms control/disarmament

OAS, 22, 123, 128, 137, 138, 180, 188
Obasanjo, President Olusegun, 23,
 25–26
Obote, Milton, 182, 200
Obuchi, Keizo, 167–68, 173
Ogata, Sadako, 154
oil, 119
Open Society Institute, 222
Organization for Economic Cooper-
 ation and Development, 10, 22,
 240 *n*44
 antibribery convention, 11, 31–32, 43
 Multilateral Agreement on Invest-
  ment, 10, 227
Organization of African Unity, 154
Organization of American States,
 22, 123, 128, 137, 138, 180, 188
organized crime, 13–14 *n*6
Ottawa Convention, 166–67, 218
Ottawa Process, 157–63, 173, 216
Oxfam, 93

Pakistan, 28–29
Parliamentarians for Global Action,
 52, 56
Partial Test Ban Treaty, 54, 56
Patkar, Medha, 105
Pax Christi, 125, 151, 195
Peace Action, 53, 64, 66, 69, 71, 81 *n*31
Peace Brigades International, 118,
 124
peace groups, 9–10. *See also* arms
 control/disarmament
Peace Research Institute, 65
Perreira, Fernando, 59
Pezullo, Lawrence, 130, 133
Philippines, 192–93, 196
Physicians for Human Rights, 133,
 146

Physicians for Social Responsibility, 66, 68, 71, 81 *n*31

Pinochet, Augusto, 2–3, 177–78, 181–82, 194–95

Plutonium Challenge, 68, 81 *n*31

Poder Ciudadano, 17–18

policy analysts. *See* expert advisors

politicians, 36–37, 72–73, 173. *See also* governments

polls, 123

Polonoreste dam project, 97–98

Pope John Paul II, 154

population growth, 3

Posey, Darrell, 98

power, 10, 12, 213–16
 big dam projects, 106–7
 corruption, 21–22
 human rights, 177, 203–4
 land mines, 172, 174
 "soft ...", 14–15 *n*22
 transnational society, 186

Preston, Lewis, 102

Princess Diana, 168

private sector, 235–36. *See also* business community

Probe International, 93

professional leadership
 arms control/disarmament, 52, 57, 68–72
 Greenpeace, 59
 Transparency International, 34
 See also expert advisors

Programme for Promoting Nuclear Non-Proliferation, 5, 72–74, 77, 81 *n*37

Project for Ecological Recovery, 93

protests. *See* direct action

Public Citizen, 227

public disclosure, 88–89

Public Education Center, 81 *n*31

public organizations. *See* grassroots organizations

public interest, 231–32

public opinion, 11, 214, 236–37
 Greenpeace, 58–63
 human rights, 193–95, 204
 land mines, 147–48, 153–59
 Transparency International, 26–30, 42

Putnam, Robert, 20–21

"A Question of Survival" (D'Monte), 111 *n*10

Rainbow Warrior, 59–62

Ramos-Horta, José, 196–97

Reagan administration, 183, 200

Red Cross organizations, 9, 141–42, 147–48, 154–55

refugees, 129–30, 132–34, 135

regional norms, 137–40. *See also* international norms

religious organizations, 8–9
 arms control/disarmament, 53
 Chiapas, 117–28
 human rights, 180, 193, 195
 International Campaign to Ban Landmines, 155
 Transparency International, 36

Reporteurs sans frontières, 223

representativeness, 233–34

repression, 192–93. *See also* human rights

research, 13 *n*2, 41, 233
 Amnesty International, 187, 192, 233
 arms control/disarmament, 51, 57, 59
 epidemiological studies, 64
 land mines, 152
 Transparency International, 34

resettlement issues, 85, 88, 95, 97–100, 103, 112 *n*26, 113 *n*32, 113 *n*41

Rich, Bruce, 91, 102

Risse, Thomas, 6, 212, 219, 233, 235

Robinson, Randall, 133

Rockefeller Brothers Fund, *viii*
Ruiz, Bishop Samuel, 119, 122–24
rule of law, 178, 197, 205

sanctions, 130–31, 133, 135, 196
San Francisco Declaration, 92, 101–2, 104
Santiago Declaration, 126, 129
Sardar Sarovar-Narmada dam project, 87, 99–101, 102–3
Schwarzkopf, General Norman, 163
Scudder, Thayer, 94–95, 108, 112*n*26
Selebi, Jackie, 164–65
Semipalatinsk, 63–64
service providers, 8, 14*n*8, 213
shaming strategies, 187–88
Sharma, L.T. and Ravi, 111*n*10
Shimizu, Toshihiro, 167
Shundahai Network, 53, 56
Sikkink, Kathryn, 189–91
Silent Valley dam project, 86–87, 90
single-issue case studies, 13*n*2
single-issue organizations, 24
slavery, 8–9, 179–80
small arms, 14*n*20, 229–30
social and economic rights, 205–6
The Social and Environmental Effects of Large Dams (Goldsmith and Hildyard), 91, 93–94, 112*n*23
Sommaruga, President, 154
Soros, George, 222
South Africa, 182, 193, 196
Southern networks, 240*n*44
de Souza, Monsignor, 36
Soviet Union, 182–83, 193, 218
spiral model of human rights change, 190–92, 191*f*
Sri Lanka, 138–39
START II, 70
Stern, Ernst, 100
strategies, 217
  big dam opposition groups, 90–94
  Transparency International, 26–41

Strombland, Jan, 104
student groups, 118
subway construction, 17–18
Suharto, President, 177–78, 194, 196–97, 200, 212
Suleimenov, Olzhas, 63–64
Summit of the Americas, 31
superpowers, 135–38
Survival International, 90, 93, 97, 100
sustainability of coalitions, 107–9, 204–6

tactical concessions, 195–99
Tarullo, Dan, 32
taxes, 10, 27, 32, 128
technology, 3, 9, 18, 61, 219–24. *See also* information
telephone access, 220
ThinkNet Conference, vii–viii
Third World debt, 84, 230
Three Gorges dam project, 106, 217–18
Tortosa, José Maria, 41
torture, 177, 181, 184–85, 196–97, 200–201, 208*n*13
trade barriers, 13–14*n*5
trade embargoes, 130–31, 133, 135, 196
trade unions, 196–97, 206–7
training, 38, 44
TransAfrica, 133
transnational civil society, 3–12, 114*n*61, 211–38
  abolition caucus, 64–65
  accountability, 232–35
  big dam projects, 90–94
  domestic civil society, 186, 217–20
  Greenpeace, 52, 61–62
  growth, 211–13
  history, 8–10
  human rights, 178, 198, 205
  land mines, 153–55, 160
  methods, 10–11

transnational civil society, *continued*
  moral authority, 186–88
  networks, vii–viii, 17–18, 52, 240*n*44
  power, 186
  transparency, 232, 237–38, 239*n*34
  See also funding; legitimacy
transparency, 232, 237–38, 239*n*34
Transparency International, 1–2, 5,
  8, 17–44, 211–13, 216–17, 224, 229,
  234
  Bribe Payers Index (BPI), 29–30, 35
  budget, 46*n*18
  coalition building, 30–35
  Corruption Perceptions Index (CPI),
    27–29, 35, 45*n*2, 233
  Council on Governance Research,
    34
  funding, 24
  Guidelines for National Chapters,
    36–37
  investigations, 37
  journalists, 38
  national chapters, 35–41
  National Integrity Systems: The TI
    Source Book, 33, 35, 38
  origins, 22–26
  politicians, 37
  process, 24–26
  strategies, 26–41
  structure, 35–41, 44*n*1
  training, 38
  World Bank, 39, 42, 236
travel bans, 133
treaties, 11, 225
Treaty Banning Nuclear Weapons
  Tests in the Atmosphere, in Outer
  Space and Under Water. *See* Partial Test Ban Treaty
Treaty on the Non-Proliferation of
  Nuclear Weapons, 5, 49–79, 73–74,
  213
  abolition caucus, 64–65
  Campaign for the NPT, 68–71

  extensions, 64–66, 72–73, 79*n*11,
    79*n*12
Greenpeace, 59
  origins, 54–55
Tuttle, Celina, 152

Uganda, 182, 200–3
Union of Concerned Scientists, 68,
  81*n*31
Union of International Associations,
  10
United Nations, 35, 180, 214–15
  access, 215–16
  Anti-Torture Convention, 177, 181,
    184–86, 208*n*13
  arms control/disarmament, 77–78
  big dam projects, 112*n*26
  CCW Convention, 144, 148, 153,
    155–56, 158–59, 171
  Commission on Human Rights,
    123, 179–80, 184–85, 195, 196–97,
    201, 215
  Conference on Disarmament,
    79*n*8, 81*n*29, 160, 163, 216
  Conference on Environment and
    Development, 101, 168–69, 225,
    231, 235–36
  Conference on Population and De-
    velopment, 225–26
  Conference on the Human Envi-
    ronment, 87, 225
  conferences, 215, 225–26
  Development Programme, 26,
    46*n*22
  Economic and Social Council, 215
  Environment Program, 240*n*44
  human rights, 178, 180, 224–25
  land mines, 144, 153–54, 162
  resettlement issues, 112*n*26
  Security Council, 133–35
  Universal Declaration of Human
    Rights, 178, 180
  women's issues, 10

United States, 217
  abolition caucus, 64–65
  Anti-Torture Convention, 208*n*13
  Arms Control and Disarmament
    Agency, 69–70, 81 *n*34
  big dam projects, 89, 97
  Biodiversity Treaty, 231
  Campaign to Ban Landmines, 152,
    163
  corruption, 24, 32, 211–12
  diaspora peoples, 116
  Foreign Corrupt Practices Act, 32,
    211–12
  Haiti, 129–30, 132–35
  human rights, 182–83, 195
  Indonesia, 196–97, 200
  Information Agency, 222
  landmines, 148–49, 156
  nuclear testing moratoria, 56, 61
  Ottawa Process, 163–66
  Ottawa Convention, 171
  Test Ban Coalition, 56
  United Nations conferences, 215
  Zapatista movement, 136–37
Universal Declaration of Human
  Rights, 178, 180, 183, 201
Urgewald, 90, 93

van Rossem, Pieter, 151, 156–57
Verification Technology Information Centre, 52, 80*n*17
Vicariate of Solidarity, 193
victims, 151–52, 155
Vietnam Veterans of America, 145,
  146, 155, 229
volunteers, 33–34
Volunteers in Technical Assistance,
  222

Wade, Robert, 96, 101
Wahid, President Abdurrahman, 197
Washington Council on Non-Prolif-
  eration, 81 *n*31

Washington Office on Latin Amer-
  ica, 118, 124, 126
Western Europe, 88, 111 *n*11, 112 *n*23
Western Shoshone Nation, 63–64
Western States Legal Foundation,
  52, 64
Williams, Jody, 141, 145–46, 173–74
  Nobel Peace Prize, 166
Williams, Philip B., 90–93
witnesses, 151–52, 155
Witness for Peace, 118
Wolfensohn, James, 33
Women's Action for New Directions,
  66, 81 *n*31
women's groups, 10, 66, 81 *n*31
World Bank, 26, 33–35, 91, 212, 214–16,
  227
  big dam projects, 87–88, 93–103,
    224–25
  corruption, 18–19
  environmental practices, 94–96,
    98–99, 102–3, 112 *n*28, 235
  Gland workshop, 104–5
  Governance, 21
  human rights, 204
  land mines, 157
  Public Information Center, 101
  resettlement issues, 113 *n*32, 113 *n*41
  Transparency International, 22–23,
    39, 42, 236
World Commission on Dams, 83, 95,
  104–7, 236
World Conference on Human
  Rights, 197
World Conservation Union, 104–5
World Court Project, 80*n*23
World Rivers Review, 92
World Trade Organization, 1, 43,
  206–7, 228
  Seattle, 1999, 1, 13–14*n*5, 227
World Wildlife Fund for Nature, 86

Ximenes, Bishop Belo, 197

Yanomami reserves, 221
Yeltsin, Boris, 60, 79*n*9
Young, Lord, 19–20

Zapatistas, 2, 6, 115–28, 136–37, 212,
  230
Zedillo Ponce de Leon, Ernesto, 119

Contributors

YAHYA A. DEHQANZADA is a researcher at the RAND Corporation in Washington, D.C.

ANN M. FLORINI is a senior associate at the Carnegie Endowment for International Peace in Washington, D.C., where she directs the Project on Transparency and Transnational Civil Society.

FREDRIK GALTUNG is a doctoral candidate at Cambridge University and was the first professional staff member hired by Transparency International.

REBECCA JOHNSON is director of the Acronym Institute in London.

SANJEEV KHAGRAM is an assistant professor at the Kennedy School at Harvard University and a former staff member of the World Commission on Dams in South Africa. The views expressed in his chapter are strictly his own and not those of the World Commission on Dams.

CHETAN KUMAR, formerly senior associate at the International Peace Academy, recently joined the Office of the Special Representative of the UN Secretary-General for Children and Armed Conflict as program officer. The views expressed in his chapter are strictly his own and not those of the United Nations.

MOTOKO MEKATA is the author of a book on the International Campaign to Ban Landmines and a member of the steering committee of the Japan Campaign to Ban Landmines. The views expressed in her chapter are solely her own.

THOMAS RISSE is a professor of international relations at the European University Institute in Florence, where he recently directed a major study of human rights networks around the world.

P. J. SIMMONS directs the Managing Global Issues Project at the Carnegie Endowment for International Peace.

Japan Center for International Exchange

FOUNDED IN 1970, the Japan Center for International Exchange (JCIE) is an independent, nonprofit, and nonpartisan organization dedicated to strengthening Japan's role in international affairs. JCIE believes that Japan faces a major challenge in augmenting its positive contributions to the international community, in keeping with its position as one of the world's largest industrial democracies. Operating in a country where policy making has traditionally been dominated by the government bureaucracy, JCIE has played an important role in broadening debate on Japan's international responsibilities by conducting international and cross-sectional programs of exchange, research, and discussion.

JCIE creates opportunities for informed discussions; it does not take policy positions. JCIE programs are carried out with the collaboration and cosponsorship of many organizations. The contacts developed through these working relationships are crucial to JCIE's efforts to increase the number of Japanese from the private sector engaged in meaningful policy research and dialogue with overseas counterparts. JCIE receives no government subsidies; rather, funding comes from private foundation grants, corporate contributions, and contracts.

Japan Center for International Exchange (JCIE/Japan)
4-9-17 Minami Azabu, Minato-ku, Tokyo 106-0047 Japan
Phone: +81-3-3346-7781
Fax: +81-3-3443-7580

URL: http://www.jcie.or.jp

Japan Center for International Exchange, Inc. (JCIE/USA)
1251 Avenue of the Americas, New York, N.Y. 10020 USA
Phone: 212-921-4260
Fax: 212-921-4356

Carnegie Endowment for International Peace

THE CARNEGIE ENDOWMENT is a private, nonprofit organization dedicated to advancing cooperation between nations and promoting active international engagement by the United States. Founded in 1910, its work is nonpartisan and dedicated to achieving practical results. Through research, publishing, convening and, on occasion, creating new institutions and international networks, Endowment associates shape fresh policy approaches. Their interests span geographic regions and the relations between governments, business, international organizations, and civil society, focusing on the economic, political, and technological forces driving global change. Through its Carnegie Moscow Center, the Endowment helps to develop a tradition of public policy analysis in the states of the former Soviet Union and to improve relations between Russia and the United States. The Endowment publishes *Foreign Policy*, one of the world's leading journals of international politics and economics, which reaches readers in more than 120 countries and in several languages.